DREAMER NATION

RHETORIC, CULTURE, AND SOCIAL CRITIQUE

DREAMER NATION

IMMIGRATION, ACTIVISM, AND NEOLIBERALISM

ANA MILENA RIBERO

THE UNIVERSITY OF ALABAMA PRESS | TUSCALOOSA

The University of Alabama Press
Tuscaloosa, Alabama 35487-0380
uapress.ua.edu

Typeface: Arno

Cover image: Freshidea—stock.adobe.com
Cover design: Lori Lynch

Cataloging-in-Publication data is available from the Library of Congress.
ISBN: 978-0-8173-2169-7 (cloth)
ISBN: 978-0-8173-6095-5 (paper)
E-ISBN: 978-0-8173-9465-3

Para Elvira Rodríguez de Castillo y Edna Rodríguez Suárez. Camino en sus pasos.

Contents

Acknowledgments

Writing this book has been a long journey, and there are many people who've helped me along the way. First and foremost, thank you to my husband, *el inigualable* Paul Goidich. You've been with me every step of the way. Thank you for your consistent love and support. Thanks also to my sons Alexei and Ignacio. You help me to believe that a better world is possible. To my parents, Jorge and Liliana Ribero, you are my home, my roots. *Los amo*. To my siblings, Paola and Juan Ribero, thanks for always being proud of me.

I've had the great fortune of making friends whom I not only love but also admire as people, scholars, writers, and teachers. To Kimberly Reinhardt, José Cortez, Sonia Arellano, and Anushka Peres, thanks for reading drafts, talking through ideas, and sharing your own work with me. Thank you to the Junior Women's Writing Salon for writing alongside me. You all kept me focused and accountable. And thanks to the Boss Ass Bitches for being, well, boss ass bitches.

My journey started in Arizona, where Adela Licona showed me the path to being a feminist scholar, teacher, and mentor. *Muchísimas gracias*, Adela. Thanks to Victor Villanueva for helping me through the many bumps I hit along the way, including many crises of confidence and bouts of imposter syndrome. You are a treasure.

To the many friends and colleagues who were generous with their time and feedback: Aja Martinez, Romeo Garcia, Cruz Medina. I am in your debt. To Peter Betjemann, thanks for giving me the exact advice that I needed to hear. You didn't let me give up. To Lily Sheehan, I revised much of this book sitting at your house during the pandemic. Thanks for making space for me. To Chris Nicholls and OSU's Center for the Humanities, thanks for always believing in my work.

Thanks to Dan Waterman and the team at the University of Alabama Press.

And, finally, thanks to the undocumented youth who continue to remind me that whenever there is oppression there is also resistance. *¡Pa'delante!*

Introduction

After more than ten years of activism, the undocumented young people popularly known as Dreamers won a much-deserved victory the day President Barack Obama announced the Deferred Action for Childhood Arrivals (DACA) program. Since 2001 young people who lived in the United States without proper documentation had been advocating for the passage of some sort of legislation that would give them respite from deportation, a method of regularization, and perhaps even a path to US citizenship. Time and time again, these Dreamers had seen their efforts go to waste. The Development, Relief, and Education for Alien Minors (DREAM) act, the piece of legislation that would help undocumented youth, continued failing to get traction on Capitol Hill, with a devastating defeat in December of 2010, when the bill passed in the House of Representatives but was narrowly defeated by filibuster in the Republican-controlled Senate. Then, on June 15, 2012, Obama did what Congress had been unable to do for ten years. DACA would provide Dreamers with temporary relief so they could establish their lives legally while Congress continued to debate a more permanent solution.[1]

In the years leading up to the DACA announcement, weary of living lives of abjectivity,[2] undocumented youth worked to place themselves in the forefront of the immigrant rights movement, using creative and passionate activism to respond to the US government's inaction and to counter the ongoing xenophobic nationalism that gained momentum after the terrorist attacks of September 11. In early 2010, in preparation for the DREAM Act's efforts in Congress, Dreamers ramped up their public presence with activism that illustrated their willingness to put their bodies on the line in order to be recognized as members of the nation. On March 10, 2010, the first "Coming Out of the Shadows" event was held in Chicago's Federal Plaza, with groups of young people publicly declaring their undocumented status in front of the offices of the US Citizenship and Immigration Services, a risky move that was unprecedented. Similar rallies continue to be held around the country in an effort not only to increase public visibility of the undocumented community but also to empower undocumented youth to live their lives without fear. The Coming Out of the Shadows rallies were followed by another defiant moment of activism: on May 17, 2010, five young people dressed in graduation caps and gowns held a sit-in in the Tucson, Arizona, offices of Sen. John McCain, demanding he sponsor the DREAM Act. Four of the protesters were arrested: three of them were undocumented. The *New York Times* reported this as the "first time students have directly risked deportation in an effort to prompt Congress to take up a bill that would benefit illegal immigrant youths."[3] It would not be the last time.

Embodying the slogan "Undocumented and Unafraid," Dreamers drew strength and knowledge from the activist traditions of Black, Indigenous, and people of color[4] (BIPOC) communities in the US—primarily the civil disobedience tactics of the Civil Rights Movement and the street performance strategies of Chicanx student activism[5]—to demand recognition as members of the nation. Dreamer activism not only made waves on the streets. Pictures of Dreamers wearing graduation caps and gowns circulated through popular media to interject Dreamers' faces—as well as their message—into the lives of the US mainstream. In a matter of years, the loosely construed group of people known as Dreamers went from being relatively unknown outside of their immediate communities to being famous (or infamous, depending on your perspective) household names. These fierce young people worked largely as a grassroots effort organizing street actions, creating and circulating media content, and sometimes butting heads with mainstream immigrant rights activist organizations that had previously dominated the scene.

As a Latinx[6] immigrant, I watched in awe as undocumented young people—fearless and rhetorically savvy—put everything on the line in order to fight for justice. As a scholar of rhetoric, I was fascinated by how Latinx Dreamers used bilingual, bicultural, and multimodal resources to craft a cogent message to a sometimes hostile audience. Dreamers demonstrated how grassroots efforts continue to effect social change, even in an era of professionalized and corporatized activism. This book reflects my desire to examine how Dreamers, through careful rhetorical moves, challenged the ways the country thought about undocumented immigrants while pushing themselves and their movement to avoid reproducing the dominant US tendency of essentializing populations of color. I wanted to understand the rhetorical choices that went into creating a movement with various, often conflicting, goals. I wanted to dive into the Dreamers' rhetorics, to think about what prompted their message, and to ponder its implications.

This book focuses on three main questions that I had as I considered

Dreamer activism. First, how did Dreamer rhetorics help create a Dreamer community? Dreamers as a community did not exist prior to being called to activism.[7] Of course, undocumented young people had lived in the US for many years. But before being connected as one group through their activist responses to specific political circumstances, these young people were for the most part individualized and isolated. The Dreamer community was created in part through online forums, live events, and face-to-face dialogue that put young people in contact with one another. However, as a community that is spread around the country (and sometimes transnationally, with some Dreamers living abroad after being deported), and that is made up of people who have been told to hide—literally and metaphorically—for most of their lives, this community was also created rhetorically. Through the stories that Dreamers shared, the images they evoked, the themes they relied on, Dreamer rhetorics helped craft and then expand the boundaries of the community. How does an extremely large group of people—which the Migration Policy Institute estimates at approximately 3.6 million—who will most likely never meet each other create community without relying on shared nation, culture, or creed?

Furthermore, while the Dream Act hasn't passed, and while President Trump targeted Dreamers in his first year in office by announcing the end of DACA,[8] Dreamer activism has led to changes in US policy and public opinion. Not only was DACA a direct result of Dreamer pressure on the Obama administration, but also opinion polls continue to attest that a great majority of respondents support legal status for Dreamers.[9] During the Obama years, one of the goals of Dreamer activism was to appeal to conservative US audiences in an effort to convince them that Dreamers deserved to remain in the country. Yet one of the biggest challenges for Dreamer activists was confronting the nationalism of the post-9/11 years, the anxiety over border security of white rural people in the heartland, and the racial resentment that would culminate in the election of Donald Trump for US president in 2016. Dreamers craftily tapped into the themes and strategies that made the most sense for this particular rhetorical situation, at times aligning themselves with neoliberal US values and presenting themselves as conventionally US American.[10] How did the rhetorics of these young immigrants try to build identification with segments of the US population that see them in many ways as their antithesis?

The conservative US public was not the only audience for Dreamers, however. Dreamer rhetorics were also responsible for keeping the community connected, alive, and active. As they sought to appeal to a conservative US public, Dreamers also worked to create and maintain the sort of community that other undocumented young people would want to join. Accordingly,

Dreamer rhetorics evolved in the Obama years. Originally, their message was geared toward people outside the undocumented community and relied on neoliberal themes and ideas that would appeal to the mainstream US: individualism, personal responsibility, US exceptionalism, etc. Later, however, as the Dreamer community grew, they began to craft a message that was directed inward—a message specifically crafted for undocumented youth. Their goal was not only about persuading the public to provide a space for them within the US body politic but also about expressing self-acceptance, confidence, and strength. Dreamer rhetorics became not only undocumented and unafraid but also unapologetic. I ask, how did Dreamer rhetorics evolve to fit the needs of its constituents?

Dreamer Nation tells the rhetorical story of how Dreamers during the Obama era creatively confronted a complex sociopolitical landscape to advocate for immigrant rights while empowering undocumented youth to proudly represent their lives and identities, all while under the ever-present threat of detention and deportation. When I claim that I am telling a "rhetorical story," I do not mean to make an argument about this particular story being uniquely rhetorical. In fact, as many have argued, stories are inherently rhetorical.[11] Stories both function as rhetorical strategies of meaning making and argumentation and are made up of rhetorical choices made by a story's author(s) and/or teller(s). Instead, I aim to tell the story of the Dreamer movement through an analysis of its rhetorics. This book presents the trajectory of Dreamer rhetorics—noting the beginnings, shifts, limitations, and possibilities. I call this work a rhetorical story.

Telling rhetorical stories is crucial to gain an understanding of social movements and activist communities. Both Sarah Bishop and Malea Powell et al. theorize the importance of storytelling to rhetorical criticism, particularly to those of us studying the rhetorics of marginalized populations. In her fascinating monograph *Undocumented Storytellers*, Bishop elucidates the role of personal narrative in understanding undocumented immigration and forwarding social change. She writes that "the future of immigration reform hinges on the power of storytelling and the political impact of these stories depends on narrative strategy and framing."[12] Powell et al., in describing the burgeoning field of cultural rhetorics, posit the specific value of stories to rhetorical knowledge: "We have to have a solid understanding of as many stories as possible if we're going to be able to say anything at all about the practice of rhetorics over the past 10,000 years."[13] My study builds on work on stories and storytelling in rhetorical criticism by engaging in a new kind of storytelling—the telling of the Dreamer movement's rhetorical story.

While other important works about undocumented immigrants tell their stories,[14] analyze their stories,[15] and theorize their rhetorics,[16] my book uniquely tells the story of the Dreamer movement through a look at its rhetorics. I find this an appropriate method because, as I make clear in the pages of this book, the Dreamer community exists not just in flesh and bone but also rhetorically—in the discourse, messages, actions, and visual representations of undocumented youth. The Dreamers' rhetorical story does not just tell the story of what happened but examines how and why it happened, attending carefully to the rhetorical and symbolic practices of Dreamer activism. Yet the rhetorical story that I tell in this book shares some of the features of narrative stories. To start, the Dreamers' rhetorical story has a narrative arc of sorts: a beginning, a middle, and an end. The protagonists of a rhetorical story are the rhetorics. And, just like the main character in a narrative story, the rhetorics in this story evolve. This book illustrates the ways Dreamer rhetorics changed as they developed over the eight years in which Obama was president. I focus this rhetorical story on the Obama years—2009 through 2016—because during this time Dreamers went from being virtually invisible as a group to being important characters in mainstream political discourse.

Obama's time in office was characterized by growing political support for immigration reform accompanied, paradoxically, by increasing anti-immigrant sentiment. These two seemingly incongruent waves in the sociopolitical climate created a complex rhetorical situation to which Dreamers had to respond. The political landscape seemed more receptive to some sort of amnesty program for Dreamers during the Obama administration. In his two terms in office, Obama and his administration often used immigrant-friendly rhetoric with a growing focus on a path toward legalization for Dreamers. Indeed, Obama called for immigration reform in seven out of his eight State of the Union addresses and advocated for Dreamers in his 2013 inauguration speech. And while he did earn the moniker "Deporter-in-chief" for deporting more than three million people during his tenure, his outward presence was decidedly pro-immigrant. In addition to Obama's immigrant-friendly appearance, Democrats had full control of the US Congress from 2009 to 2011, and of the House of Representatives until 2015. The liberal lean of the executive and legislative branches of government seemed to bode well for Dreamers who had been advocating for the DREAM Act since 2001. Finally, the Obama years also saw an expansion of access to social media and mobile digital technologies, which made it easier for young people to organize and create messages that would reach audiences across the globe. Indeed, the Obama presidency was an auspicious time for the fight for young immigrants' rights.

Notwithstanding the seemingly favorable political circumstances, the country also found itself in the throes of anti-immigrant sentiment that had been exacerbated by September 11 xenophobia. After the attacks of September 11, terrorism and immigration became part of the same conversation so that a generalized brown other was the target of US efforts to bolster simultaneously homeland security and national identity.[17] Panics about the safety of the homeland rationalized practices of national exclusion and surveillance, including the passage of the Patriot Act of 2001, the FISA amendments of 2008, and a slew of similar legislation. While anti-Latinx and anti-immigrant policies and rhetoric have been present throughout US history, the events of September 11 altered anti-immigrant and anti-Latinx sentiments by conflating these with the fear-mongering discourses of the war on terror. Under what ethnic studies scholars Mary Bloodsworth-Lugo and Carmen Lugo-Lugo refer to as "the 9/11 project," undocumented immigrants became the focus of policies and practices that sought to safeguard the nation from foreign threat, and the US-Mexico border became the locus of these efforts despite the fact that none of the perpetrators of the attacks of September 11 had entered the US through its southern border.[18] Dreamers in the Obama era were specifically responding to the offshoot of the "9/11 project," namely, the increased militarization of the US-Mexico border, the further dissemination of war discourses about the US Southwest, and, consequently, the continued criminalization of undocumented people living in the US, particularly of brown and Black undocumented folks.

The Obama era—which cultural critic Cornel West has referred to as "the last gasp of neoliberalism"[19]—also saw the expansion of corporate rights, the growth of social inequality, and the further entrenchment of neoliberal discourses in the US mainstream.[20] Neoliberalism, which Jeffrey St. Onge aptly surmises as "a highly problematic practice of democracy that dismisses collective concerns in favor of individual rights; privatizes key aspects of shared governance like health care, prisons, and potentially Social Security; and warrants hyper-antagonistic debate by positioning individualism and collectivism as fundamentally incompatible, supporting the former while maintaining a steady distrust of the latter,"[21] infiltrated all aspects of life in the US and created an insidious narrative about how US society should function. Within activist movements, neoliberal ideology ushered an important change in focus, from demanding radical change that benefits the collective, to winning individual legal battles and gaining state recognition.

It is no surprise that during this time immigrant activism was vulnerable to neoliberal ideology. The idea that Dreamers could in fact perform the role of good neoliberal US citizens was foundational in the early stages of the Dreamer movement. As many scholars have argued, the rhetorical positioning of Dreamers has often been produced by and reproduced neoliberalism—young, innovative, ready to contribute to the economy through individualized effort, and full of nationalist pride and a belief in the merits of a free market economy through the narrative of the American Dream (indeed, the term "Dreamer" not only denotes a connection to the DREAM Act but also connotes an allusion to the American Dream).[22] The Dreamer rhetorics I outline in this book are reflective of the discursive limits of the neoliberal milieu of the Obama years.

And yet their activism also demonstrates that Dreamers during the Obama years struggled with neoliberalism and the ways in which it reproduces the social stratification that oppresses those most vulnerable. Dreamers voiced their dissatisfaction with the ways neoliberal ideology limited how they were represented in outward-facing media and the arguments they could make to advocate for themselves. So, they often used neoliberalism strategically, highlighting certain aspects of themselves that would appeal to neoliberal US values, while simultaneously challenging neoliberal notions of acceptability, respectability, and individual responsibility. Take, for example, the Tucson, Arizona, sit-in I mention earlier in this chapter. Dreamers sat in McCain's office wearing graduation caps and gowns in an effort to cast themselves as students. In neoliberal discourse it is quite common to cast young adults as students; the student persona not only helps to differentiate them from full adults (who are most often cast as consumers) but also assigns them value in a neoliberal society that sees education as the preferred route to social assimilation. Because the four activists could not cast themselves as consumers (due to their youth and limited purchasing power), they strategically cast themselves as students in order to signify their belonging to the neoliberal nation-state.

While I provide more examples of Dreamers' strategic use of neoliberal rhetoric in the chapters that follow, my argument in this book is that despite arising out of a neoliberal moment, Dreamer rhetorics worked to disrupt neoliberal discursive constraints through activism that troubled the primacy of the nation-state and citizenship, that refused to adhere to respectability politics, that forwarded embodied identity and transnational belonging, and that looked for liberation in community—not solely in legislative action. I show how through their rhetorics, Dreamers transcended neoliberalism to imagine a radically different world. Both *of* and *beyond* neoliberalism, Dreamer rhetorics evidenced a rhetorical flexibility—a "both/and" nature—that allowed Dreamers to vacillate between neoliberal tropes and radical arguments.

I propose that this rhetorical versatility is illustrative of the Dreamer's *nepantla* rhetorics—what Gloria Anzaldúa refers to as "the overlapping space between different perceptions and belief systems."[23] Anzaldúa describes her own *nepantla,* which comes from being pushed and pulled among multiple worlds: the queer, Chicana, feminist world; the Mexican and Indigenous patriarchal worlds; and the white academic world. She writes, "In *nepantla* you are exposed, open to other perspectives, more readily able to access knowledge derived from inner feelings, imaginal states, and other events, and to 'see through' them with mindful holistic awareness."[24] In *nepantla* no way of knowing or living overpowers another, so one's understanding of truth becomes flexible. *Nepantla* is not necessarily a comfortable state: it is a positionality in crisis, a tearing of the self, a wound that does not heal. Anzaldúa writes, "In *nepantla* we undergo the anguish of changing our perspectives and crossing a series of *cruz calles,* junctures, and thresholds, some leading to a different way of relating to people and surroundings and others to the creation of a new world."[25] Indeed, this is precisely what I intend to show in this book: that Dreamer rhetorics can create *mundos nuevos* at the limits of what's possible. Dreamer rhetorics reimagine a new future for undocumented immigrants. *Nepantla* is "the locus of transition" toward new possibilities.[26]

Chicana feminist Chela Sandoval describes this ambivalent position as "differential consciousness," which "permits functioning within, yet beyond, the demands of dominant ideology."[27] As an activist strategy, differential consciousness serves as "tactical weaponry for intervening and shifting currents of power."[28] As I show in this book, Dreamer rhetorics have the flexibility to move among different ideological positions to strategically respond to the present forms of domination. Their differential consciousness stems from their liminal positionality between (at least) two states, cultures, languages, and worlds. They live in the interstices between their countries of birth and the US. And while the country of birth remains important in many Dreamers' lives, often providing their mother tongue and some foundational cultural ties, their day-to-day lives are influenced by and experienced in the US cultural context, language, and value system. This "in-betweenness" allows Dreamers to understand and use rhetoric flexibly to negotiate with the various, often conflicting, audiences in which they have stake. Anzaldúa writes, "Torn between ways, we seek to find some sort of harmony amidst the *remolinos* of multiple and conflictive worldviews."[29] Trying to make sense of the turbulent winds of their lives, Dreamers make new worlds with their rhetorics.

Sarah de los Santos Upton writes that the concept of *nepantla* is not just theorized in classrooms and within academia, but also guides lives, identities, and approaches to activism.[30] Relatedly, I propose that *nepantla* drives Dreamers' approach to rhetoric, identity, community building, and worldmaking. Dreamers develop rhetorics with which to straddle rhetorical borders between neoliberalism and radicality. Because Dreamers are in the transitional space of *nepantla*, pulled between worlds, they have the critical vision to examine and question their and others' practices of worldmaking. Anzaldúa writes, "Seeing from two or more perspectives simultaneously renders those cultures transparent . . . you glimpse the sea in which you've been immersed but to which you were oblivious, no longer seeing the world the way you were enculturated to see it."[31] In *nepantla* the mind becomes more critical and skeptical of truth claims and their implications. In this unstable positionality, Dreamers are able to see through the limitations of neoliberal discourse and the promises of the nation-state, and to produce rhetoric that dares to imagine a world without borders, detention, or deportation.

SITUATING MY STUDY IN THE EXTANT LITERATURE

Dreamer Nation is a book about the activist rhetorics of Latinx Dreamers. Whereas there's been a great deal of work about Dreamers from across the disciplines,[32] this book is one of the first to specifically focus on the form and function of the rhetoric, language, and symbolic practices of undocumented youth. Delving into an underexamined rhetorical field of inquiry, I demonstrate how the Dreamer community and identity were produced rhetorically through the linguistic and embodied symbolic practices of undocumented youth.

My rhetorical approach to Dreamer activism is a unique contribution to the long trajectory of scholarship on the rhetorics of undocumented immigration.[33] As Lisa Flores reminds us, "The symbolic [rhetorical] and political terrains of immigration are never neatly distinct."[34] Consequently, the study of rhetorics of immigration seeks to understand the form and function of meaning making about and by immigrants so that we understand the political implications of their lives. For example, in her study of representations of Mexican immigrants by journalists and politicians in the 1920s and 1930s, Flores finds that early twentieth-century rhetoric about Mexican immigrants reinforced the idea that Mexicans should always be denied a permanent place in the nation. Flores outlines two simultaneous conflicting narratives of the time—the narrative of need, which painted an image of Mexicans as docile peons willing to be exploited, and the narrative of the Mexican problem, which painted Mexicans as dangerous and Mexican immigration as significant and out of control. Flores concludes that despite these conflicting depictions, one idea was clear in the US national conversation—Mexicans "had no permanent place in the national body."[35] Thus, Flores's work implies that rhetorics about Mexican immigrants had a role in shaping the nation, with tremendous consequences that still endure.

Importantly, studies on the rhetorics of immigration have found that the meaning-making practices of immigrants can call into question issues of exclusion, including racialized hierarchies of citizenship and the criminalization of immigration. Indeed, rhetoric scholars have argued that immigrant rhetorics can trouble normative definitions of citizenship and push for new conceptualizations of the nation. Such work illustrates the ways that immigrant rhetorics challenge normative definitions of citizenship yet remain preoccupied with citizenship's supposed liberatory potential. The concept of cultural citizenship, for example, has long been useful in understanding how marginalized Latinxs, including the undocumented, reframe the idea of belonging to claim citizenship for themselves. Cultural citizenship, as defined by Latinx studies scholars William V. Flores and Rina Benmayor, describes the "broad range of activities of everyday life through which Latinos and other groups claim space in society and eventually claim rights."[36] Flores proposes that the struggle to create community and claim rights makes Latinxs into citizens, not necessarily citizens with documentation but citizens as community members who contribute to culture and knowledge, who feel belonging in a certain space, and who deserve rights.[37] In this way Latinxs "deposed the limited concept of citizenship as a restrictive category and replaced it with the much more inclusive notion of 'citizens' as public actors and as 'subjects' of public action."[38] Cultural citizenship—a sort of citizenship without the nation-state at its center—"includes how groups form, define themselves, define their membership, claim rights, and develop a vision of the type of society that they want to live in."[39] The Dreamers that I write about in this book surely engage in such practices of cultural citizenship. Yet, I argue, there is more in their rhetorics—citizenship becomes a site of contestation in which they dare to imagine a radically different world.

In his study of immigrant rhetorics as practices of citizenship, Josue David Cisneros argues that undocumented immigrants create new ways of forming community and perform different ways of being citizens through their activism. The author posits that much immigrant activism creates hybrid performances of citizenship with which to respond to increasing policing and bordering practices that make life more difficult for the undocumented. These hybrid performances of citizenship "[fuse] multiple national traditions, diverse cultures and languages, different political identities, and various constituents."[40]

Contemporary immigrant activist rhetorics, Cisneros explains, reframe belonging partly through a performance of cosmopolitan identity that "[transcends] the nation-state and [roots] belonging in an ethic of hospitality and shared humanity."[41] He proposes that immigrant activist rhetorics disrupt citizenship as monolithic and legitimated by paper.

Similarly, Tania Unzueta and Hinda Seif argue that undocumented immigrants have a role in defining citizenship and belonging. Reflecting on her personal experience as an undocumented activist, Unzueta proposes that the activism of undocumented youth helps them to "contest hegemonic citizenship definitions" and "perform strategies to claim citizenship rights."[42] The alternative vision of belonging that undocumented youth activism can forward presents a more flexible definition of citizenship so that the largest number of undocumented folks can access its rights, including the right to live and work in the US.[43] It is noteworthy that these and other studies of undocumented activist rhetorics see citizenship as performative. If citizenship is not a given for anyone but instead is something one performs, then those without citizenship papers can still claim this social location through its performance. Yet even this more capacious view of citizenship is still tethered to exclusion and oppression. I find Amy L. Brandzel's work on citizenship helpful in thinking about citizenship's limitations. She writes: "Citizenship is, inherently, a normativizing project—a project that regulates and disciplines the social body in order to produce model identities and hegemonic knowledge claims. Moreover, it is a violent exclusionary operation, one that relies upon and reproduces a multipronged, gatekeeping apparatus that works to create, retain, and imbue citizenship with meaning at the direct expense of the noncitizen."[44] In this book I read Dreamer rhetorics for the ways they reproduce citizenship—both traditionally construed and otherwise—as well as for the possibilities these rhetorics present for different frameworks of being-in-belonging.

Extant scholarship on immigrant rhetorics also highlights the ways that Dreamers and other immigrant activists have often relied on neoliberal rhetoric to argue for their inclusion. In their analysis of the Dream Action Portal, an online space helping Dreamers to connect, Claudia Anguiano and Karma Chávez found that Dreamer rhetorics reproduced the myth of the American Dream and employed a rhetoric of exceptionalism to deemphasize Dreamer similarities with other undocumented communities.[45] The authors propose that the very identity of the American Dreamer (written as DREAMer in allusion to the DREAM Act) is bound in the tropes of the US meritocracy and the bootstraps narrative of the immigrant in the land of opportunity. In turn, Unzueta describes the meritocratic standards that undocumented youth reproduce in their antideportation activism, including in the fight against her own deportation. A rhetoric of respectability painted undocumented youth as being "good and deserving," having "strong test scores, civic engagement," "talent," and "hard work."[46] Undocumented youth thus served as examples of the "acceptable heterogeneity"[47] that could be included in the nation-state, in opposition to other immigrants who did not meet these standards. Unzueta claims that Dreamers stuck to such "hegemonic messaging" because of their sense of collective responsibility, meaning that they didn't want to ruin the chances for other undocumented youth to gain documentation by relating their own stories and experiences if they did not measure up to respectability standards.[48] They felt that deviating from the message would hurt everyone's chances of gaining legalization.

Neoliberalism and essentialism were also found to be key elements in rhetorics about undocumented immigrants in the media. Multiple rhetorical studies have focused on the portrayal of immigrants in news and popular media, illustrating how immigration has long been part of the mainstream national conversation. In their seminal book *Shifting Borders: Rhetoric, Immigration and Proposition 187*, Kent Ono and John Sloop found that in media coverage of the issue, neoliberal rhetoric was central in both pro and con arguments.[49] Ono and Sloop explain how immigrant rhetorics in news media relied on neoliberal tropes to both defend and make arguments against Proposition 187.[50] In particular, undocumented immigrants were primarily referred to as "human capital"—either an economic benefit that merited basic social services (e.g., education, health care, food assistance, etc.) or a financial drain that took dollars out of the pockets of US citizens and legal residents.[51]

Such simplistic portrayals of the immigrant experience were also present in the popular media that Stacey Sowards and Richard Pineda analyzed. The authors found that immigrant representations in popular media create sympathetic yet ultimately neoliberal and stereotypical narratives about immigrant life, relying on stories about illegal border crossing and bootstraps narratives, and on themes of individual fault, hard work, and personal responsibility.[52] Even in stories that were meant to present sympathetic portrayals of undocumented Latinxs, the narratives focused on stereotypical experiences in ways that exacerbated anti-immigrant sentiments or created what Sowards and Pineda call "unmotivated sympathy"—sympathy with the individual but without any motivation to call for structural change.[53]

In this book I argue that Dreamer rhetorics in the Obama years were at times caught up in the idea that liberation would come via citizenship and belonging in the nation-state. I also show how citizenship and belonging eventually became less prevalent in the rhetorics, signaling its decreasing priority for Dreamers. As Roberto Gonzales posits, the neoliberal narratives of wasted immigrant talent and exceptional Dreamers failed to persuade congress to pass the DREAM Act.[54] I propose that as Dreamers realized that neoliberal messaging was not benefiting them as a community, their rhetorics moved away from neoliberalism and from the belief in finding freedom in citizenship. Instead, Dreamer rhetorics moved toward more radical, critical, and decolonial modes of engaging their community, the US government, and the media. Indeed, as Veronica Terriquez et al. argue in their work on the undocumented youth movement, Dreamers gravitated toward the concept of intersectionality as it helped them to understand their multiple levels of oppression and to see their intersectional identities as a resource with which to create more inclusive communities, organizations, and activist movements.[55]

Dreamer Nation is unique in its focus on Latinx Dreamers with the goal of expanding what we know about Latinx rhetorics, connect the study of Latinx rhetorics with the study of social movement rhetorics in the US, and advocate for further inclusion of Latinxs in rhetorical criticism. Studying the rhetorics of Latinx Dreamers allows me to explore the rhetorically rich Spanish-language, bilingual, and bicultural activism of this segment of the population. Additionally, the study of Dreamer rhetorics contributes to understandings of Latinx rhetorics by exploring how rhetoric accounts for the ways resistant subjects employ diverse strategies of meaning making—alphanumeric, visual, aural, embodied, etc.—to assert their desired place in society. This understanding of rhetoric—as ideological, political, and tremendously consequential—is quite fitting as a lens with which to view the rhetorical productions of Dreamers, a population that has employed rhetoric to create an identity and a community in order to claim their place in society and argue for social change.

My study is situated within the constellation of scholarship on Latinx rhetorics, which demarcates a subfield of rhetorical studies that explores the rhetorical productions of Latinxs throughout the history of the Americas. Latinx rhetorics emanate from a particular yet diverse positionality. Latinxs are first and foremost hybrid subjects, regardless of the racial mixture in our blood. We navigate many different cultures, as we stubbornly refuse to assimilate completely to the US way of life. We are the subjects of conquest. While we often carry the blood of the Spanish colonizers who raped and pillaged what is now Latin America, we are also descendants of those who were colonized and enslaved—of the Indigenous peoples that first inhabited what we now call America and of the African peoples that were bought and sold in this continent. Many of us are subjects of miscegenation, whether this mixture happened willingly or forcibly. Our presence in the US is complex. We are the immigrant, the colonial subject, the one who has been here the longest, the one who crossed the border, the one whom the border crossed. We have close cultural ties to our birth countries, to the land of our ancestors; or maybe we don't. Either way, we live in a country that simultaneously loves and hates us. Our home is this nation that fetishizes our music, art, and food, that depends on our labor, yet is willing to name us their scapegoat. In this way we are "*ni de aquí, ni de allá*." Inevitably, our rhetorics are interstitial: Latinx rhetorics are hybrid, speak truth to power, aim for social transformation, and articulate the rage and frustration of a people who have been dismissed throughout US history.

As a Latina academic, my intellectual lineage comes from Chicana feminist Gloria Anzaldúa, who was not formally a rhetoric scholar, yet whose ideas have greatly influenced the study of Latinx rhetorics. Anzaldúa's notion of *mestiza* consciousness has been largely adopted by scholars of Latinx rhetorics to explain the form and function of rhetorics that challenge the various oppressions faced by Latinxs in the US,[56] despite the fact that she writes from and about her specific positionality as a queer Tejana Chicana. A *mestiza* consciousness, Anzaldúa proposes, allows subjects to invent from the interstices of languages, nations, cultures, and identities. Epistemologically flexible and tolerant of ambiguity, a *mestiza* consciousness makes possible new identities, texts, and ways of thinking that are "proudly defiant" of the dominant culture.[57] When relating to the study of rhetoric, Anzaldúa's new *mestiza* is a positionality that brings forth innovative oppositional rhetorics from a hybrid nondominant perspective. As Anzaldúa writes in her interview with Andrea Lunsford, "Any mark we make on [this territory] has to be made in relationship to the fact that the [dominant culture] occupies the space."[58] Accordingly, as a diverse population that is positioned as the always already other of the US nation-state, the rhetorical productions of Latinxs often seek to insert non-normative folks into the narrative of the nation through subversive rhetorical interruptions. I contend that Dreamer rhetorics are one of the most important Latinx rhetorical productions of our time and must be positioned alongside the activist histories of Latinxs in the US.

While I write about Latinx Dreamers, I am not claiming that all Dreamers are Latinx. Although a great majority of Dreamers descend from Latin America, they also come from many other countries around the world. The statistical significance of Latinx Dreamers is only part of the reason why this book features only the rhetorics of Latinx Dreamers. An important reason for limiting my scope to Latinx Dreamers is that the US popular imagination sees undocumented immigrants as always already Latinx. Even second- and third-generation

Latinxs are questioned about their belonging. I focus on the rhetorics of Latinx Dreamers to analyze how they respond not only to the marginalization and oppression of Latinx undocumented folks but also to the exclusion and marginalization of *all* Latinx folks—particularly those with brown or black skin. Latinx Dreamers are not just fighting for themselves: they fight for all of us. During the Obama era, Latinx Dreamers were at the forefront of the Dreamer movement. Their bodies were the most visible. Their lives were most at risk. This book recognizes the magnificent effort of Latinx Dreamers by attending to their rhetorical choices.

WHO ARE THE DREAMERS?

Just like the label "Latinx" holds within it a diversity of people and experiences, the label "Dreamer" also describes a complex and diverse population. Even though the moniker "Dreamer" is widely used in popular discourse to describe undocumented youth at large, I must specifically explain who it is that I am referring to when I use the term "Dreamer" and why I've chosen to use this term despite its neoliberal baggage.

As I'm using it in this book, the Dreamers are a group of young people, older than twelve but younger than thirty years of age, who arrived in the US during their childhoods and have been living here ever since. Many Dreamers have resided in the US for most of their lives and have never returned to their birth countries because they lack the paperwork for re-entry into the US. They attended US schools, speak English, and are familiar with the country's cultural norms and values. Dreamers also remain culturally connected to their countries of origin. While a large majority of those who could be considered Dreamers were born in Mexico, they come from many countries around the world and represent difference races, ethnicities, genders, sexual orientations, ages, abilities, and experiences.[59]

Despite their differences, their similar experiences with the immigration system unites them. Without proper documentation, they have little to no access to affordable college education or high-paying jobs. Their experiences of exclusion from mainstream US society guided their creation of the Dreamer community and forced them to develop a political consciousness. As Dreamers started talking to other similarly situated undocumented young people in meetings and social media forums, they became aware of the shared aspects of their lived experiences and fired up to do something to change them.[60] When I use the word "Dreamer" in this book, I am specifically referring to the politicized segment of this community, to those who engage in activism whether in the streets, in writing, or through their art. The label "Dreamer" for me reflects how this community of young people developed a public presence and a clear voice in the public sphere, rather than retreating into the shadows as would be the expectation in contexts of state hostility.[61] The Dreamer is an activist, even though their cause has evolved over time.

As I mentioned previously, the Dreamers as a group first came to the US political scene in support of the DREAM Act. The DREAM Act was introduced in the Senate by Senators Dick Durbin of Illinois and Orrin Hatch of Utah on August 1, 2001, as a way to provide legal relief for undocumented young people who were brought into the US by their parents as children. Although the DREAM Act has changed since its initial drafting, the primary elements include permanent resident status and, in the more ambitious versions, a pathway to citizenship for undocumented immigrants who meet the following conditions: "they entered the country before the age of 16; they have lived continuously in the US for five years or more; they have 'good moral character'; they graduated from a US high school or received a GED; and they have been accepted to a 4-year university or completed 2 years of military service."[62] More than two decades later, this legislation is still an important part of the ways Dreamers are positioned in popular discourse. While none of its provisions have become law, the DREAM Act today symbolizes the hope of legal status for undocumented young people and unites many in the undocumented youth community under a common goal.

During their DREAM Act activism, Dreamers argued for their inclusion in the US civic body through what Walter Nicholls calls "niche openings," "legal, economic, and moral ambiguities that question the extent to which *all* undocumented immigrants should be considered fully illegal."[63] The particular niche opening that Dreamers took advantage of was located at the intersection of two changes in the ways the country viewed undocumented immigration in the late 1990s. The first was the result of overburdened immigration enforcement agencies. With limited resources, immigration enforcement agencies wanted to be able to triage immigration cases by prioritizing deportation of immigrants who were seen as more of a threat to public safety or who represented a more egregious disregard for the rule of law. Cases of lower priority, such as those of undocumented students who were for the most part culturally assimilated, could be given temporary reprieve from deportation on humanitarian grounds.[64] The second change taking place had less to do with the US government and more to do with a change of perspective in the US public. As Nicholls describes, during the late 1990s, segments of the population were starting to question whether all undocumented immigrants were created equal. The passage of the Illegal Immigration Reform and Immigrant

Responsibility Act of 1996 (IIRIRA) brought harsh new penalties for undocumented entry into the US as well as restrictions on the sorts of public assistance for which undocumented folks could apply. Included in this act were restrictions on in-state tuition for undocumented applicants at public universities. As stories of undocumented students unable to access higher education began to surface, the idea that perhaps not all undocumented immigrants should be treated with equal severity started gaining traction.[65] These two changes in the immigration climate created a niche opening for Dreamers. As immigration agencies sought to triage enforcement, why not deprioritize the deportation of undocumented students, a population with which the nation was beginning to sympathize?

The first stories about Dreamers that made it to mainstream US media used essentialist narratives to present Dreamers as a coherent group that could fit the available niche opening. The rhetorical goal was to show that Dreamers were different from other undocumented immigrants and therefore should be treated differently. Gayatri Chakravorty Spivak has referred to this rhetorical tactic as strategic essentialism.[66] Spivak implies that it is counterproductive to completely reject essentialism, as it occludes the possibility of collective action for justice.[67] In other words, if oppressed peoples do not cohere around a set of supposedly shared characteristics, albeit generalizations and universalizations, how can they move forward with the work of dismantling the oppressor? The public narrative about Dreamers relied on exceptionalism to appeal to a conservative US mainstream. First, Dreamers were shown to be quintessentially US American. During the initial support of the DREAM Act, immigrant rights organizations played up stories that showed Dreamers behaving like average young people in the US. They were cheerleaders and football players. They were the girl and boy next door. Secondly, Dreamers were also supposed to be the "best and brightest" of their generation. High school valedictorians and honor students were prominently featured in news stories about the Dreamers. Finally, it was emphasized that Dreamers had immigrated to the US "through no fault of their own." By reminding the US public that it was the Dreamers' parents who had crossed the border illegally, Dreamers could be remade innocent. These three traits initially defined Dreamer identity. However, as the Dreamers' mainstream narrative began to spread, there were disagreements in the group about the long-term benefits of portraying Dreamers in this way. Indeed, some Dreamers felt that capitalizing on the binary logic that pits "good immigrants" against "bad ones" only served to divide the undocumented community. Although Dreamers initially organized in the fight for their own legalization, this moment was but a catalyst for their continued political mobilization under broader goals of immigrant justice. As journalist Eileen Truax eloquently describes it, "Theirs is a struggle for civil rights, for recognition of one's personal dignity, and for one's place in the world."[68] Dreamers want the country to recognize undocumented immigrants as human beings with unalienable rights.

Dreamers have more recently fought for wide-ranging immigrant justice through intersectional appeals that recognize the complexity and diversity of the undocumented population. These appeals no longer just look out for those who best fit US society but instead advocate for the most vulnerable—for queer and trans undocumented folks who face disproportionate rates of violence, for unaccompanied minors, for asylum seekers fleeing violence. Dreamers have come together under new labels that reflect their intersectionality. For example, the coalitional term "undocuqueer" speaks to specific experiences at the intersection of being undocumented *and* queer, and seeks to recognize the central role queer BIPOC take in the push for social change.[69] The label "undocuqueer" also shows how Dreamer activism has expanded to include cultural critique as it challenges the homonormative narrative of cis-gendered whiteness.[70] While some young activists who identify as undocuqueer may or may not identify as Dreamers, I include them when I speak about Dreamers in an effort to map out the ways the undocumented youth movement has evolved over time.

The term "Dreamer" tracks the astounding history of activism that this population has achieved in a relatively short period of time. Yet, for some young activists, the label harks back to an earlier stage of the movement, a stage that some activists are happy to move beyond. While the word is now easily associated with undocumented young people, the moniker was strategically given to undocumented youth by the professional immigrant rights organizations that were working toward passage of the DREAM Act.[71] Because the term does not have grassroots origin, it is in a way antithetical to the bottom-up approach to activism that Dreamers adopted during the Obama era. After 2010 Dreamers sought to take control over the ways they were represented to the US public and to the immigrant community. Consequently, the "Dreamer" moniker is not universally adopted by undocumented youth, and some of them outright reject it.[72] In my time researching Dreamer rhetoric, I have pondered whether another label may be more appropriate. Instead of a Dreamer whose driving force is internal and individual (dreaming, after all, is a solitary action), perhaps the image associated with this community should reflect the strong coalitions these young activists have built and the fearlessness with which they have spoken truth to power. Words are important, and there is much room for revision here. I choose to use the term "Dreamer" in this book, aware of its limitations.

ABOUT MY METHODS

I draw on the primary method of my discipline: rhetorical analysis. Rather than searching for the ways rhetors find the available means of persuasion, I borrow from Victor Villanueva's take on rhetorical analysis. He writes: "There is no necessary textual artifact that undergoes analysis in this brand of rhetorical criticism, this brand of rhetorical analysis; rather we look to the ways in which ideology is present in the language, forming tropes that surround us."[73] In this book I analyze the ways Dreamer rhetoric makes meaning, explore how this rhetoric is a product of a particular sociohistorical context, and discuss the ways its impact reverberates beyond the intended effects of its creators. Through my analysis of Dreamer rhetorics, I demonstrate how every rhetorical choice is largely conscripted by the discursive limits of the moment.[74] When Dreamers chose to highlight a particular narrative, they were doing so, at least in part, in accordance with discursive forces well beyond their control or even beyond their ken. Similarly, the effects of that rhetorical choice will span further than they ever imagined.

My approach to rhetorical analysis also considers the material and cultural aspects of multimodal composition. As Sara Alvarez et al. argue, the process of composing "should not be separated from bodies. This includes the bodies of composers and it includes the bodies of consumers, readers, and viewers."[75] The bodily implications of rhetoric are particularly relevant for the study of social movements, as activists often put their bodies on the line to make a point. While many of the texts that I analyze in this book were circulated digitally, they are all directly connected to Dreamer actions. In this way Dreamers' rhetorical choices can never be considered outside of the connection to their bodies, their safety, and their mobility. In my analysis I attend to the connections between Dreamer rhetorics and Dreamer lives. Whether videos created while in an immigrant detention center or art condemning anti-immigrant political discourse, Dreamer activist texts work to improve their ability to work, study, eat, play, and perform other behaviors necessary for life to thrive in this country.

Dreamer Nation pushes the boundaries not only of how we see undocumented Latinxs in the US but also of how we understand the rhetorics of vulnerable minoritized populations. Throughout this book I draw on relevant critical cultural theories, primarily from feminists of color, to propose a re/vision of the form and function of Dreamer rhetorics. While Dreamer rhetorics have often been criticized for adhering too closely to neoliberal models of acceptability, I read Dreamer rhetorics through a feminist-of-color lens to expose the radical and revolutionary undercurrents in the Dreamers' rhetorical choices. Even in texts that rely on US exceptionalism to argue for immigrant rights, the rhetorics hide a radical message that can be decoded only when read alongside the theories and ideas of communities of color. This sort of rhetorical analysis is akin to what Adela Licona describes as a practice of "reading between the lines" to understand the layers of meaning hidden within the rhetorics.[76] This book also acknowledges that scholars of rhetoric must continue to cross disciplinary boundaries in order to help fill the gaps in our knowledge and theorizing. While the analysis of the minoritized rhetorics of BIPOC has a rich history, with Jacqueline Jones Royster, Victor Villanueva, Ellen Cushman, and Jaime Mejía among those who paved the way, we still have a long trek ahead inasmuch as we see diversifying and complicating the study of rhetoric as our goal. This book crosses disciplinary lines to infuse rhetorical analysis with the knowledges of communities of color, yet it remains grounded in the foundational belief that rhetoric is a practice of meaning making with the power to change the world.

THE DREAMERS' RHETORICAL STORY: CHAPTER BREAKDOWN

The chapters in this book relate moments in Dreamer activism and the texts—written, recorded, performed—that helped construct those moments. Each chapter presents a different rhetorical situation within the US "crisis" of migration and the rhetoric that Dreamers used to respond to it. This book thereby shows the diversity of Dreamer rhetoric. Throughout the Obama years, Dreamers had to learn from and adapt to their ongoing encounters with legislators and mainstream audiences. The pages that follow illustrate the rhetorical savvy of young Dreamers, the innovative ways in which they confronted and challenged the dehumanization of undocumented immigrants in the US, and the powerful ways in which they used rhetoric to create and maintain their community.

The book is organized chronologically, although not every year in Obama's eight-year tenure is covered. I begin with the 2010 effort to pass the DREAM Act through the US Congress. Illinois senator Dick Durbin and eight other members of Congress had introduced a new version of the DREAM Act that had managed to pass the house. DREAM Act activists and supporters had learned their lessons in 2007 when, despite the support from a majority of Senators, the bill was killed via a filibuster that included eight Democrats. On July 20, 2010, undocumented youth held sit-ins in Washington, DC, in order to push senators to vote for the DREAM Act. The sit-ins brought new attention to the Dreamer movement, showing the US mainstream that these young people were in the fight of their lives. Expectedly, their activism also received criticism, from conservative pundits for sure, but also from the organizations that had previously led the fight for immigrant rights. On September 21, 2010, Dreamer activists responded to the criticism and outlined their argument in support of the DREAM Act in an online essay cowritten by four young Dreamers. The essay was angry and bold. It showed Dreamer frustration at being rejected not only by the mainstream US but also by their own communities in their efforts to make better lives for themselves.

Chapter 1 takes up this Dreamer letter; that year's Dreamer hunger strikes in New York City, Los Angeles, and San Antonio; and the first Coming Out of the Shadows rally in Chicago, to analyze how Dreamers were situating themselves in those early years. Of course, Dreamer activism in support of the DREAM Act had been going on long before 2010. However, I propose that 2010 marked the beginning of a new phase of Dreamer rhetorics that presented a both/and approach to persuasion. Chapter 1 analyzes how the events of 2010 grounded Dreamer rhetoric on a belief in the rule of law (e.g., their support for the DREAM Act and their hope for legislative action) yet also evidenced a dissenting rhetoric and an irreverent spirit that would help push Dreamer rhetorics beyond its assimilationist tendencies.

In chapter 2 I analyze a moment of activism that is indicative of the rhetorical move away from appeals to legislative action. On July 22, 2013, a youth-led grassroots activist network, the National Immigrant Youth Alliance (NIYA), led nine Dreamers to the US-Mexico border to protest the family separation caused by deportation in what became known as the Dream 9 action. Almost a year after Obama created DACA, undocumented young people continued to live lives of uncertainty. While some of them were able to benefit from deferred deportation due to DACA, their parents were still being detained and deported at very high rates. In addition some young people who had left the US just before DACA was enacted were looking for ways to return to the US and take advantage of this new program. With a set of actions titled the Bring Them Home campaign, NIYA sought to argue that it was in the interest of the US to recognize the Dreamers' place in the nation-state. While this rhetoric entailed rhetorical choices that highlighted Dreamers' affective citizenship and national belonging,[77] chapter 2 argues that the Bring Them Home Campaign also posited an argument for the freedom of movement, a denouncement of dehumanizing immigrant detention practices, and a critique of citizenship.

Continuing my analysis of the Bring Them Home campaign, chapter 3 analyzes the rhetoric surrounding the Reforma 150 action, the third and final major action of Bring Them Home. Unlike the previous actions of the Bring Them Home campaign, Reforma 150 mobilized immigrants of various ages and backgrounds to petition for reentry into the US as asylum seekers. Accordingly, Dreamer activists had to shift their strategy and rhetorical tactics to fit this new constituency. In this chapter I focus specifically on how gender played out in the rhetorics of Reforma 150. With a focus on mothers and children, Reforma 150 took advantage of mainstream associations of motherhood with virtue to present undocumented immigrant mothers as acceptable to the nation. I argue, however, that there is also a decolonial, revolutionary, and queer undercurrent in the rhetorics of Reforma 150—a whisper of dissent that becomes apparent when the rhetorics are read through a women of color feminist lens. Accordingly, in this chapter I draw on women of color and queer women of color feminisms to outline how the theme of motherhood in the rhetorics of Reforma 150 connotes the forms of resistance that undocumented women must engage in to survive. The stories of immigrant mothers who were separated from their children by deportation and self-deportation highlight the ways in which, for undocumented women, motherwork[78] incorporates the struggle against state forces that seek to separate them from their families.

As Dreamer rhetorics continued to evolve, so did representations of undocumented youth. Dreamers began to more openly express their disdain for the Dreamer label and its heteronormative connotations. The label/identity "undocuqueer" gained a more central place in the movement for immigrant rights. Chapter 4 examines undocuqueer rhetorics and focuses on how undocuqueer youth drew on ideas of the erotic, desire, and love to forward their activism. I first analyze the video "UndocuQueer Manifesto" created by the Queer Undocumented Immigrant Project. This text uses bilingual and bicultural terms and concepts to constitute a rhetoric of undocuqueer love with the goal of social transformation and liberation for queer and trans undocumented youth. The "UndocuQueer Manifesto" demonstrates the remnants of hope during the Obama years—the hope that through love, acceptance, and community the US would learn to welcome and perhaps even to love undocuqueer youth. Contrastingly, the chapter then turns to the "artivism"[79] of undocuqueer graphic artist Julio Salgado to outline the ways that it draws on ideas of desire and the erotic to express a rhetoric of radical undocuqueer pleasure. As the Obama years waned, undocuqueer rhetorics began to reject the structures of inequity that produce the nation instead of arguing for love and acceptance within them. Through my analysis of Salgado's artivism, I demonstrate how undocuqueer rhetorics opened up the possibilities to express a refusal to engage in appeals for belonging. Chapter 4 argues that Salgado's 2016 artwork directly challenged the undocumented community to rethink their investment in the nation, national borders, and notions of acceptability. This rhetoric of radical undocuqueer pleasure portends the grim times around the corner for undocumented immigrants: the election of Donald Trump as US president, a candidate who ran largely on an anti-immigrant platform.

This book ends by looking to the possibilities of Dreamer rhetoric in challenging continuing anti-immigrant sentiments and politics in the US. The concluding chapter contextualizes some of the new obstacles that Dreamers experienced with the election of Trump and considers the lessons learned from activism in the Obama years. From the push for a "clean DREAM Act," to protests against "tender age" immigrant detention camps, Dreamers remained active during the Trump presidency, even as they were (re)made vulnerable through Trump's attacks on DACA. I ask, What rhetorical lessons can be gleaned from Dreamer activism in the Obama years? This chapter synthesizes the characteristics of Dreamer rhetorics and looks to the new rhetorical paths that grew out of this movement. In moments of darkness, even a small flame can be blinding. Dreamers have been the fire at the heart of some of the most important activist moments of the twenty-first-century US. Their flame will not be extinguished.

1

Dreamers' *Nepantla* Rhetorics and the Push for the DREAM Act of 2010

> *"We are undocumented youth activists and we refuse to be silent any longer."*
>
> —Neidi Dominguez Zamorano et al. "DREAM Activists: Rejecting the Passivity of the Nonprofit, Industrial Complex"

On September 21, 2010, undocumented activists Neidi Dominguez Zamorano, Jonathan Perez, Jorge Gutierrez, and Nancy Mesa published an essay titled "DREAM Activists: Rejecting the Passivity of the Nonprofit Industrial Complex" in the independent news website TruthOut.org (hereafter referred to as "the TruthOut letter") that presented the status of the Dreamer movement, their reasons for supporting the DREAM Act, and their frustration at the current mechanisms of mainstream immigrant rights activism. Connecting themselves to the Civil Rights Movement through an allusion to Martin Luther King Jr.'s "Letter from Birmingham Jail," the Dreamers stated: "Youth DREAM Act activists stopped waiting. We organized ourselves and created our own strategy, used new tactics and we rejected the passivity of the non-profit industrial complex. At a moment when hope seemed scarce, we forged new networks of solidarity. We declared ourselves UNDOCUMENTED AND UNAFRAID!"[1]

The goal of the letter, a manifesto of sorts, was largely to explain and defend the Dreamers' position as an independent movement by and for undocumented youth. Importantly, they called out the criticism they had received, not only from conservatives whom they call "racist, sexist, and homophobic" but also from liberals and progressives: "The nonprofits, think tanks, the privileged and self-righteous activists who comprise the social justice elite have had their hand in stopping the DREAM Act from being introduced, and at times, they have been more vicious than the right. WE DO NOT WANT IMMIGRATION RIGHTS 'ADVOCATES' SPEAKING FOR US ANY LONGER. WE DEMAND THE RIGHT TO REPRESENT OURSELVES!"[2]

The publication of this letter came as Dreamers had been ramping up activism in an effort to pass the 2010 DREAM Act. The letter illustrates the rhetorical exigencies these Dreamer activists were facing as another possible vote on legislation that would change their lives loomed near. Even though 2010 seemed as auspicious a time as any for the passage of the DREAM Act, Dreamers had learned their lesson from their experiences in 2007 when the act had been narrowly defeated in the Senate. After this defeat the Dreamers displayed distrust for the traditional mechanisms for legislative change (e.g., mainstream activist organizations and their relationships with policy makers). The TruthOut letter presented a new voice for Dreamers as independent from the mainstream immigration rights movement and much more fierce. They wrote, "We are building the DREAM Movement action-by-action, city-by-city, and campus-by-campus. . . . Repeatedly, undocumented youth have risked the threat of physical violence, incarceration, and deportation by engaging in acts of non-violent direct action in order to push the immigrant rights movement forward."[3]

At this time, Dreamers were also facing the usual opposition to the DREAM Act—that it was an amnesty program, that it was too broad and opened up legalization for undocumented criminals, that it benefited those who had not obeyed the law and disadvantaged those who were "waiting in line" for legal immigration. This opposition was being fueled not only by the usual Fox News talking heads but also by a white paper titled "Ten Things You Need to Know About S.3827, the DREAM Act" being circulated in Congress by Alabama senator Jeff Sessions. Among other criticisms of the DREAM Act, "Ten Things" claimed that the bill would legalize "criminal aliens"; take money from "hard-working, law-abiding Americans" by providing Dreamers access to in-state tuition at public universities, federal student loans, and federal work-study programs; and lead to an increase in immigration through family sponsoring programs.[4]

In this difficult political context, Dreamers were not taking any support for the DREAM Act for granted. Even while they supported what they describe as a "less-than-perfect piece of legislation," Dreamers mobilized their activist energy and creativity to do whatever it took to give the DREAM Act a fighting chance. In this chapter I begin to tell the rhetorical story of the

Dreamer movement by exploring the activist rhetoric in the push for the 2010 DREAM Act. The pages that follow assert that Dreamers used rhetoric that was risky, forceful, and even radical in their support of a bill that reproduces the neoliberal nation-state. I argue that the activism of 2010 in support of the DREAM Act illustrates the Dreamers' *nepantla* rhetorics: their ability to be *of* neoliberalism and still push against it to fight for a different world. I do this by analyzing three different yet related moments of activism: the aforementioned TruthOut letter; the Dreamer hunger strikes in California, New York, and Texas; and that year's Coming Out of the Shadows (COTS) rally in Chicago.

In the TruthOut letter, Dreamers confronted neoliberalism in the same text and often in the very same sentence in which they conceded its power over their lives. Their support for the DREAM Act despite its military option demonstrated how Dreamers argued for government recognition and legalization while simultaneously contributing to and critiquing US militarism. Thus, the TruthOut letter reminds us that *nepantla* is not always an ambivalent position. While ambivalence can be construed as uncertainty or indecisiveness, *nepantla* is a position that confidently acknowledges the limitations and possibilities on all sides.[5] Even though Dreamer rhetorics often reproduced neoliberal tropes of the nation, particularly those that forwarded the DREAM Act as solution for Dreamers' precarity, their activism also made room for critique of the government's treatment of undocumented folks, the power of the deportation regime,[6] and the congressional failure to help Dreamers achieve livable lives.

SOCIAL MOVEMENTS AND ACTIVIST MOMENTS

In this chapter I tell the rhetorical story of Dreamer activism in 2010. The activist moments that make up this chapter were all part of the activism in support of the 2010 DREAM Act. Each of these moments presents a different point in the constellation that was the Dreamer movement during that particular year.

My methods in this book illustrate how the rhetorical story of a social movement is told through an analysis of moments. What I mean is that in telling the Dreamers' rhetorical story I don't aim to be comprehensive. I do not see it as necessary (or possible) to analyze every moment of activism in order to tell the Dreamers' rhetorical story. Perhaps this is because there is not a single story but multiple stories. It is my goal in this book to tell one of these stories. To do this I present a deep look at some activist moments, not a wide look at the whole of the Dreamer movement.

I propose, therefore, that social movements can be understood as collections of activist moments—specific instances of action, particular texts, particular communications, etc. Activist moments are themselves made up of a constellation of interrelated texts, including street protests, manifestos, social media, and/or artivism. Therefore, a social movement is much more than a single protest or even a group of protests. It is a constellation of "texts" that work together to express the values, priorities, and goals of a movement. I draw inspiration here from Karma Chávez and her work on coalitional moments. In her influential monograph *Queer Migration Politics: Activist Rhetoric and Coalitional Possibilities*, Chávez examines the inner workings of what she terms "coalitional moments." She writes, "A coalitional moment occurs when political issues coincide or merge in the public sphere in ways that create space to reenvision and potentially reconstruct rhetorical imaginaries."[7] I find her treatment of the concept of a "moment" particularly useful: "A moment possesses both temporal and spatial qualities, and the specific nature of the spatial dimension to a moment implies a coming together or *connection* whereby there is a possibility for change."[8] An activist moment takes place in a particular moment in time, but it also reflects the trajectories of time that it took to get there and the connection of those trajectories. An activist moment is not just a single moment in time but the intersection of many moments in time that led to this particular *coyuntura*.

According to the Real Academia Española, a *coyuntura* is defined as the "*combinación de factores y circunstancias que se presentan en un momento determinado*" (combination of factors and circumstances that make themselves visible at a particular moment).[9] I use the word *coyuntura* here to reflect the web of events, actions, texts, etc. that come together at any particular activist moment. In her work Chávez describes something similar: "Moments taken this way reveal that time's passage and the meaning assigned to time need not reflect normative assumptions."[10] In my work a *conyuntura* allows me to see and acknowledge the many paths that converge in a particular activist moment. A moment, in this way, is not a singular point but instead looks like as asterisk: each line of the asterisk representing a line in time/space that converges in an activist moment. Moments, as Chávez writes, also have a spatial component that implies a coming together with the goal of change. The *coyuntura* of an activist moment takes place *somewhere*—whether in physical or digital space—and involves a collection of *someones*. This sort of coming together makes it possible to see the coalitional aspects of activism, the long-running labor that occurs before and after any particular activist strategy, and the multiplicity of rhetorical strategies, texts, and meanings that shape any one moment.

NEPANTLA IN THE DREAMERS' TRUTHOUT LETTER

When the TruthOut letter was published, the Dreamers were preparing for the final push of the DREAM Act. The DREAM Act of 2010 had been incorporated as an amendment to the National Defense Authorization Act; the logic was that the DREAM Act's military option (the provision that in lieu of higher education, Dreamers could qualify for benefits if they served in the military) made this piece of legislation crucial to the operation of the US armed forces. Unsurprisingly, the DREAM Act's military option had drawn critique from activist and ally communities, especially in a time of increasing US involvement in overseas armed conflicts. In a short essay in the journal *Latino Studies*, Chicano studies scholar Jorge Mariscal condemns the military option as benefiting desperate military recruiters at the expense of the lives and safety of undocumented youth. He asks, "Won't the vast majority of undocumented youth find the college path simply too difficult and the military path deceptively simple? How many . . . will end up as cannon fodder in the next unnecessary war?"[11]

The TruthOut letter helps Dreamers to contextualize their position in support of the DREAM Act, despite its military option, and to defend their prerogative for backing it. Yet their position was not one of uncritical support. The ways they defend their support for the DREAM Act illustrate their complex and informed stance on the issue. The authors write: "It has been argued that the military option will funnel thousands of young people into the military. We disagree with this argument. Military recruitment in our communities will continue whether the DREAM Act passes or not. In 2007, the DREAM Act did not pass, but the military recruitment in communities of color continued unabated."[12] With these words they outright reject the idea that the DREAM Act's military option will create military recruitment and enlistment practices that aren't already happening. Their position accepts the tempting incentive of trading military service for a green card and a pathway to citizenship (indeed, the Migration Policy Institute estimated in 2010 that approximately 31,000 DREAM Act beneficiaries would take advantage of the military option[13]). However, in the same sentence authors also call out what they see as disproportionate recruitment of poor communities of color by the US military.

Furthermore, the authors also show that they are aware of how politically persuasive the military option can be, especially in an era of continued military conflict. They write, "Moreover, who in this current anti-immigrant climate would step forward to sponsor a reconfigured DREAM Act without a military option? A military option could easily be introduced as a stand-alone bill. Let's be honest. We all know that the Democratic Party refuses to be painted as 'unpatriotic,' especially with mid-term congressional races looming. A DREAM Act shorn of its military option, sadly, is an impossible proposition."[14] Here, Dreamers challenge the idea that a perfect DREAM Act, one that doesn't require undocumented youth to adhere to neoliberal ideas of their value (as students or as members of the military) is practically impossible. And even though their tone sounds forceful, their statement evidences their perception of the DREAM Act as a negotiation with the US government. The authors acknowledge that they need to take advantage of the convergence of their interests and those of the Pentagon and the Democratic Party.[15] I contend that Dreamers see their own lives as directly connected to the interests of white US citizens. In this text Dreamer rhetorics were not trying to create a moral crisis that would persuade Congress to pass the DREAM Act. Their rhetorics show their recognition that Dreamers are an asset to the US government, not just in the cultural and economic sense but also as bodies to fight wars.

Of course this sort of perspective is precisely why other activists, allies, and scholars criticized the Dreamers in the run up to the 2010 vote on the DREAM Act. Indeed, the idea that equal rights should be exchanged for military service is greatly problematic. As sociologist Tamara Nopper writes in the radical queer collection *Against Equality: Don't Ask to Fight Their Wars*, "The inclusion of more gays and lesbians and/or undocumented immigrant youth in the U.S. military is not an ethical project given that both gestures are willing to have our communities serve as mercenaries in exchange for certain rights, some of which are never fully guaranteed in a homophobic and white supremacist country. Nor is it pragmatic. By supporting the diversification of the U.S. military we undermine radical democratic possibilities by giving the military state more people, many of whom will ultimately die in combat or develop PTSD and health issues and/or continue nurturing long-term relationships with the U.S. military, including a political affinity with its culture and goals."[16] Nopper contends that the DREAM Act not only promises rights in exchange for risk to life and limb but also threatens progressive goals of radical democracy by propagating militaristic ideologies.

Nevertheless, I don't read Dreamers' stance on the DREAM Act's military option as uncritical or desiring to blindly reproduce military culture and values. The TruthOut letter does not forward a romanticized story of military service. There is no mention of patriotism or of wanting to spread the US value system across the globe. Instead, the authors' stance in support of the military option is a practical quid pro quo. They know that a white dominant and nativist society will not grant them legalization if Dreamers don't first offer a sacrifice. That is why the support for the military option in the letter comes with a critique of military recruitment and a reminder that "many of the DREAMers have organized in high schools and universities against military recruitment and done anti-military recruitment education with thousands of women and youth of color."[17] This is how Dreamer rhetorics can be neoliberal and radical at the same time. Their adoption of a neoliberal solution to the problem of undocumented youth acknowledges their limited possibilities in a neoliberal US society. They ask, "So should we wait until there are no more wars? Should we wait until our public school systems are perfect? Should we wait until a perfect politician introduces the perfect bill?"[18] With these sarcastic rhetorical questions, the authors use *nepantla* rhetorics to critique the failures of US society while asking for space for themselves inside it.

I momentarily pause my analysis here to outline how I understand the word "radical" in this book. A radical social movement demands change at the core of society. In the process of analyzing Dreamer rhetorics, I often wonder whether a movement can be called radical if it moves toward neoliberalism. My main argument in this book is that Dreamer rhetorics are both radical and otherwise. I come to this conclusion by understanding Dreamer rhetorics as having radical threads. There are times when Dreamers are making radical arguments that challenge the foundational core of the US nation-state. Then there are times when they are reproducing the status quo. Therefore, I can't claim that the Dreamer movement is radical. But Dreamer rhetorics, at their best, are radical indeed.

In the letter's closing, the authors' emphasize their radical critique of US society and repeat their support for the DREAM Act. They write, "We must look to the women and men in the DREAM movement, undocumented queer and transgender young activists with emerging ideologies that challenge the capitalist, heterosexual and misogynistic systems here in the United States. . . . We must fiercely challenge privilege and oppression, whether located among allies or the opposition. . . . Our fight is for the legalization of all people, and *the DREAM Act is a vehicle towards that goal*."[19] These statements are a fascinating illustration of the rhetorical versatility of Dreamer rhetorics. With the TruthOut letter, Dreamers affirm their willingness to capitulate to neoliberal priorities through their support of the DREAM Act. Yet in these few sentences they also align themselves with those who challenge oppressive systems in the US—the very systems buttressed by neoliberal values and practices.

Dreamer rhetorics of 2010, however, also betray naiveté on the part of the Dreamers. Although the DREAM Act is a piecemeal approach to immigration reform, the authors of the TruthOut letter see it as a path toward freedom for all undocumented folks. Their belief that the DREAM Act would eventually lead to widespread immigrant legalization drives the activism of 2010. It illustrates their ultimate belief that the legislative channels of social change are willing to be swayed.

NEOLIBERALISM AND RHETORICAL EXTORTION: DREAMER HUNGER STRIKES OF 2010

The hunger strikes that took place around the country that year reflected the Dreamers' belief in the American Dream and the possibility of social change through legislative action. In a demonstration of *nepantla,* these strikes also raised the stakes of the activism of 2010 by engaging in the "weaponization of life"[20] to create a moment of rhetorical extortion. In the hunger strikes, Dreamers wielded their lives, health, and well-being to demand support for the DREAM Act, in essence creating a life-or-death hostage situation to support legislation that "retrofits" Dreamers into "a homogeneous culture and social order that maintains their unequal position in society."[21]

My reading of the Dreamer hunger strikes of 2010 illustrates the moment of "rhetorical extortion" in which Dreamers used implied threats to demand support for the DREAM Act. While the Dreamers participating in the hunger strikes did not intend to die for the cause, many of them experienced the illness and physical discomfort that comes from prolonged hunger. Their sacrificed corporeal integrity sought to force the hand of legislators by implying that any harm to the Dreamers' well-being would be, in essence, a result of legislative inaction. By targeting specific legislators, the Dreamers' use of rhetorical extortion became much more cutting: a (very) small group of legislators were put under the spotlight so that their support for the DREAM Act, or lack thereof, would be directly connected to the deteriorating well-being of the young hunger strikers.

I propose that this moment of rhetorical extortion had two rhetorical effects in addition to asking for DREAM Act support. First, the hunger strikes waged a critique of the US's power over Dreamers' lives. The hunger strikes emphasized the power differential between the Dreamers and the US government. Dreamers put their corporeal well-being in the hands of a targeted group of legislators and thus reminded their audiences that Dreamer lives are always subject to the whims of government. Second, the strikes were an affirmation of the Dreamers' humanity. Their embodiment of the pain and vulnerability suffered in hunger reminds audiences that the Dreamers are human and should be treated as such. This radical activist strategy condemns the dehumanization of undocumented youth and demands that the lives of Dreamers be given value.

However, the hunger strikes were also framed through neoliberal discourses of deservability, with participants alluding to the idea that because they had been obedient neoliberal subjects thus far, they deserved a path to citizenship via the DREAM Act. The themes of hard work, education, contribution, and the American Dream were present in much of the media coverage of the hunger strikes. Such rhetoric helped Dreamers to position themselves on a neoliberal measure of "Americanness" that seeks to persuade audiences that Dreamers are, indeed, US Americans.

With the aim of continuing to tell the Dreamers' rhetorical story, I first describe some of the different Dreamer hunger strikes that took place in 2010 in support of the DREAM Act, as reported on the *New York Times*, the race-focused news website Colorlines, and other popular news outlets. I explore some of the neoliberal themes that circulated in Dreamer rhetorics during these activist moments. Then I draw on work on the rhetorical power of hunger strikes to analyze how the Dreamer hunger strikes worked to create meaning and to argue for governmental action through a last-resort rhetoric of extortion. Although my analysis of Dreamers' use of hunger strikes as an activist rhetoric is limited to fasts taking place in California, New York, and Texas, their use of hunger strikes was widespread in 2010. Indeed, hunger strikes were an important part of Dreamer rhetorics during the Obama years, illustrating the urgency of the movement and the willingness of Dreamers to use their bodies as sites of political struggle.

Despite the long and diverse history of fasting and hunger striking as strategies for social and political change, the rhetorical meaning of contemporary hunger strikes is largely influenced by the famous fasts of Mahatma Gandhi, the Indian nationalist and father of nonviolent resistance. As political scientist Johanna Siméant writes, the Gandhian fast had a "broad palette of meanings . . . [including] calling on the exemplarity of the striker risking their life for the cause; shaming their adversaries; establishing a power struggle; and at the same time adopting a rigorous practice of physical asceticism."[22] The complex rhetorical meanings assigned to a hunger strike make it a tactic whose rhetorical force is difficult to pin down. For example, in his struggle for India's independence from British colonial rule, Gandhi took part in multiple fasts and hunger strikes both as acts of penance for the sins of his community and as actions that push for the end of British colonial rule.[23] For Gandhi, the hunger strike served both as a sort of self-flagellation directed inward to purify and atone, and as a method of political action directed outward to demand change. This matrix of meanings is the rhetorical antecedent of the Dreamers' hunger strikes. The Dreamers who engaged in hunger strikes were evidently rich in resolve and commitment to the cause; however, they were also at their wit's end and seeking a—surely desperate—strategy that would help them accomplish that which had thus far eluded them.

Yet the limited scope of the Dreamer hunger strikes, the scant attention they received from mainstream media, and the neoliberal discourses that framed them affected Dreamers' ability to accomplish their goal of forcing the hands of US legislators. Therefore, the Dreamer hunger strikes raise questions about the rhetorical efficacy of a hunger strike that does not culminate in death. If the strikers are not ready to make the ultimate sacrifice in order to achieve their goals, then what is the rhetorical force of such a strategy? If the starving body is not visible to mass audiences, can the hunger strike create change? My analysis here seeks to answer those questions.

Hunger Strikes in New York City, Los Angeles, and San Antonio

On June 10, 2010, a hunger strike began in front of Democratic senator Charles F. Schumer's midtown Manhattan office calling on him to support the DREAM Act. Schumer was chair of the Senate subcommittee on immigration at the time. The strike was led by the Dreamer activist group the New York State Youth Leadership Council. Gabriel Martinez, age twenty-seven, one of the hunger strikers, told the *New York Times* that the strike would last "as long as we can hold."[24] Martinez told ABC News, "I don't think there's another way, unless we want to escalate to violence."[25] The strike lasted ten days and ended after several participants became ill.[26]

A neoliberal rhetoric of respectability and deservability was clearly visible in the ways Dreamers contextualized their choice to participate in the hunger strikes. Having recently graduated from Columbia University with an architecture degree, Yadira Alvarez, age twenty-two, told ABC News that she participated in the New York hunger strike because, "I just can't sit around anymore and watch how my dream is being killed. . . . Even though *I've done everything right*; I got good grades in high school, I finished college, I was a good student, I behaved. I did everything right and now this dream can't continue because I don't have documents."[27] Alvarez forwards the idea that education is characteristic of a model US citizen by basing her "good behavior" on her academic success. Dreamers become valuable to the nation because their education gives them the ability to contribute to the US economy. Alvarez argues that because she "did everything right," which means that she received good grades and finished college, she deserves a pathway to citizenship. In this way she proposes that her potential contribution to the US economy supersedes the fact that she is undocumented.

Similar neoliberal ideas about Dreamers' deservability and Americanness were present in the rhetoric surrounding the hunger strikes in front of Democratic senator Dianne Feinstein's Los Angeles office. The fifteen-day hunger strike, which took place from July 21 to August 5, 2010, asked for Feinstein to support the DREAM Act, which she had done in the past. According to the Southern California Public Radio station KPCC, the strike began with ten students and ended with five.[28] Carlos Amador, one of the strike participants, described Dreamer deservability: "We grow up as Americans; attending public schools, becoming involved in sports, and excelling in our education. Our American Dream suddenly faces a social, economic, and legal barrier as soon as we turn eighteen."[29] Amador presents a picture of the all-American boy next door, even including the typical US American involvement in sports, so that this radical activist moment is overlain with the quintessence of US American youth. Jeff Kim, another hunger striker, connects US citizenship to education, using the logic that education leads to contribution and negates criminality. He states, "We just want our rights, to be educated and to contribute to this country. . . . We are not criminals."[30]

And finally, fifteen undocumented students from the University of Texas in San Antonio began a hunger strike in early November 2010 asking Republican senator Kay Bailey Hutchinson to support the DREAM Act.[31] They were later joined by more students and received support from universities in Arlington, Houston, Austin, and Dallas.[32] The protest was organized by the Dreamer activist group United We Dream.[33] Lucy Martinez, one of the hunger strikers at UT San Antonio, repeated the themes of hard work and contribution that also framed hunger strikes in New York and Los Angeles: "We want to let Sen. Hutchison know that we want her to recognize our sacrifice and *hard work. That we want to contribute to this country.*"[34]

On November 29, almost three weeks after beginning the strike, the San Antonio protesters were arrested for criminal trespassing when they refused to leave Senator Hutchinson's office after being told to do so by San Antonio police.[35] Upon their release, after twenty-seven days of consuming only water and juice, the strikers met with San Antonio Mayor Julián Castro who asked them to stop the strike. Castro agreed to call Hutchinson personally and stated that "[Dreamers] have played by the rules and gotten an education and want to work hard for America. . . . They are on the right side of the issue."[36] Castro's words illustrate the circulation of the neoliberal rhetoric that Dreamers used during the hunger strikes and in other contemporary moments of activism: Castro reproduces themes of education, hard work, and contribution, and presents Dreamers as deserving of the DREAM Act because of their neoliberal potential. Nevertheless, Hutchinson did not end up supporting the DREAM Act, even though the San Antonio strikers lasted a total of forty days without food.

While Dreamers' use of neoliberal rhetoric during the hunger strikes matched the sorts of frames that had been previously employed to push for the DREAM Act,[37] it is worthwhile to note how these frames reproduced damaging ideas about undocumented youth. As I discuss in this book's introduction, neoliberal ideology positions Dreamers on the good side of the "good immigrant/bad immigrant" binary. The idea that Dreamers deserve legalization because of their academic success implies that those who have not achieved academic success will not be able to contribute to the nation and therefore, do not deserve reprieve. Such rhetoric also legitimizes normative notions of what it means to be US American. As my descriptions above illustrate, Dreamer rhetorics during the hunger strikes defined US Americans as educated, law-abiding, and even athletic, and therefore reproduced white, middle-class, and ableist understandings of who legitimately belongs in this country.

However, my analysis of Dreamer rhetorics during the hunger strikes also exposes how these radical moments of activism highlighted the severely unequal power dynamic between the state and the Dreamers, called out government inaction via a rhetoric of extortion, and countered dehumanizing discourses by enacting Dreamers' humanity. The analysis that follows shows the "both/and" logic of Dreamer rhetorics: Dreamer hunger strikes are *both* neoliberal *and* radical. I outline the *nepantla* nature of Dreamer rhetorics by reading the hunger strikes outside of the toolbox of nonviolent resistance and instead within what political theorist Banu Bargu terms as "the weaponization of life." Bargu describes the weaponization of life as "the tactic of resorting to corporeal and existential practices of struggle based on the technique of self-destruction, in order to make a political statement or advance political goals."[38] She writes:

> As a tactic, the weaponization of life encompasses a series of practices that range from varieties of nonlethal self-mutilations (which include forms of amputation, maiming, infection with disease, sewing of eyes and mouth, *temporary starvation,* all inflicted by and upon oneself) to more fatal actions of self-immolation (understood as setting oneself on fire), *temporally indefinite hunger strikes,* fasts unto death, self-killing (through a variety of methods including hanging, drinking pesticide, slitting wrists, overdosing on medication, and swallowing cyanide capsules), and forms of suicide attack (involving, again, different forms of actions such as the detonation of bombs strapped upon the body,

> driving a loaded vehicle into a target to induce explosion, participation in military assaults with no chance of survival, and so on).[39]

While hunger strikes and other "self-destructive forms of resistance" have gained popularity in detention centers throughout the world,[40] this activist strategy is still located in the fringes of other less extreme tactics of civil disobedience, including marches, sit-ins, and protests. When read alongside other practices that weaponize life, the Dreamers' hunger strikes, which in the aforementioned list might be defined as "temporary starvation" or "temporally indefinite hunger strikes," become much more radical positions against state power.

Rhetorically, the hunger strikes helped make the issue of Dreamer rights a matter of life or death and therefore created a moment of rhetorical extortion. Extortion is "the action or practice of extorting or wresting anything . . . from a person by force or by undue exercise of authority or power."[41] I understand rhetorical extortion as the purposeful creation of meaning to force another to act in one's desired way. Because rhetoric is a practice of meaning making, in rhetorical extortion the hunger strikers seek to endow their bodies with a particular meaning in order to get the targeted audiences to concede to their demands. I call this a rhetorical act of extortion, not with the aim of disparaging the Dreamers who planned and participated in the hunger strikes. Instead I present it as extortion to note the radical and confrontational aspects of this bodily activist strategy as used by the Dreamers. In the hunger strikes, the body becomes a site of political struggle.[42] It is a body whose pain, vulnerability, and suffering are used rhetorically. While the Dreamer hunger strikes of 2010 were not death fasts, they were still significant, particularly the San Antonio hunger strike lasting forty days. Bobby Sands, the famous twenty-seven-year old Irish nationalist hunger striker, died after sixty-six days without food. Even though the time it takes for someone to die by starvation depends on factors like body type, age, and health, forty days without substantial nourishment is not to be taken lightly.

Even though the hunger striker can often be read as occupying a position of passivity especially compared to activists participating in more dynamic forms of activism like protests or rallies (indeed images of Gandhi as a skeletal, bedridden hunger striker abound in the collective imagination), the hunger striker is not passive. James Chase Sánchez writes that hunger strikes, like self-immolation, inhabit a liminal space between violence and nonviolence. While a hunger strike is a nonviolent activist strategy, it also takes part in violence "because the literal stage of hunger, of one's body eating itself from the inside, is a type of violence as well."[43] Dreamer hunger strikers realize the potential of the weapon they are wielding. They expect that no politician would want to be associated with a Dreamer's death or severe illness by starvation, and they are willing to use that knowledge to move their audience to action. Gerard Hauser refers to this as "passive aggression." In writing about Bobby Sands and the H-block hunger strikers, Hauser describes passive aggression as "the prisoner's use of the body to establish physical relationships that accentuate the power differential with the penal institution."[44] In other words, passive aggression is a form of violent action that makes visible the chasm between the power of the state (in my analysis, the US government) and the hunger strikers (in my analysis, the Dreamers). The Dreamer hunger strikers highlight the power that the US government has over their lives in order to show US audiences the human costs of governmental inaction. The government has the power to save Dreamer lives by passing the DREAM Act. In this context their inaction is reprehensible and even murderous.

As the hunger strikes illustrate the excess of state power over Dreamers' lives, they also highlight Dreamers' suffering to reaffirm the humanity of undocumented people. In a hunger strike, "the body in pain is a rhetorical site."[45] The pain of hunger, which is most often a form of private suffering, is made public. The hunger-striking body accepts pain willingly in order to embody and therefore make visible the suffering of those it represents. In the hunger strikes of 2010, the pain of the hunger-striking Dreamers symbolized the pain of all Dreamers living the precarious lives of the undocumented. And because suffering is inherent to the human condition, I read the pain, vulnerability, and suffering of the Dreamer hunger strikers as rhetorical affirmation of their humanity. In a context in which undocumented Latinxs are continuously dehumanized, Dreamers embody suffering to remind audiences that they are indeed human. This reaffirmation of humanity through suffering frames the urgency of passing the DREAM Act as an issue of human rights.

Yet, like other rhetorics, such a radical technique still has persuasion as an end goal. And here is where the Dreamer hunger strikes faltered. The targeted senators did not yield to the Dreamers' extortion. I propose that the hunger strike is inherently of problematic reception, particularly for its difficult and tenuous connection to rationality. Because it goes against the human survival instinct, it is difficult for a hunger strike to be considered a rational tactic. Instead, it can be understood as a purely emotional and embodied expression of anger and frustration without a productive end. Potential supporters are forced to pick a side on the reason/emotion binary and this often results in that hunger strikes are not fully appreciated by possible allies of the struggle.

For example, Senator Hutchinson, a republican with an anti-immigration voting record but who showed particular concern for the plight of Dreamers, stated through a spokesperson that she believed Dreamers should abandon the hunger strike and "pursue *safer* and more *constructive* methods of promoting their cause."[46] And Senator Schumer, a supporter of the DREAM Act, refused to even meet with the hunger strikers.

Furthermore, the striking body needs an informed witness to its suffering. If the body's decay has no witness or if it's starvation is not given context, its rhetorical power is lost. Hauser writes that "self-starvation is inexplicable without a frame," meaning that if the audience does not know why the hunger strike is happening, they will not understand its rhetoric.[47] I note that media attention is important here. Although there were multiple hunger strikes going on during the final push for the 2010 DREAM Act, they garnered very little attention from the media and from the community at large. There were some articles in major publications, mainly the *New York Times*, but overall the starving Dreamer bodies elicited very little press. A thorough description of why the Dreamers were striking was largely missing from media coverage. Importantly, there was no iconic image of starving young bodies that could circulate the Dreamers' intended rhetorical meaning. Without the sort of pressure that media attention can evoke, the legislators were able to ignore the Dreamers' demands.

Finally, I propose that the neoliberal aspect of the strikes also contributed to their failure to achieve legislative action. Because Dreamer rhetorics worked to present the hungers strikers as US Americans, their willingness to endure severe sickness and pain for the cause was called into question. Legislators trusted that no Dreamers would give up their lives for the cause. That sort of sacrifice does not happen very often in the contemporary US. Legislators saw no need to participate in this moment of extortion. In essence, they called the Dreamers' bluff. And this is a shortcoming of the hunger strike's rhetorical power. As Bargu suggests, "The technique of self-destruction as the basis of political action is radical and enigmatic in general . . . because it renders difficult, if not altogether impossible, the achievement of political ends through means lesser than death."[48] Since Dreamers were not willing to die for the cause, since they still believed in achieving their American Dream, their hunger strike was ineffective in forcing the hand of legislators.

A LIVABLE LIFE IN "COMING OUT OF THE SHADOWS"

Some of the main concerns for Dreamer rhetorics during the hunger strikes were questions of what conditions make life unlivable and what risks are worth taking to make life livable again. By denying themselves sustenance, hunger strikers used their bodies to argue that death or illness is better than their unlivable undocumented lives. In this way the activist strategy of hunger striking is similar to that of coming out of the shadows: protesters take great risks to work toward lives that are livable. Of course, in coming out of the shadows, Dreamers are not compromising their physical well-being for the struggle. But they are claiming to be prepared for deportation to a country they often have not seen since their emigration, a fate for some akin to a sort of death.

In this section I argue that Dreamer rhetorics in COTS were based on the assumption that a life in fear is a life unlivable. I draw on four videos of the event that were uploaded on YouTube to outline the form and function of Dreamer rhetorics during the event. The videos show portions of the speeches given by the seven speakers, as well as part of the march to Federal Plaza and some of the audience's reactions. While other scholars of COTS have focused on big-picture rhetorical frames,[49] my analysis reads closely the language that COTS participants used at the rally in order to look for evidence of Dreamers' *nepantla* rhetorics. Consequently, I find that even as Dreamers argued that lives in fear are lives unlivable, they also insisted that a livable life is characterized by professional and academic success.

My analysis also contributes to understandings of Dreamers' coming-out rhetoric by putting this activist moment in conversation with Nicholas De Genova's concept of the deportation regime and Yen Le Espiritu's concept of differential inclusion. I argue that Dreamer rhetorics in COTS defied Dreamers' differential inclusion and challenged the power of the deportation regime, while maintaining its grounding in neoliberal themes of citizenship, hard work, education, and contribution. Furthermore, in another illustration of both/and rhetorical strategies, Dreamers argue that undocumented people are not free in the US, thus critiquing the idea that the US is a "free country," while also positing that freedom can be effected only through citizenship.

The Dreamers' unique cultural capital—the familiarity with US culture that comes only from living in the country for most of their young lives—gave them the impetus to defy the power of the "deportation regime," the matrix of policies and practices that keep undocumented folks in the shadows for fear of detention and deportation.[50] Tania A. Unzueta and Hinda Seif ascribe Dreamers' rhetorical force in part to the fact that "the sociopolitical positioning of young undocumented immigrants is at points distinct from their parents, or those who migrated to the United States as adults."[51] By seeing themselves as equals to their US-born peers, Dreamers more clearly understood the ways that under the deportation regime the fear of deportation controls the lives of undocumented folks, essentially influencing every decision they make. The COTS events, in which Dreamers revealed their undocumented status in front of a crowd that often included activists, supporters, and immigration law enforcement agents, signaled an escape—if only momentary—from the power of the deportation regime.[52] Their evasion of the deportation regime highlighted a generational gap between Dreamers and their elders, as evidenced by the words of Dreamer activist Angy Rivera in the trailer for the PBS documentary *No le digas a nadie* (Don't Tell Anyone). Rivera, who participated in one of the first COTS events in New York City, states, "My mother raised me in an environment where speaking out about your status is wrong. She taught me the same fear. 'No le digas a nadie,' she would say. 'Don't tell anyone.' But I started seeing things differently."[53] In coming out of the shadows, Dreamers declared their singular rejection of the paralyzing fear that comes with the constant threat of deportation.

The COTS rally, which took place in Chicago on March 10, 2010, was primarily organized by the undocumented youth activist group the Immigrant Youth Justice League. Protesters met in Union Park in the Near West Side of Chicago and marched to Federal Plaza, near Homeland Security and other federal law enforcement offices. Once at Federal Plaza, the rally featured seven Dreamers who, despite Homeland Security vehicles being parked at the protest site, spoke openly to protesters about their experiences living in the US undocumented. Dreamers discussed the idea that risking deportation is better than continuing to live in the shadows, that they were willing to give it all up. Each speaker ended his or her story by unambiguously coming out as undocumented: "My name is _____. I am undocumented, and I am not afraid!"[54]

I read the COTS rally in Chicago not as a rejection of Dreamers' exclusion from the nation-state but as a refusal of their differential inclusion. Ethnic studies scholar Yen Le Espiritu describes differential inclusion as "the process whereby a group of people is deemed integral to the nation's economy, culture, identity, and power—but integral only or precisely because of their designated subordinate standing. Edward Said has described such outcast populations as people whose existence always counts, though their names and identities do not; *they are valuable precisely because they are not fully present*."[55] The place of undocumented immigrants in the nation is always dependent on their ability to serve the economy's need for cheap labor in agriculture, manufacturing, food processing, and the service industry, which requires them to remain silent and complacent while they live their lives in the shadows. While Dreamers at first seem outside of this "acceptable" role because of their US education, even those who attend college often struggle to get jobs outside of the service sector.[56] Thinking about Dreamers as differentially included, rather than entirely excluded, makes visible the ways in which racialized immigrants—undocumented and documented—are made part of the nation as perpetual others through "legal subordination, economic exploitation, and cultural degradation."[57] Thus, Dreamers are not necessarily entirely excluded from the nation-state. They are included but only as long as they exist in the shadows of society, experiencing only the limited economic and social opportunities that shadow living provides, and always subject to the fear that makes their lives unlivable. Dreamers' coming out signifies a rejection of their differential inclusion and a demand for full inclusion. Dreamers insist on being fully included or risk being excluded altogether.

The refusal of the deportation regime and of the differential inclusion that it facilitates highlights the intersection of these two tactics of domination. The deportation regime causes undocumented people to endure precarious living and working conditions because they fear that speaking out may result in being reported to immigration authorities.[58] Undocumented workers are compelled to accept their subordinate status—their differential inclusion—and thus contribute to the US economy through their much-needed, low-wage labor. A life under the deportation regime is a life of hiding in darkness, fearful of the state and accepting of its abuse.

The intersection of the deportation regime and of differential inclusion is evident in the story of Nico, a speaker during the COTS event in Chicago. Nico told not only his own story of living undocumented but also of his mother, who died of cancer after working at a poorly ventilated factory where she was exposed to harmful chemicals. Nico began his speech with a direct rejection of the deportation regime: "I stand here to tell you that I'm no longer afraid to come out of the shadows."[59] He then described his and his mother's differential inclusion via the deportation regime—the fact that his mother endured abhorrent work conditions for many years for fear of being deported. He stated, "Here in the United States, my mom worked in a dark windowless fume-filled room for twelve years with her *compañeras* side by side, not realizing that her lungs were being filled with harmful chemicals. Anyone who had proper documentation would not work under those conditions."[60] Nico ended his speech by assigning responsibility for his mother's death to the US immigration system: "*La migra* never came, but the broken immigration system took my mother from my family. She died of cancer two years ago and at that point I realized that I wasn't going to let my mother die in vain. I made the choice to fight and I'm here to say that I am not afraid anymore. My name is Nico and I'm undocumented!"[61] Nico's story highlights how the deportation regime can lead to death, even for those who will never be deported. Nico's refusal to let his mother "die in vain" signals his unwillingness to live under differential inclusion or remain silent in the face of the dehumanization that the deportation regime advances.

While deportation works to define the borders of the nation-state by deciding who is allowed to be inside and who must be put out, it operates most harshly on the majority of undocumented immigrants who are susceptible to deportation but who have not yet been deported.[62] The fear that the undocumented youth described at the COTS event evidences the power of the deportation regime. These young people lived in fear that they and/or their loved ones could be deported at any time. The fear caused by the deportation regime controlled their lives, shaped their decisions, and curtailed their movements. The rhetoric of COTS presents Dreamers' rejection of state power over their lives through their refusal of the deportation regime and their acceptance of—yet never their complacency with—their potential deportation.

Hugo, one of the event's speakers, described the fear that characterized his life under the deportation regime and then expressed his refusal to live in fear any longer. Having lived in a predominantly immigrant neighborhood with his undocumented mother, Hugo recalled a childhood haunted by the fear of deportation. At the COTS rally, he was the only speaker to address the audience in Spanish. Here I transcribe and translate portions of the speech he delivered in Chicago:

> *Pero mamá nunca me dijo que para vivir en este país tendríamos que hacerlo con miedo. . . . Es el mismo miedo que hace que tu estomago se apriete . . . el mismo miedo que yo empecé a tener cuando tenia nueve años y había visto enredadas en mi barrio, un barrio mayormente hispano y vietnamita. Yo y mis hermanos nos quedábamos encerrados en nuestro apartamento con las ventanas y las puertas y las luces apagadas orando y pidiéndole con todo lo que podíamos para que no agarraran a nuestra madre esta tarde y pudiera regresar a nuestra casa. . . . Estoy dispuesto de dejar todo lo que yo tengo, dejar mi miedo y salir fuera de las sombras. Hoy estoy cansado de tener miedo.*

> But Mom never told me that to live in this country, we must do so in fear. . . . It is the same fear that makes your stomach tighten . . . the same fear that I started having as a nine-year-old when I saw immigration raids in my neighborhood, a neighborhood that was primarily Hispanic and Vietnamese. Me and my siblings would stay locked up in our apartment with the windows and doors and lights off, praying and asking Him with everything that we could that our

> mother would not be taken and that she would be able to return home. . . . I am ready to give up everything I have, to give up my fear and to come out of the shadows. I am tired of being afraid.[63]

Hugo's story illustrates one of the most significant rhetorical moves of COTS, the idea that giving up fear and coming out of the shadows also means being ready to relinquish life in the US. Both of these actions are concurrent because when undocumented people no longer live in fear of being deported, they may also do things that might bring forth their deportation, such as publicly revealing their immigration status. These simultaneous rhetorical moves forward the idea that life under the deportation regime is unlivable. In choosing to live in the open, Hugo and the other undocumented youth who came out of the shadows that day and who have continued to come out of the shadows every day since, refuse the power of the deportation regime and accept their potential deportation.

Despite the rejection of state power implied by the rhetorical move of coming out of the shadows, Hugo's story outlines the concept of a livable life for undocumented youth based on neoliberal and normative notions of the American Dream and of the US as a color-blind meritocracy:

> *Cuando mi madre, una mujer soltera, me trajo a este país, me dijo que esta era la tierra donde yo podría trabajar duro y realizar todos mis sueños. Pero mamá nunca me dijo que para vivir en este país tendríamos que hacerlo con miedo. . . . Es el mismo miedo que sigo teniendo al saber que tengo que dejar mis sueños, mi sueño de tener ese trabajo que va a hacerme levantarme* [*sic*] *todos los días en la mañana y sentirme como alguien exitoso. Es el mismo miedo de tener que dejarlo [mi sueño] después de haber trabajado duro cuando me gradué del colegio con honores después de tanto trabajo. . . . No quiero seguir diciéndole no a mi futuro, al bienestar de mi familia, y sobre todo a los valores de democracia, libertad, y justicia que este país nos ha enseñado.*
>
> When my mom, a single woman, brought me to this country, she said that this was the land where I could work hard and realize all of my dreams. But Mom never told me that to live in this country, we must do so in fear. . . . It is the same fear that I still have knowing that I have to give up on my dreams, my dream of having a job that will make me wake up every morning and feel successful. It is the same fear that I have to give it up [my dream] after having worked hard when I graduated from school with honors, after so much work. . . . I don't want to keep saying no to my future, to the well-being of my

> family, and most of all to the values of democracy, freedom, and justice that this country has taught us.[64]

The concept of dreams is woven through this portion of his speech not only to connect this activist moment to the Dreamer movement and the DREAM Act but also to reproduce notions of the US as the land of opportunity and of the American Dream. In his story of immigration, Hugo taps into a narrative theme common to the US mythos as an immigrant nation: that in the US you can realize your dreams if you work hard. Consequently, dreams in Hugo's story are defined by academic and professional success. And the ability for Hugo to realize his dreams becomes the measure for his happiness. He speaks of this job as the reason for waking up in the morning. Giving up his dream of having a good job fills him with fear. A livable life for Hugo is defined solely as being able to work hard and reap the (professional) fruit of his labor. Success and happiness as promised by the nation-state are characterized by the acquisition of wealth and middle-class status that supposedly can be attained only through hard work in school and profession. Hugo seems to maintain this belief in the US as meritocracy despite the evidence that systemic racism dispels any meritocratic fantasy.

It is also worth noting how the ideas of democracy, freedom, and justice play out in this text. On the surface, democracy, freedom, and justice are tropes that quickly advance romanticized notions of US essentialism. For example, I read Hugo's mention of freedom alluding to the unalienable rights mentioned in the US Declaration of Independence: life, liberty, and the pursuit of happiness. Yet freedom in Hugo's story also implies the nation's broken promise: the US's failure to live up to the idea that all people are created equal. Hugo calls out the US on its broken promise and disrupts the belief that the US is a free country. He challenges a foundational trope of the nation-state and thus makes a radical rhetorical move.

Whereas Hugo implies that the US in not a free country, Tania, another one of the speakers, directly states that a life in fear is not a free life. She states, "Every time that I want to take a step forward in my life, I have to consider that my actions are limited because in this country I am not free. We are not free. . . . Even as I stand here, my hands shaking, my heart racing, my voice breaking, I do it knowing that the risks that we are taking are necessary so that one day we can all be free."[65] Arguing that the US is not free, or that it is not free for all, is a radical critique of the myth of US essentialism. If there are people who do not live freely in this country, then the US is not a free country, it is not special, it is not better or worse than any other place. Tania challenges

US essentialism at its core by being living proof that this is not a free country. Yet her apparent belief that citizenship or even legalization will bring freedom reinvests in the power of the US nation-state. In Tania's rhetoric, freedom is subject to legislation. It is not an unalienable right—it is a right granted by the state.

RHETORICAL BEGINNINGS

The rhetoric used in Dreamer activism of 2010 set the stage for what was to come. The hunger strikes and COTS events that year allowed Dreamers to gain power in representing themselves and to decide what that representation would entail. The TruthOut letter specifically refers to their move away from the traditional activist machine: "The Nonprofit Industrial Complex is a network of politicians, the elite, foundations and social justice organizations. This system encourages movements to model themselves after capitalist structures instead of challenging them. In this manner, foundations control social movements and dissent; philanthropy masks corporate greed and exploitation."[66]

In the years that followed, the Dreamer movement worked to maintain its independence from the "nonprofit industrial complex" through strategies and actions that separated them from other immigrant activists. Many of these new bold tactics are the focus of this book. The Dreamer movement with its radical rhetorics succeeded in recentering immigration in the US political conversation. They instilled new energy to an exhausted immigrant community and pushed the US mainstream to reconsider its stance on undocumented immigration. As the manifesto states, "In a time when the entire immigrant community is under attack, and increasingly demoralized, stripped of our rights, the DREAM movement has injected life, resistance and creativity into the broader immigrant rights struggle."[67] They did this through a youth-centered, Dreamer-made approach to activism that focused on empowering youth via self-representation and control of their rhetorics.

Ironically, such activism often challenged the behavioral stipulations of the DREAM Act. While the DREAM Act asked that potential beneficiaries fit into neoliberal models of US citizen behavior—school attendance, military service, good moral character—Dreamer activists in the TruthOut letter, the hunger strikes, and COTS deviated from this straight-arrow image. Instead, through their rhetoric they demonstrated the ways that Dreamers would never be docile subjects. Their experiences of oppression, fear, and differential inclusion under the deportation regime had made them fierce.

Dreamers in 2010 demonstrated how US American they really are, not in the blindly patriotic and neoliberal sort of way, but instead in the tradition of protest of the Civil Rights, Black Power, Chicano, Native, and queer rights movements. While Dreamer rhetorics often have neoliberal notes, it is my view that this also shows the Dreamer movement as uniquely US American. Dreamers, unlike other undocumented immigrants, are culturally from this country. They were raised in the US and therefore have internalized the foundational rhetoric of this nation—myths and all. Their unique positionality mobilizes their *nepantla* vision. Like rhetorics of the borderlands, Dreamer rhetorics have a foot on each side, not of the US-Mexico border necessarily, but of neoliberal and radical ideologies.

The ways that the Dreamers' *nepantla* continued to shape their rhetorics became apparent in the activism that followed. After 2010 the focus of Dreamer activism was not on legislative action. They for the most part abandoned general solutions to the perils of undocumented immigration. Dreamers instead began to look for ways to help individual undocumented folks by, for example, stopping singular deportations and helping small groups of immigrants to cross the border. They also focused on empowering undocumented youth by creating a more robust and diverse Dreamer community. They maintained the critique of the nation-state that they waged in 2010, even as they acknowledged its power to assuage their precarity.

2

Dreamer Rhetorics in the Dream 9 Action

On the unusually cool Monday morning of July 22, 2013, nine young Dreamers wearing graduation caps and gowns walked hand in hand to the US port of entry in Nogales, Arizona, and asked the US government to let them come in.

The Dream 9, as they would come to be known, had all been born in Mexico but had immigrated to the US as children; some of them were no more than a few months old when they made their way across the border. After living in the US for a large portion of their young lives, they had returned to Mexico for a variety of reasons and now wanted to go back to the US, the country they thought of as their home. Three of the nine Dreamers, Lizbeth Mateo, Lulu Martínez, and Marco Saavedra, were members of the National Immigrant Youth Alliance (NIYA), the activist network that was organizing this border crossing, and had returned to Mexico deliberately to take part in the action. The stakes were high for this group of Dreamers. Lizbeth was supposed to begin law school at Santa Clara University in California in the fall term. Lulu had just applied for DACA. That summer they put their lives on hold to send a message to the US government about its inhumane immigration laws.

The other six Dreamers did not identify as activists prior to this momentous morning. Some of them had been deported back to Mexico, some had left to reunite with deported family members, some had gone in search for access to higher education, and some had crossed the border into Mexico because they no longer wanted to live under the constant threat of deportation. Luís León joined NIYA's Dream 9 action with the hope of returning to the US to pursue his studies after trying unsuccessfully to attend college both in the US and Mexico.[1] He had crossed the border without papers and been caught by Border Patrol four times before becoming one of the Dream 9.[2] In June 2013, while working a customer service job in Cancún, Luís received a text message from an acquaintance who told him about the opportunity of reuniting with his family by crossing the border with the Dream 9.[3] Luís remembers saying yes immediately. Recalling the events he says, "I had nothing to lose at the point. I had already lost it all."[4] For Luís, as for the other Dreamers, this moment of activism was a last chance, a final attempt at regaining the US life they had left behind.

Young and defiant they risked detention and permanent exclusion from the country they thought of as their home in order to shed light on a broken immigration system and on the lives that are shattered by it. The Dream 9 were not only asking for their own paths toward legalization in the US; their actions were also meant to condemn the Obama administration's skyrocketing deportation rate and the family separation that resulted from it.

At a more practical level, the short-term goal of the action was to get the Dreamers on US soil so that lawyers could argue for them to stay.[5] Long-term, the nine Dreamers desired paperwork that would allow them legal residency in the US. The legal strategy for the Dream 9 action, as devised by attorney Margo Cowan, a Pima County, Arizona, public defender who had agreed to work for the Dream 9 pro bono, was to ask that the Dreamers be given humanitarian parole by showing that there was a "significant public benefit" in their return to the US. Knowing that this request would most likely be denied, Cowan also asked the Dreamers to prepare asylum applications that would require them to show they had "credible fear of persecution or torture" if they returned to Mexico.[6]

Pictures of that fateful morning in mainstream and independent news sources show Dreamers confidently walking up to the US port of entry, aware of the risks yet not fully knowing what would happen to them in the next few hours, days, and weeks. NIYA organizers had trained them on what to say to border agents, how to behave in front of the TV cameras, and what to do if—and this was almost a certainty—they were taken to a detention center. The road would be long, but ultimately all nine Dreamers would be released onto US soil pending asylum hearings after spending two weeks in detention.

In this chapter I examine this activist moment to argue that Dreamer rhetorics in the Dream 9 action constituted the rhetorical identity of Dreamers in ways that challenged conventional understandings of US citizenship and moved to claim space for Dreamers within the US body politic. I illustrate how Dreamer rhetorics in the Dream 9 action had overt neoliberal connotations. When glimpsed from afar, much of Dreamer activism is based on the idea that these young people are exceptional and therefore can contribute to the nation in ways that other immigrants cannot. Their belonging is transactional; their contributions to the nation are paid for through the privilege of acceptance. However, I propose that a close examination of the Dream 9 action unveils its radical potential. Dreamers make the argument that they belong to a nation that has never wanted to include them. Logically, this argument implies that the nation needs to change.

Through an appeal to citizenship—in particular citizenship's affective characteristics[7]—the undocumented youth of the Dream 9 positioned themselves as rightfully belonging in the US. Indeed, one of the main rhetorical goals of the Dream 9 action was to show that Dreamers were for all intents and purposes US American and that they were outstanding young people that could contribute to the US economy. Additionally, the Dreamer identity also purposefully took on a radical ethos that challenged the existing immigration practices of detention, deportation, and family separation. Both neoliberal *and* radical, the rhetorics of the Dream 9 action are a beautiful display of the Dreamers' use of *nepantla* in their organizing. As I show in this chapter, the message that Dreamers conveyed in the first stage of this action—while they attempted to cross the border—was quite different from the message in the second stage—once they were put in detention. While acting as a small group of nine Dreamers asking for asylum, they presented themselves as the "good immigrants" who were already assimilated to US culture and happy to contribute to the US economy. However, in detention the Dream 9 harnessed the power of the undocumented community to—well—raise hell. Along with other detained immigrants, the Dream 9 called out the inhumane practices of detention, made visible the hypocrisy of deportation, and argued that freedom of movement is akin to life.

In the pages that follow, I relate the events of the Dream 9 action by exploring the rhetoric in the constellation of texts that made up this activist moment. The Dream 9 movement was not only composed of one day's worth of action. It was accomplished through strategic media outreach, social media campaigns, and in-person actions, all created by the nine Dreamers that took part in the action, as well as by supporting activist and allies. The proliferation of texts about the Dream 9 helped to craft the Dream 9's message of Dreamer belonging. The Dream 9 action reverberated through space and time via the circulation of texts that were created before, during, and after the nine Dreamers crossed the US-Mexico border. Through a rhetorical analysis of many of the texts involved in this action—a streamed video of the event, a talk given by one of the Dream 9 to a University of Portland audience, activist videos, and radio interviews, I outline how the rhetoric of the Dream 9 action constituted a unique Dreamer identity that encompassed neoliberal and patriotic tropes while also waging critique of the state. While the event was discussed by journalists in small as well as large publications, my goal is to explore how Dreamers represented themselves and their arguments. Of course their representations were also influenced by the discourse of immigration that surrounded them. Still, in order to argue that Dreamer rhetorics are rhetorics in their own right, I devote these pages to the analysis of media that was made by undocumented young people.

SOME BACKGROUND: NIYA AND THE "BRING THEM HOME" CAMPAIGN

The Dream 9 action was organized by the National Immigrant Youth Alliance, a network of activist organizations led by undocumented youth who believe that the immigrant-rights fight in the US is to be fought on the streets as well as in the halls of government. Committed to "achieving equality for all immigrant youth, regardless of their legal status,"[8] NIYA advocated for a grassroots effort based on civil disobedience that positioned undocumented youth at the forefront of the immigrant movement. Their most famous action was the Bring Them Home (BTH) campaign of the early 2010s, which aimed to highlight the family separation resulting from federal deportation policies and state laws that encourage "self-deportation" such as Alabama's House Bill 56 and Arizona's State Bill 1070.[9]

What made NIYA extraordinary was its attempt to redefine the US as a *home to return to* for undocumented immigrants. NIYA's rhetorical innovation was not in framing the US as the Dreamers' home; it was the *return home* that set them apart. BTH mobilized previously deported or "self-deported" undocumented immigrants to ask for reentry into the US based on their previous lives and connections in this country. Asking to return home was a rhetorical maneuver that allowed NIYA to highlight Dreamers' affective citizenship by showcasing the personal and emotional connections that these young undocumented Latinxs had with the US. In a more practical sense, this move allowed Dreamers to take advantage of laws regulating asylum and humanitarian parole. There are not many laws that allow undocumented immigrants already in the country to regularize (legalize) their immigration status. Other than the U visa, which provides legal status to victims of certain crimes who are willing to work with law enforcement, there just are not many ways for someone who is in the country illegally to become legal, at least not since Ronald Reagan's amnesty program of 1986. This is why the argument that undocumented immigrants should just "get in the back of the line" is invalid and, quite honestly, uninformed. Being outside of the country, however, allowed Dreamers to apply for legal entry through humanitarian parole and/or asylum. If denied humanitarian parole, Dreamers would be able to wait in the US for their asylum hearings, which could take months or even years. Meanwhile, they would have legal residency and an end to the immediate threat of deportation.

In the Dream 9 action, the nine Dreamers asked for entry through humanitarian parole but were denied. They then applied for asylum and were taken to detention. After two weeks in detention, immigration officials decided that all nine Dreamers faced credible fear of persecution or torture if they were returned to Mexico. They were released and allowed to return to their homes in the US and continue their lives while awaiting their asylum hearings.[10]

It is an understatement to say that the Dream 9 action was risky, particularly for Lizbeth Mateo, Lulu Martinez, and Marco Saavedra, who crossed the border south specifically to take part in the Dream 9 action. These Dreamers risked losing their lives in the US in order to participate in this moment of activism. While it could be argued that all activism by undocumented immigrants puts their US lives on the line by making them subject to detention and deportation, Dream 9 activists took this risk to the next level by purposefully crossing the border from the US into Mexico in an act of "self-deportation." The US government would literally have to do nothing to rip these young people from the lives that they'd built in the US.

The risks of the Dream 9 action, however, were somewhat mitigated by the strong social media presence with which NIYA activists hoped to protect the border crossers. NIYA purposefully created a conspicuous online presence, using social media to increase awareness of its actions and to humanize each crosser with videos of their stories posted on YouTube. In the days before the Dream 9 action, activists created videos that presented a sympathetic character to their audience and contextualized the upcoming action. During the event Dream 9 organizers encouraged audiences to share information about the demonstration on Facebook, Twitter, and Tumblr. The prolific Dream 9 presence in social and digital media helped raise the stakes for the US government by providing NIYA activists with names, faces, and stories, and therefore making it more difficult for the US to quietly ignore their pleas for return. NIYA was essentially challenging the US government to see if it would be willing to deny reentry to such a highly visible group of Dreamers. The pressure seemed to work. On July 29, 2013, thirty-five US members of Congress signed a letter to Obama asking him to allow the Dream 9 to return home.

AFFECTIVE CITIZENSHIP AND THE NATION-STATE

In this chapter I show how Dreamer rhetorics develop the argument that young undocumented Latinxs possess affective citizenship and that this form of belonging should be considered reason enough to allow their legal residence in the US. As I refer to it in this chapter, affective citizenship is not its own type of citizenship. Instead, I understand affective citizenship as highlighting the affective dimensions of citizenship. In this way, affective citizenship helps me to think about how national belonging can be defined through emotional connections, practiced through affective behaviors, and regulated and policed by affect management.[11] Dreamer rhetorics in the Dream 9 worked to position the affective dimensions of citizenship as more important than its legislative dimensions. A major goal of the Dream 9 action was to emphasize that the nine Dreamers *felt* US American and therefore should be considered as such.

The concept of affective citizenship intimates that there is an embodied experience of being a citizen and that citizenship is much more than a legislative status or even a set of cultural practices. Citizenship is felt in the body; it incorporates the feelings, emotions, and behaviors that arise from an affective experience. Sharon Yam writes that "citizenship remains a politically and *emotionally powerful* heuristic on how we understand our reality, identities, and relationships with others" (my emphasis).[12] Affective citizenship points to the ways belonging is externalized through emotions (discursive representations of affect). Political theorist Danielle Allen describes this sort of national identification as a friendship built on the recognition of "a *shared* life—not a 'common' nor an identical life—only one with common events, climates, built-environments, fixations of the imagination, and social structures."[13] Allen theorizes the nation as a kinlike community of citizens built on shared experiences and their resulting common "feelings."

Affective citizenship confronts the limits of citizenship as birthright and provides a multidimensional understanding of belonging that makes space for undocumented youth in the nation-state. Citizenship in this conceptualization marks not one form of belonging but the intersection of many forms: all interwoven and influencing one another. I use the term "citizenship" here, despite its neoliberal, exclusionary, and settler colonial baggage, because it acknowledges that citizenship has multiple dimensions with varying levels of importance. For undocumented young people, for example, it isn't enough to *feel* a sense of belonging or have their affective citizenship validated. They also need the legal papers to live lives removed from the fear of (at least their own) deportation.

I want to also call attention to the exclusions that come from any consideration of citizenship, including of its affective dimensions. Yam contends, "Citizenship . . . is interpreted through intimate familial values, and that grants justification for selective inclusion and exclusion of subjects based not on democratic deliberation, but on sentiments and feelings that support the dominant national imaginary."[14] The feelings of citizenship don't only connect citizen subjects to the nation-state and to its members but also become a way to measure who belongs and who doesn't. The affective dimensions of citizenship help us to know the other as other; we feel in our bones that the other is a stranger. As Sarah Ahmed argues, "The figure of the stranger is far from simply being strange; it is a figure that is painfully familiar in that very strange(r) ness. . . . We recognize somebody *as a stranger*, rather than simply failing to recognize them."[15] It follows that the affective dimensions of citizenship help to rationalize the other's exclusion and to draw and defend the boundaries of the nation. Like other dimensions of citizenship, affective citizenship can work as a tool for exclusion that depends on its boundary limits; in this case some forms of affect and the feelings they produce are deemed to be acceptable for citizenship, while others are not. This "code of conduct" for good affective citizens, not surprisingly, is delineated along lines of race, gender, ability, sexuality, and class.[16]

The Dream 9's affective citizenship unveils the gap between those who *feel* like citizens and those who are given the benefits and privileges with which citizenship supposedly comes. Regardless of feeling like citizens of the US, Dreamers are not seen as such by the law. In this way, thinking about affective citizenship can show that the current legislative model of citizenship is unworkable as it does not account for people positioned simultaneously within the nation and at the limits of the state. As queer migrations scholar Siobhan Somerville describes it, "the state . . . is usually understood to be a juridical formation within some territorial component. In contrast, 'nation,' derived from the Latin root *nasci* (to be born), has traditionally been associated with a sense of kinship, a primordial belonging."[17] This difference highlights why affective citizenship may be a way to better understand the liminal positionality of Dreamers—a position that is rejected by the US government (the state) despite its embodied and emotional connection to US culture (the nation).

"WE ARE AMERICANS*": AFFECTIVE CLAIMS OF HOME AND BELONGING

In June 25, 2012, *Time* magazine's cover featured Jose Antonio Vargas, the Pulitzer Prize–winning journalist who had just the previous year disclosed his undocumented status on the pages of the *New York Times Magazine*. The *Time* cover also presented thirty-five other undocumented young people from various countries, along with the headline in capitalized and bolded red text, "We are Americans*." In smaller white text, the corresponding asterisk provided the caveat "*just not legally." This issue of *Time* introduced the faces of undocumented young people into mainstream US living rooms with an unequivocal argument: we are here to stay.

In the accompanying article titled "Not Legal Not Leaving," Vargas tells about life as an openly undocumented immigrant. He describes how as a child he learned to pass as a US citizen, "right down to cultivating a homegrown accent."[18] He relates some of the most common questions he gets from US citizens as he travels the country doing immigrant activism ("Why haven't you gotten deported?" and "Why don't you become legal?" are perhaps the most obnoxious two), and he reminds readers, "We love this country. We contribute to it. This is our home."[19] Vargas ends his essay with a poignant question for the US readers: "When will you realize that we are one of you?"[20]

The idea that Dreamers are US American is perhaps the most important line of argument in pleas for legislative solutions to Dreamers' liminal position. Throughout their activism Dreamers have made rhetorical choices to present themselves as quintessentially US American with the goal of convincing a US public to view them as equal. As I described in the introduction to this book, framing Dreamers as US American has often involved using strategic essentialism to create an idealized notion of undocumented young people as model neoliberal subjects and therefore natural citizens. Highlighting that Dreamers are essentially US American was a key feature of Dreamer rhetorics in the Dream 9 action, and the theme of the Dreamers' "US Americanism" was ubiquitous in texts related to the Dream 9. In this portion of the Dreamers' rhetorical story, I analyze how Dreamer rhetorics constituted Dreamers as US American through appeals to US exceptionalism by positing that the US is the only country that can provide a home for Dreamers. The rhetorics also show how the Dream 9 action framed Mexico as a place of departure for Dreamers. Thus, Dreamer rhetorics worked to denounce Dreamers' birth country as unsafe and unfit, and to renounce it by eschewing the identity of "Mexican." I hope to show how emphasizing affective citizenship is a complex rhetorical exigency that Dreamers respond to by appealing to US exceptionalism.

Denouncing Mexico: US Exceptionalism and Safety

US exceptionalism contributes to the Dreamers' claim of affective citizenship, and this theme is carefully woven through Dreamer rhetorics, particularly in statements that denounce their birth country.[21] This is a logical move in Dreamer rhetorics since their affective citizenship connotes an emotional connection with the US even as they continue to be relegated to the shadows and threatened with detention and deportation. This means that Dreamer rhetorics must appeal to US exceptionalism by at times disregarding US oppression and instead focusing on the shortcomings of sending countries, particularly around the issue of safety. By focusing their narratives on the dangers of Mexico, the nine Dreamers constitute the US as their home, a place that transnational feminist scholar Chandra Tapalde Mohanty describes as "where one lives within familiar, safe, and protected boundaries."[22]

In a video made by NIYA and posted on YouTube before the Dream 9 action, Claudia Amaro, one of the nine Dreamers, describes how she and her family did not feel safe living in Mexico. I find Claudia's story interesting because it illustrates how migration is not a linear process but instead can be characterized by repeated movement across international and national boundaries. Claudia's family immigrated to the US after her father was killed during a family vacation in Durango, Mexico, when she was just ten years old. Her widowed mother took Claudia and her four sisters to the US with hopes of a life without fear. Some time later, the family moved to Wichita, Kansas, where Claudia met and married her husband and gave birth to their son. In 2005 her husband, also undocumented, got pulled over by the police while he was driving to work, an encounter that resulted in his deportation. Claudia and her son, who was five at the time, moved to Mexico in order to keep the family together.[23]

When she joined the Dream 9, Claudia and her family had been living in Mexico for seven years. In a narrative familiar to those paying even cursory attention to immigrant stories, Claudia wanted to return to the US not only to finish her own education but also to provide her US-citizen son a better life. She says in the video, "I don't want you to get me wrong. Mexico is a good country in many ways, but it's just not my home."[24] Claudia then goes on to describe her ideal home by telling the camera about Mexico's many shortcomings; she frames the US as her home by explaining why Mexico could never be her home. In Mexico, she states, her family has been victim to many (unspecified) crimes. In addition, her son has suffered from bullying from peers and teachers. The entire family is in therapy to cope with the stress of their living situation. "I don't feel safe," she says. "I don't feel safe at all."[25] Claudia's narrative ends emotionally: "I feel that I have no past because where I live right now [in Mexico] I don't have any past. I don't have a present because I'm not happy and I'm not leaving it. And I don't see a future."[26] As a viewer, it is easy to hear the despair in her voice and see the frustration in her eyes. Unlike other immigrant-story videos that are limited rhetorically by the ways each testimony fits into established narrative scripts, Claudia's story seems raw, and it is this realness that gives it its strong persuasive appeals. Claudia is unable to imagine a future for herself outside the US. The audience is left wondering what will become of Claudia if she cannot return to her life in Wichita. Interestingly, her narrative vacillates between stating that Mexico is a good country and then stating why it is not enough for her and her family. She seems to be saying that Mexico is okay—for Mexicans. And, in her heart, she is not Mexican. She is US American.

Throughout the Dream 9 demonstration, the US is framed as having the power to fix the Dreamers' situation by providing regularization and recognition within dominant conceptualizations of citizenship. The US is presented as agent, actor, and savior with the power to "give them papers" and "bring them home" (these were popular slogans during the demonstration on the US-Mexico border while the nine Dreamers were attempting to cross). This is the powerful and benevolent nation that Claudia is counting on when she states, "My dream is, if you guys support me. . . . if President Obama let [*sic*] us come home, I wanna finish my career so I can serve my community."[27] This rhetoric of US exceptionalism puts hope in the US and in Obama but ignores the ways US immigration policies along with the nation-state's dependence on cheap migrant labor contribute to immigrant precarity.

The theme of an unsafe Mexico contributes to the rhetoric of US exceptionalism in many of the other nine Dreamers' narratives and bolsters their claim to affective citizenship. For example, during a talk at the University of Portland on November 14, 2013, Luís describes the prejudice he experienced when he returned to Mexico to go to college. He states that he was bullied by a professor and that his peers called him *pocho*[28] and told him to go back to the US.[29] The feeling of alienation that many Dreamers describe points again to the affective aspects of citizenship. While some Dreamers may *actually* face dangers in Mexico compared to the US, it is important to note that the *perception* of danger is just as meaningful for Dreamers who grew up creating an emotional connection to the US. They may be just as unsafe in the US as in Mexico; but they *feel* safer in the US. In a radio interview with Los Angeles radio station KCRW's program *Sonic Trace* on October 8, 2013, Lizbeth talks about the six Dreamers who were already in Mexico when they took part in the Dream 9. She says, "Some of them left the [US] for different reasons and then realized that they just didn't fit in in Mexico, and they were just, you know, really wanted to come home, to *be safe* with their families in the US."[30]

The feeling of safety is more of a perception of the potential for safety. In actuality, Dreamers in the US are not safe from the deportation regime,[31] from abusive labor practices, and/or from outright anti-immigrant violence. Yet there is the idea that they can be safe in the US, whereas they cannot imagine being safe in Mexico. This is one of the ways citizenship can be affective. Affective citizenship is made up of an embodied intuition that *this* is one's place of belonging. However, this feeling may not match up with the reality of one's life in that country.

Renouncing Mexico: US Exceptionalism and Belonging

Dreamer rhetorics of the Dream 9 also forward the idea that the US is the only home for Dreamers by making moves that renounce other national affiliations. During his talk at the University of Portland, Luís describes how before the Dreamers presented themselves at the US port of entry, they marched around Nogales, Sonora, as the first group of "undocumented students that grew up in the US and were going to protest from the Mexican side, asking to come home."[32] Luís refers to the Dreamers as undocumented students, even though in Mexico they are not undocumented: they are Mexican. While Luís had lived in Mexico for over a year at the time he joined the Dream 9, he still rhetorically locates himself in the US. Indeed, the Dreamers' positionality is always rhetorically US based. Luís's words are telling, and they match the ways Dreamer rhetorics position the Dreamers in relation to Mexico. Although Nogales, Sonora, could be read as a space of belonging for them as Mexican nationals, the Dreamers march around this border city not only to garner the support of those on the Mexican side of the border but also to highlight the idea that the US—not Mexico—is their home. As they walk around Nogales, the activists are constituting the border city as the place to leave behind: a reminder of their US belonging. There are no voiced regrets about leaving Mexico, only the desire to "come home" to the US.[33] Framing Mexico as the place of departure fulfills the narrative present in dominant discourses of migration in which Mexico and other countries of origin are described as unable to fulfill the migrant's emotional and economic needs in opposition to the exceptional US: the land of freedom and opportunity.

A similar argument was intimated in other videos that presented various aspects of the Dream 9 action to the wider public. A thirty-six-minute video recording of the US side of the border at Nogales was filmed by NIYA and streamed live as a way to reach those who could not participate in person and get them involved, albeit virtually, in the day's events. It was captioned as follows: "Deportations have exploded in recent years, topping 400,000 in 2012, more than double the number seven years earlier. US lawmakers are debating an overhaul to the country's immigration system that could include a fix for immigrants who were brought in illegally as children. Many have grown up in America and have no recollection of life in another country, but they have no legal status in the US."[34]

The captioning text functions to identify the Dream 9's affective US citizenship. Stating that Dreamers have no recollection of their lives in other countries, the video's accompanying text seeks to present Dreamers as solely US American by denying the transnational belonging experienced by many undocumented young people who identify with the US *and* with their countries of origin even if they have not visited the latter since emigrating. Downplaying immigrants' complex national allegiances has been a common move in immigrant rights activism.[35] What is different here is the complete denial of a conscious life before the US with the words "no recollection of life in another country." The rhetorical positioning of Dreamers as solely US American helps not only to downplay another national allegiance but also to position the US as the only nation that can provide a home for undocumented young people.

And yet there are ways in which the Dreamers' claim of affective citizenship is cognizant of the contradictions that occur when you love the nation but the nation doesn't love you back. This is where the Dreamers' *nepantla*, their ability to inhabit "both/and" ways of thinking and being, is most visible in their rhetorics. In the Dream 9 action, Dreamers argue that they are US American, but they also understand that even affective citizenship is a two-way street. They call the US their home and reject their birth countries. They feel a strong emotional connection to this land. Claudia finishes her video by saying, "My father told me, the land of a person is where you are happy or where you are successful. . . . Wichita, Kansas is my home and I wanna go home."[36] As I've stated, this connection is an important part of the affective citizenship that Dreamers are claiming. However, they also admit to feeling rejected by the US government. Ceferino Santiago, who moved to Lexington, Kentucky, with his brothers when he was thirteen and returned to Mexico to visit his parents says in a video filmed from Mexico, "Now I wanna go back home to Kentucky to be with my brothers, but the government of the United States *may not want me*."[37] Similarly, Lizbeth says, "I came to Oaxaca knowing that the US government may not allow me to go back."[38]

Somerville critiques the ways in which the trope of the immigrant who desires the US fails to reflect how the nation-state through its policies and practices decides whether that desire will or will not be fulfilled. She asks, "To what extent, for instance, does the construction of a desiring immigrant obscure the ways that the state itself, through immigration and naturalization policy, sets the terms of this imagined love, actively distinguishing between which immigrants' desire will be returned and which will be left unrequited? To what extent does the presumed lovability of the United States distract us from, among other things, the state's own construction of certain immigrants and citizens as 'lovable,' and others as inappropriate objects for the nation's love?"[39] These Dreamers acknowledge that the US government does not want them; there is a palpable sadness in this feeling of rejection. It is the feeling that Dreamers are all too familiar with and an important motivation of their activist rhetorics. The state's standards of acceptability are drawn along lines of race, gender, sexuality, language, and immigration status. Dreamers, positioned at the intersection of many of these lines, face state rejection. And even though they continue to claim affective connection to the nation, their patriotism is not blind. They are patriotic *despite* the US government's rejection of them and their families. Their desire for the nation highlights the importance of the separation between the nation and the state in Dreamer rhetorics. The nation is home, even though the state as gatekeeper keeps shutting the door.

"THAT'S ALL WE EVER WANTED:" DREAMERS AS NEOLIBERAL SUBJECTS

Scholars have described how neoliberalism functions as an ideology based on free-market principles that reaches all aspects of social and political life. Political theorist Wendy Brown proposes that neoliberal ideology "disseminates the *model of the market* to all domains and activities—even where money is not at issue—and configures human beings exhaustively as market actors, always, only, and everywhere as *homo oeconomicus*."[40] In a neoliberal society, all aspects of life are shaped by a capitalist market model that values individualistic competition and a maximized return on investments.

Ironically, the vast expanse of neoliberal ideology has reached activism that advocates to end income inequality and racialized injustice. Enticed by the promises of neoliberalism, such activism forgoes radical possibilities in exchange for state recognition and regularization. In the Obama era, some mainstream activism refocused their goals from demanding radical change to winning individual legal battles and electoral politics at least partly due to the influence of neoliberal ideology. Immigrant activism during this time was not immune to neoliberalism's appeal. Within US neoliberal society, Dreamers who would benefit from radical change were often limited to asking for regularization into exclusionary neoliberal systems of income inequality.

On the surface the Dream 9 action is an illustrative example of the ubiquity of neoliberal ideology in Dreamer rhetorics of the Obama era. The neoliberal subjectivity of Dreamers is created through rhetoric that strategically highlights individualism in order to rehumanize Dreamers while also helping them fit into normative definitions of acceptable citizens. Dreamer rhetorics present the Dreamers as individuals, putting a face and name to a statistic as a (re)humanizing strategy. For example, activists at the border during the Dream 9 action held signs that asked for each Dreamer to be "returned home" by name. Signs stating, "Bring Lizbeth Home," "Bring Adriana home," etc. are visible in pictures of the event. In order to be the truly neoliberal subject, the figure of the Dreamer must be first and foremost an individual. In this way the figure of the Dreamer appeals to a sort of postracial rhetoric of colorblindness in which immigrants are accepted into or rejected from the nation not on the basis of race, ethnicity, or national origin but on an individual basis. This appeal hinges on the idea of a meritocracy in which individuals on their own are acceptable because of their individual merits.

Dreamer rhetorics' investment in the individual is also evident in the slogan "Undocumented and Unafraid," one of the most highly used slogans by Dream 9 demonstrators, as visible in the livestreamed video, and in Dreamer activism at large. Education scholar René Galindo writes that "Undocumented and Unafraid" is much more than a slogan: it is a political subjectivity with which Dreamers rejected being relegated to living in the shadows.[41] As a political subjectivity, "Undocumented and Unafraid" helped to interject Dreamer lives and stories into the mainstream US political discussion. I read "Undocumented and Unafraid" as a statement of the Dreamers' desire to be recognized by the country and the world on their own terms. It shows pride in undocumented subjectivity and willingness to fight to be seen. However, I suggest that the slogan also reproduces the neoliberal emphasis on individual responsibility. The stance of being "unafraid" gives the Dreamer the duty of fighting fearlessly for the end of immigrant precarity. Dreamers are expected to be tough and pull themselves up by their bootstraps—not only in the upward-social-mobility kind of way, but also in the activist, fight-for-your-rights kind of way. Those undocumented young people who fail this neoliberal imperative, who cannot be unafraid, are not worthy of inclusion in the nation-state (because they didn't fight for their rights) and not worthy of inclusion in the movement (because they didn't toe the line of fearlessness). The slogan "Undocumented and Unafraid" downplays the fact that many of these young people do actually fear their own detention and deportation and/or that of their loved ones and takes the focus away from the state's responsibility in perpetuating immigrant vulnerabilities.

Photographs of the Dream 9 illustrate how neoliberal respectability politics permeate Dreamer activism. As they marched around Nogales, Sonora, toward the US port of entry, eight young Latinxs donned graduation caps and gowns (the exception was Mario Félix, who joined the group at the last minute, making the group the Dream 9) and walked arm-in-arm so that their human chain took up most of the city's dilapidated downtown street. Behind them walked a small group of adults, including a priest and a couple of journalists. The young activists smiled brightly; in their hands they held the legal documents that requested their humanitarian parole. They did not look like undocumented activists about to challenge the entry laws of the most powerful country in the Western Hemisphere. They looked like college graduates celebrating.

The student identity was purposefully deployed through the use of graduation caps and gowns to symbolize the Dreamers' potential to become productive members of US society and counter the narrative that undocumented immigrants are a drain on the state. This rhetorical strategy positioned the Dreamer as the stereotypical college-educated citizen—belonging to the middle class and invested in neoliberal models of meritocratic advancement. Selecting the graduation cap and gown as the sartorial symbol for Dreamers reveals that young undocumented activists are savvy about how images circulate in a digital economy. The image of the graduating student circulates quickly in digital media and is easily recognizable by a US audience that values success in education as the measure of merit and the indication of hard work. Images and illustrations of the Dream 9 wearing caps and gowns abound online. The Dream 9 were even wearing these same caps and gowns when they were released from the Eloy Detention Center two weeks later. By purposefully highlighting their identities as students, the Dreamers implied that they too are invested in the meritocracy and in state forms of social management through institutions like the university, the military, and even the heteronormative family. "That's all we want, just go to college, sit in a classroom like this and study. That's all I ever wanted," Luís reminded the students of the University of Portland.[42] Because the Dream 9 action (and, it could be argued, Dreamer activism in general) frames the Dreamers as primarily concerned with education, this moment of activism can be read as doubling down on the good immigrant/bad immigrant binary that separates Dreamers (the good) from other undocumented immigrants (the bad).[43]

AFFECTIVE CITIZENSHIP AND THE FREEDOM OF MOVEMENT

In describing the form and function of the deportation regime, Nicholas de Genova attests the importance of freedom of movement for human life. He writes, "Human life, in its most apparently 'biological' and socially undifferentiated or unqualified (animal) sense, is inseparable from the uninhibited capacity for movement which is a necessary premise for free and purposeful exercise of creative and productive powers."[44] De Genova describes the restrictions to mobility effected through the regime of deportation against those deemed deportable as a form of enslavement connected to capitalist production. He continues, "The freedom of movement remains the freedom of life itself, not merely the mundane necessity to make a living but *the freedom to truly live*. Deportation, as a more or less juridical, more or less arbitrary, exercise of state power, is therefore an exquisitely concentrated abnegation of that freedom, one more usurpation by the state of the sovereign power of humanity itself."[45] I propose that the Dream 9 action calls attention to the ways the deportation regime restricts Dreamers' freedom of movement across national boundaries and results in their alienation from their birthplaces. The results of restrictions to their freedom of movement are noteworthy. First, maintaining transnational communication and kinship with one's birth country can be particularly important for many Latinx immigrant populations. In a society that often under- or misrepresents Latin American history and culture, a close connection to one's birth country can be life affirming. Second, it is the curtailment of Dreamers' freedom of movement that buttresses their claims of affective citizenship. Perhaps one of the reasons that these Dreamers *feel* so US American is that they have not been allowed to visit Mexico and build a connection to its land, people, and culture *as Mexicans*. The deportation regime thus helps to produce culturally liminal Dreamers with strong ties to the US and wavering knowledge of their birth countries.

When the three activist Dreamers—Lizbeth, Lulu, and Marco—crossed the border into Mexico to take part in the Dream 9 action, they were there also to connect to their estranged homeland. However, they were not in Mexico to stay. Crossing the border into Mexico was intended to help constitute the US as the Dreamers' home. While they were in Mexico, the three Dreamers made videos checking in, telling their stories, and talking about the upcoming activist event. These videos were posted on the NIYA YouTube channel to bring attention to the Dream 9 action and to contextualize the Dreamers' reasons for participating in the event. I argue that the videos also served as a critique of their curtailed freedom of movement and as an emphasis of the affective citizenship that they had developed due to their inability to travel internationally.

In their videos Lizbeth, Lulu, and Marco, the three activist Dreamers, comment on how crazy it is that they are actually in Mexico. Marco begins his video by stating, "If you're watching this, it's because I am currently in Mexico, as crazy as that sounds."[46] Marco says this as he stares into the camera, the sound of an ominously ticking clock in the background. Marco's statement itself portends misfortune, as it sounds similar to messages left by someone who has faced mortal peril (i.e., "If you are seeing this, it's already too late"). Lizbeth, in a lighter yet more vulnerable tone, begins her check-in video by stating, "I'm making this video from Mexico. I know that's gonna sound a little crazy, and, to be honest, I still can't believe that I'm here."[47] Lulu, eyes filled with tears, echoes these comments in her own check-in video.[48] The statement that it is crazy that they are in Mexico conveys two important claims of Dreamer rhetorics. First, it works to frame the US as the Dreamers' rightful place. The repetition of the word "crazy" invites viewers to see it as unbelievable that the Dreamers are in Mexico. Their presence south of the border is denaturalized: it is extraordinary and inconceivable. The Dreamers' natural habitat is in the US.

Secondly, commenting on how abnormal it is for Dreamers to be in Mexico makes a statement condemning the inability of Dreamers to move freely across borders. None of these Dreamers had visited Mexico since their initial emigration, because of the fear of not being able to return to their lives in the US. Each video makes a point of listing how many years it has been since each Dreamer was in Mexico: "more than twenty years"[49] for Lulu, "since he was three years old"[50] for Marco, and "more than fifteen years"[51] for Lizbeth. While the Dreamers' main argument is that they belong in the US, theirs is also an argument for the freedom of movement. This argument is made through rhetorical choices that emphasize the experience of being reunited with a birthplace. Lulu states, "To be honest, I think it's even crazier that I had to wait fifteen years to see my family."[52] Lizbeth states, "I got to see where I was born; I got to see where my dad grew up. I got to see my cousins who are my age."[53] In this way Dreamer rhetorics critique the US immigration system that keeps young Dreamers trapped on one side of the border because the risks of crossing it are too high.

I see the deportation regime extending its arms into Dreamers' lives, not in keeping them from migrating to the US but instead in preventing them from freely crossing the border to see their cultural homeland without risking their lives in the US. The regime of deportation works in a very specific way for Dreamers. Sure, deportation is a constant threat that through fear keeps them from living their lives fully. However, it is also a threat that stops them from creating transnational connections to other cultural homes. Being ripped away from the place of one's ancestors is a devastating reality that Dreamers must learn to live with. And yet, when they reach for their adopted homeland—the

US—this nation refuses to account for them. This is the Dreamers' cruel liminal space and the reason their affective citizenship sometimes seems to me a desperate attempt at feeling connected, rooted, belonging to some place.

"¡EL PUEBLO UNIDO!" COMMUNITY BUILDING AND GESTURES OF COALITION

The Dream 9 finished their walk around Nogales, Sonora, and arrived at the Mariposa port of entry, the largest in Arizona. The nine Dreamers entered the port of entry, and when they could not show the relevant visas or paperwork, they were arrested, questioned, and then taken to the Eloy Detention Center to be processed as asylum seekers.[54] They were held at Eloy for two weeks.

The Eloy Detention Center is a 1,600-bed immigrant detention facility owned and managed by CoreCivic (formerly the Corrections Corporation of America). The center houses male and female immigrants who are being detained for immigration violations.[55] When they entered the detention center, Dreamers' positionality changed from innocent undocumented young people asking to come home to infiltrators demanding justice for the wider undocumented community. It is while in detention that the Dream 9 began to argue that part of affective citizenship is holding the state accountable for its actions. Their emotional connection to the US gave them the warrant for calling out its wrongdoings.

The Dreamers' dissident positionality is evident in the phone calls that the Dreamers made from detention. NIYA recorded at least some of the phone calls and posted them, along with pictures, slides, and moving images, on their YouTube channel as part of the BTH campaign. In Maria Inez Peniche's check-in from Eloy, NIYA specifically claims this new infiltrator positionality for the Dreamers, overlaying Maria Inez's voice with a black slide with white bold text stating, "Phase 2 Infiltration begins. Our work begins inside organizing our friends and families."[56] Interestingly, Phase 2 of BTH was never referenced in outward-facing messaging before Dreamers were put in detention. This makes sense, since announcing their plans to bring their activism to the detention center may have derailed NIYA's efforts to get the Dreamers across the border. However, the mention of a new, previously undisclosed phase in the campaign positions Dreamers as covert agents looking to do damage from the inside. Whereas before entering detention, the Dreamers had been portrayed as good neoliberal subjects of the nation-state, after entering detention they were presented as troublemakers. Additionally, it is important to note the caption's use of the words "our friends and families." It is irrelevant whether or not the nine Dreamers actually knew someone that was being detained at the Eloy

Detention Center. Their aim is to gesture to the undocumented community at large and to the work of organizing with and advocating for the other immigrants in detention. In fact, in an interview with the radio program *Latino USA*, Maria Inez states that when she entered the detention center, her perspective shifted: "Being in contact with the other detainees, the other women, listening to their stories, made me see the bigger picture, made me realize that this is bigger than myself."[57] It is at Eloy that the Dream 9 action moves beyond aiming to help the nine Dreamers: it is now aimed at the entire undocumented community.

Based on the Dreamers' actions (particularly the women's) inside the detention center, Phase 2 of the Dream 9 action involved researching conditions inside the center and organizing the detained immigrants to demand better treatment and even bonded release. While in detention the Dream 9 disturbed the status quo, risking worsening their condition within the center, and perhaps even damaging their asylum cases, in order to create community and organize. Both Maria Inez and Lulu were put in solitary confinement (or, euphemistically, "disciplinary isolation") because they attempted to organize the detainees. According to a phone call by Claudia Amaro, Maria Inez and Lulu stood on tables in the cafeteria, handed out the contact information of an immigration attorney to the detained women, and started a chant of "¡El pueblo unido, jamás será vencido!" and "¡Sin papeles, sin miedo!"[58] The two young women were then handcuffed and separated from the rest of the population. Claudia describes how after that encounter Maria Inez and Lulu were accompanied by two guards each whenever they moved around the center.

Karma Chávez's notion of the "coalitional gesture" is useful in thinking about what Dreamer rhetorics do here. Chávez writes that sometimes coalition is not "an avowed relationship, but instead a space of convening that points toward coalitional possibility."[59] I see the Dreamers' presence at Eloy as this sort of space. In being locked up with other immigrants, the Dreamers have the opportunity to personally connect with them and to see the possibility for coalition. They decide to advocate for the other immigrants in detention and to use their activist training to help them. I suggest that Dreamer rhetorics interpellate the other immigrants in detention as part of the Dreamer community—their families, their friends—in a gesture of coalition.

More specifically, the slogans of "¡El pueblo unido, jamás será vencido!" and "¡Sin papeles, sin miedo!" work together to integrate the Dreamer community with the rest of the undocumented community. "¡Sin papeles, sin miedo!" is the Spanish translation of "Undocumented and Unafraid," a slogan that, as I mention above, was coined by the Dreamers and usually used to refer to Dreamers coming out of the shadows. "¡El pueblo unido, jamás será vencido!" on the other hand, is a protest slogan with histories in Latin America and in the US Latinx community.[60] Putting these two slogans together is a coalitional gesture with the entire Latinx community in the US and with traditions of protest in Latin America.

I must take a small detour here to discuss some of the implications of immigrant detention in order to set the context for the rhetorical situation that Dreamers were responding to inside the Eloy Detention Center. It is common practice for ICE to detain undocumented immigrants found living in the US while in deportation proceedings. It is also common practice for ICE to detain asylum seekers who arrive at US borders, even if they have broken no laws. In 2014 ICE was filling 34,000 beds in immigrant detention centers every night, as mandated by US Congress. Indeed, as legal scholar Anil Kalhan writes, in the decade before Obama was elected to his first term, immigrant detention skyrocketed from approximately 6,000 immigrants in detention per day in 1994 to an average of 33,000 per day in 2008.[61] This same time period saw a growth in private prison corporations like CoreCivic, which has 120 facilities currently under its management in the US, including prison, jails, and so-called detention centers.[62] The IIRIRA of 1996 extended the list of crimes that counted toward mandatory detention of undocumented immigrants and made it standard practice to detain asylum seekers. Undocumented immigrants who have committed certain crimes face mandatory detention, even if they have already served time for their crime or even if they were never sentenced to serve time for their crime. Undocumented immigrants and asylum seekers who have been deemed inadmissible are also held while ICE processes their removal. So are asylum seekers who have "credible fear" yet are unable to pay their bonds (although it must be noted that many immigration cases have no bond hearings; parole and bond decisions are often made at a categorical level, not on a case-by-case basis). Finally, people with deportation orders can be detained for an extended period of time while "judicial review is pending or ICE is attempting to effectuate removal."[63]

The Sixth Amendment guarantee to a speedy trial does not apply to immigration proceedings, so many immigrants end up being held for long periods of time while the backlogged immigration court system functions.[64] Conditions under which immigrants are held in the United States approximate conditions of criminal incarceration, so that the phrase "immigrant detention" is used euphemistically to refer to incarceration or imprisonment of people who have often committed no crime.[65] According to Kalhan, "overcrowding and lack of adequate telephone access, visitation hours, ventilation, food, clean quarters, and functioning showers and toilets have long been documented, and verbal and physical abuse have also been common."[66] So has inadequate health care. The ACLU reports that LGBTQ immigrants detained by the Department of Homeland Security face disproportionate levels of violence and sexual abuse while in custody, and that prolonged isolation for LGBTQ immigrants in "protective custody" is common practice.[67] The Eloy Detention Center has not been immune to allegations of inhumane treatment and negligence. In 2015 approximately two hundred of those being held at Eloy were participating in a hunger strike to protest inhumane and abusive conditions, including inadequate mental and medical care, lack of access to legal resources, and the exploitation of detainees' work. The hunger strike was sparked by the mysterious death of José de Jesús Deniz-Sahagún while being held in Eloy.[68]

During their time at Eloy, the Dreamers called out inhumane—and perhaps unconstitutional[69]—practices of immigrant detention. Importantly, this calling out works to rhetorically broaden the Dreamer community by incorporating immigrants who do not fit the Dreamer mold into their activism, particularly women/mothers. The Dreamers express how women are scared into submission at Eloy through threats and dehumanization. In a phone call from Eloy, Lizbeth describes how the women in detention are reticent about speaking to the Dream 9 about their living conditions. They are afraid that they will be put in solitary confinement or have their phone calls restricted. She states, "I don't know what they've done to the women here."[70] A phone call from Claudia describes how the guards at the center "tell [the women] that they are nobody."[71] By putting the Dream 9's phone calls from Eloy on their YouTube channel, NIYA is expanding the scope of their activism and incorporating gender issues into the primary concerns of Dreamer rhetorics. This is significant, especially since Dreamers were in the early 2010s called "entitled" and "selfish" by some mainstream immigration activists for centering issues that concern only immigrant youth.[72]

I write in much more depth about Dreamer rhetorics' focus on women/mothers in the following chapter; however, there was one phone call made while the nine Dreamers were at Eloy that serves as an example of how Dreamer rhetorics of the Dream 9 gestured to a wide immigrant coalition that paid particular attention to women's suffering inside the detention center. The call is not from a Dreamer and has little to do with the undocumented youth community, yet NIYA published the entire phone call on their YouTube channel and connected it to the other videos from the Dream 9 action. The call is from a woman named Thelsa Zelaya Trejo. In it she talks about the conditions of her detention and her despair at having been locked up for an entire year. Her phone call is in Spanish, but on the YouTube video her text has English subtitles and features the NIYA logo and information about BTH. I quote her at length here, in the English translation, not only because this text illustrates the ways that the Dreamer community expanded to incorporate non-Dreamers, but also because I think it is important to give Thelsa a voice in this book. Most people in the US don't know a person who has been detained as an undocumented immigrant. Many of us are unfamiliar with conditions in immigrant detention centers and in prisons in general. I think it is important for students and scholars to listen to the voices of immigrants in detention and to try to understand the reality in which they live.

Thelsa's narrative incorporates themes of gendered dehumanization and invites the inclusion of women/mothers into NIYA's priorities. I include Thelsa's words to help readers come to terms with what the US government is doing (or at least condoning) in the name of its citizens.

> My name is Thelsa Zelaya Trejo. The women from *Dream 9* and all the people at Eloy are being treated like criminals . . . they don't treat us like people, like mothers, they treat us as if we were nothing. It's not fair. . . . We are mothers, we are grandmothers, we are daughters. We are here because of our children. Because we want a better life for them. A young lady hung herself here. . . . She hung herself because a guard treated her badly and that same guard is still working here. They treat us like the worst dogs. . . . Even the guards laugh at us. . . . I can't take being here anymore. . . . The women that don't speak English are forced to speak English because if they don't [the guards] won't give them things and they yell at them, they shut doors on them. . . . We have decided to do something but we don't know who will protect us. Because we are afraid they will deport us, especially me because I don't have a lawyer. . . . More than anything, I'm afraid. . . . We are tired of this. We are not criminals. We are people who came here because of our children. To work, not to steal from anybody. I have lived here for 20 years and I have never been a thief, a drug addict, a drunk. I am only a mother who wants the best for her children. I only want to work and make a better life with my children. . . . I have been [in detention] for a year and two people have died because they gave them the wrong medicine, medicine that wasn't for them, medicine for a different person, a higher dose than the one prescribed for them and both of them died. There was also the woman who hung herself and a man who hung himself. . . . Because a dog has more worth here than us as human beings, as mothers. I can't take it.[73]

Even though in our current era the notion of incarceration is so inseparably linked to the idea of punishment that we are unable to imagine a society without it,[74] there is something exceptional about the imprisonment of immigrants. As I read Thelsa's narrative, I consider what it says about US society that a person can live in this country for 20 years, make a life, and then all of a sudden be locked up, her freedom restricted for over a year without having done anything specific to break the law other than living her life across a man-made border. Thelsa's very being is illegalized and criminalized, just like the rest of the Dream 9. And her supposed illegality rationalizes her dehumanization—indeed, she describes being treated lower than a dog.

Thelsa's narrative makes visible the gendered dehumanization of women at Eloy. Her repetition of the gendered roles of "mothers," "grandmothers," and "daughters," highlights the value of womanhood/motherhood and positions these gendered roles as characteristics of humanity. Because they are mothers, Thelsa claims, their dehumanization is even more egregious. In the same way, the rhetorics at work in Thelsa's narrative illustrate how immigrant detention works as a machine of dehumanization where women/mothers are treated as animals, or worse. Her repetition of the word "dog" frames Eloy as the place where immigrant women/mothers become nothing more than beasts in the eyes of the state. This injustice is the driving force for Dreamer rhetorics at the end of the Dream 9 action.

To return to affective citizenship, I suggest that Dreamer rhetorics from within Eloy highlight a different affective component of citizenship: anger at the nation for having betrayed and disappointed. When Dreamers become detainees, what they see and hear from inside the detention center turns them into angry dissidents. Their rhetorics in action reflect their rage.

CONCLUSION

As of 2015, at least eight of the nine Dreamers were living in the US while they waited for their asylum hearings.[75] The Dream 9 protest, however, had implications beyond the nine Dreamers' lives. In the Dream 9 action, Dreamers not only made arguments for their belonging, but also dared to imagine the sort of nation they'd like to belong to: a nation where people are treated with empathy and love. Coming from a group of people who have experienced oppression and seen the suffering of their loved ones at the hand of the state, this imagining is no small feat.

Perhaps it is their attachment to affective citizenship—although, of course, they do not refer to it by this name—that gives the Dream 9 the flexibility and creativity for such a national imagining. Indeed, in the Dream 9 action, affective citizenship is a strong rhetorical claim for immigrant belonging because it allows Dreamers to express love for the nation without foreclosing the possibility for critique. As my analysis of the Dream 9 action illustrates, affective citizenship is not necessarily romantic or naïve. It is felt, embodied, and sensitive to the nation's whims. It can be exhilarating, like I imagine was the case for Lulu and Maria Inez when they stood on the tables in the Eloy cafeteria and led chants of "¡Sin papeles, sin miedo!" It can also be extremely painful, as we hear in Claudia's voice when she fears not being able to return to Wichita. Like any relationship, affective citizenship requires a give and take. The affective citizen can demand that the nation return the love she has given it. Of course, there are no guarantees that this love will ever be requited.

On the other hand, the Dream 9 action is a reminder of how any attachment to citizenship is associated with inclusions and exclusions. Citizenship is a club to which Dreamers argue they belong. In the Dream 9 action, they perform the affective behaviors that are legible as citizenship: love for the nation, democratic engagement, neoliberal individualism, even social critique. In performing the affect of a citizen, Dreamers also stipulate what is *not* considered appropriate citizen behavior. In creating the boundaries of affective citizenship, they also decide who will be excluded from the citizenship space. The consequences of citizenship's exclusions are evident in Thelsa's narrative from detention, as we see the ways those who are deemed not to belong cannot even expect for the state to regard them as humans.

3

Rhetorics of Immigrant Motherhood in Reforma 150

After the relative success of the Dream 9 action, NIYA organizers learned that they could emphasize the vulnerability of deported Dreamers as a way to bolster asylum-seeker claims of credible fear of torture or persecution. In the Dream 9 action, all nine Dreamers had successfully argued that they would face danger if returned to Mexico specifically because of their Dreamer identity. In other words, Dreamers claimed that they were particularly vulnerable to violence, bullying, and extortion in Mexico because they were Dreamers. With this idea in mind, NIYA organized another action—the Dream 30—which would push "for a new 'Dreamer' particular social group to be defined as a protected ground under asylum laws."[1] NIYA organizer Mohammad Abdollahi succinctly expressed the main premise of this activist strategy: "[Dreamers] are getting persecuted [in Mexico] because as soon as they speak Spanish people know they're American."[2] On September 30, 2013, approximately thirty-four undocumented immigrants walked to the US port of entry in Laredo, Texas, wearing graduation regalia and, echoing the words that the Dream 9 had used just a few months earlier, asked the US to let them return home.

Yet this activist strategy was insufficient when Dreamer activists attempted to help larger groups of immigrants of diverse ages, backgrounds, and life stories. As I conclude in chapter 2, when the undocumented youth were detained at the Eloy Detention Center in Arizona, their rhetorics began to gesture to a wider Dreamer community that includes other detained undocumented women. Consequently, in NIYA's subsequent action, Reforma 150, Dreamer organizers focused on helping a more diverse immigrant population. In Reforma 150, approximately 150 undocumented immigrants asked for asylum at the Otay Mesa port of entry in San Diego, California, in March 2014. The immigrants were of various ages and nationalities, many of them parents, with or without their children.

Taking advantage of the importance of family reunification for immigration decisions during the Obama presidency[3] and of the weight that rhetorics of family values held and continue to hold in the US mainstream, Reforma 150 highlighted the familial bonds of the border crossers in order to argue for their entry. For example, the parents of Maria Inez Peniche, one of the Dream 9, crossed as part of Reforma 150. Her brother had already crossed the border into the US as part of the Dream 30. Allowing the Peniche parents to come into the US would effectually reunite the entire family. Isabel Martinez crossed to reunite with her daughter Sarai, a US citizen living in Chicago. Dolores Lara, a father of two, was one of the first ones to cross as part of Reforma 150. Although he was returned to Mexico almost immediately, he was able to spend a brief moment with his daughters, whom he hadn't seen since he was deported three years previously.[4] The narrative was that these asylum seekers were members of families, raising children and working hard to build lives in the US.

As they worked to build community—a main purpose of Dreamer rhetorics—Dreamers developed and used rhetorics that sought to create space for undocumented people who did not fit the Dreamer mold. For example, by framing the women who took part in Reforma 150 as "*our* mothers," Dreamers were taking advantage of their (albeit limited) political capital to help undocumented women and, in turn, expand the Dreamer community. In this way, Dreamers wove the concerns of undocumented women and children into their own narratives, centering Dreamers rhetorically in order to capitalize from their relative appeal to the US mainstream. This rhetorical move is why I propose that Reforma 150 is an example of Dreamer rhetorics that push beyond what such rhetorics are commonly considered. As my analysis shows, Dreamer organizers made careful strategic and rhetorical choices to maximize the success of this action and to present a diverse group of undocumented people as part of one vast undocumented *familia*.[5]

Instead of crossing as a single group, Reforma 150 participants crossed in groups of thirty to forty over the course of eight days. The groups were purposefully created to maximize the possibility of all family members being admitted into the country, not returned at the border or detained indefinitely. For example, on one particular day, the group featured only mothers and children seeking asylum. As NIYA organizer and Dream 30 participant Rocio Hernandez Perez explains in a video of the events on March 18, 2014, having entire families cross together would prompt ICE to detain and/or deport the fathers, granting parole only to the mothers, who could enter the US with their children. Crossing each parent separately with a child, when possible, would make it more difficult for the US to deport the fathers, because they have at least one of their children in tow.[6] While some of the Reforma 150 participants were returned to Mexico the same day on which they crossed, others were paroled into the US over the next few weeks, awaiting asylum hearings.

Gender takes shape in a very particular way under this new activist strategy. The need to show fear of torture and persecution in Reforma 150 requires rhetorics that highlight immigrant vulnerability, which is often read as a feminine characteristic. The vulnerable woman, the damsel in distress, is a well-rehearsed patriarchal trope that has found its way into all sorts of rhetorical contexts, from white supremacy to human rights.[7] Dreamer rhetorics emphasize vulnerable femininity, particularly in mothers and children, to argue for asylum. Similarly, the need to frame the nation as home (as in "Bring them Home") has important implications for how gender and sexuality work in Dreamer rhetorics of Reforma 150. When the nation is portrayed as a home, women's rhetorical position is in large part restricted to roles ascribed by heteropatriarchy: heteronormative, domestic, mothers.

With rhetorics that focused on the family—the building block of the nation—NIYA organizers in Reforma 150 argued that because these immigrants belonged to heteronormative nuclear families, they logically belonged in a nation that claims to respect traditional family values. Ethnic studies scholar Lisa Marie Cacho notes that in seeking to replicate normative models of US life, undocumented immigrants often align themselves with the ultimate structure of normativity, the nuclear heteropatriarchal family.[8] In immigrant narratives of Reforma 150, the heteronormative family became the measure of acceptability into the nation. NIYA's heteronormative family rhetorics sought to frame undocumented immigrants, particularly women, as acceptable, somewhat relatable, and decidedly nonthreatening. Undocumented women were framed as acceptable in their adherence to heteronormative roles, relatable in their performance of conventional motherhood practices, and nonthreatening in their supposed subservience to the patriarch(y). The figure of the mother rhetorically can accomplish all of these goals.

Such appeals, however, reify the assumption that Latinx women are and should be primarily subservient to men and white women in US society. Rhetorics that privilege motherhood as the main legitimate identity for immigrant women can result in Latinx women being understood as part of the nation first and foremost as members of the private sphere. As Sara McKinnon writes, in asylum cases, women are most often placed in the private side of the public/private binary, a side that occludes their political subjectivity and makes them unintelligible as anything other than domestic.[9] Similarly, because immigrant women are rhetorically legitimated primarily through their role as caretakers of the home, the rhetorics of motherhood reify the private/public binary in which Latinx immigrant women are limited to the private realm, while white women "citizens" can enter the public sphere. Ergo, in dominant US discourses, Latinx immigrant women are legible only in the private realm, where they will leave no mark on the homogeneous national image, but where they *will* be found in the private homes of white women cleaning the house and taking care of white children.

As a Latinx woman, I am exhausted by this seemingly perpetual limitation in the ways that brown women are portrayed in US whitestream culture. As a Latinx feminist, I am also troubled by how our own communities reproduce patriarchy and heteronormativity—themselves colonial constructs.[10] And yet, as Amalia Pallares argues, "we should not assume that a politics that relies on a reproduction of conventional norms always means or implies a lack of emancipatory potential."[11] Therefore, as I analyze the rhetorics of Reforma 150, I look for alternative imaginings of Latinx immigrants. While highlighting motherhood in Reforma 150 may be rhetorically auspicious, women of color feminisms have shown that motherhood is not a universal experience.[12] Motherhood in some contexts might be associated with the private sphere, but for Latinx mothers it can incorporate public demonstrations of *fuerza*.

In this chapter, my analysis explores how the particular function of gender and sexuality in discourses of vulnerability and family can result in rhetorics that confront patriarchal assumptions. I propose that in Reforma 150, gender and sexuality work in ways that present possibilities and limitations in the rhetorics. In the pages that follow, I argue that in centering gender and sexuality in immigrant activism, Dreamer rhetorics have the potential to construct feminist subjectivities that disrupt normative narratives of undocumented Latinxs. Dreamer rhetorics create ruptures in patriarchal discourses to make room for radical feminist positionings. Such ruptures, however, are often hidden behind heteropatriarchal discourses of respectability. These layered meanings demonstrate the rhetorical complexity of Dreamer rhetorics and are the driving force for my desire to read these rhetorics against the grain.

Like Anzaldúa's *nepantla* and Sandoval's differential consciousness, Dreamer rhetorics inhabit a flexible way of being and thinking, a "tolerance for ambiguity" that allows not only for the transgression of borders but for the existence of new and dissident positionalities. Therefore, I follow a "both/and" methodological approach, an analytic that rejects singular readings and instead looks for *both* the possibilities *and* the limitations that come from appeals of belonging that are based on the heteronormative family.[13] I draw on Latinx and Black feminisms to unveil the layers of meaning in the rhetorics of Reforma 150 and propose a re/vision of this activist moment. I illustrate how these activist rhetorics can be read as having *both* heteropatriarchal *and* radical connotations. I posit that in centering the family in immigrant activism, the rhetorics of Reforma 150 did much more than simply reproduce heteropatriarchal ideas of women. Indeed, I argue that such rhetorics have the potential to construct feminist subjectivities that disrupt normative narratives of undocumented Latinx women both inside and outside the Latinx community.

I ground my analysis largely on María Lugones's concept of the coloniality of gender. The coloniality of gender refers to the ways in which the dichotomous system of gender categorization (i.e., understandings of gender limited to only male or female subjects) was imposed via colonization as a way to dehumanize colonized subjects.[14] This process of gender subjectification was imposed on colonized peoples who subsequently internalized it; this means that the gendered rhetorics of oppressed peoples often function on this colonial gender binary. Lugones argues that the coloniality of gender works to dehumanize the oppressed by denying them gender and therefore humanity.[15] Women are positioned as human only in their relation to white men, meaning that in colonialist discursive formations only white women are considered to be human.[16] Under this system colonized females are "nongendered, promiscuous, grotesquely sexual, sinful."[17] As a frame with which to analyze the rhetorics of the Reforma 150, the coloniality of gender prompts a decolonial re/vision of colonized woman as an informed and resisting agent. Dreamer rhetorics gesture toward what Lugones refers to as "decolonizing gender" by framing immigrant women as more than subjects of the coloniality of gender. If the pervasive coloniality of gender posits that only white females are women/human, then by producing themes of Latinx womanhood, Dreamer rhetorics may indeed be subverting the legacies of colonization.

The terms "decolonial," "decolonization," and "decoloniality" have been differently defined and approached by various scholars, from Latin American philosophers to Chicana feminists. In my use of the concept, I draw primarily on Latinx feminism to understand decoloniality and its derivatives. I also consider the landmark text on decoloniality by Even Tuck and K. Wayne Yang, "Decolonization Is Not a Metaphor."[18] I understand decolonization as a response to the legacy of settler colonialism and the mechanisms with which it continues to attempt to eliminate the Indigenous people of this hemisphere.

From an academic perspective, decolonization is a practice that dislodges some of the assumptions of settler colonialism by making visible subaltern ways of knowing and being while remaining attentive to the scholar's own complicity with settler colonialism. As an activist practice, decolonization involves the reappropriation, recasting, and reframing of previously subjugating settler colonialist terms and concepts. Decolonization understands that "resistance [is not] the end or goal of political struggle, but rather its beginning, its possibility."[19] As such, it is an ongoing practice that "implicates and unsettles everyone."[20] Decolonization denotes a practice to dismantle settler colonialism and the privileges of land and knowledge that it continues to assign to the settlers in the settler-native-slave triad of relations.[21]

To engage this decolonial reading practice, I return once again to the idea I develop in chapter 1: that activist moments are made up of constellations of texts. As I mention in chapter 1, an activist moment makes meaning beyond the time and space of the action. The meaning-making capacity of activist moments such as, for example, Reforma 150, begins long before the first activists hit the streets. In fact, much of the meaning that is made by an activist moment, not to mention an entire movement, is done before and after the on-the-street action, in the texts that surround the primary activist focus. In this chapter I analyze videos created before the Reforma 150 actions. I look for the decolonial possibilities in these texts and outline how they construct a resistant Latinx mother ethos that counters heteropatriarchy inside and outside the Latinx immigrant community. I pay careful attention to how the rhetorics in these texts shift and stretch among differing ideological positions and challenge the stability of meaning.

SOMOS MADRES: MOTHERHOOD, MOTHERLY DUTY, AND RESISTANCE

As a precursor to the Reforma 150 events, NIYA created a three-minute video titled "Bring Our Mothers Home #WeAreElvira" to introduce some of the mothers and children who would take part in the action. This video features a large room with approximately ten women and their children sitting in front of a blue banner of the hashtag #BringThemHome. The letter "o" in the word "home" is the red, white, and blue rising-sun logo from Obama's presidential campaigns. During the video some of the women share their stories of migration, talking about their reasons for returning to their countries of origin after having lived in the US undocumented, and about their desire to now go back to the US.

This text illustrates how discourses of nation and home are gendered so that female positionalities help craft what transnational feminist scholar Chandra Tapalde Mohanty describes as nationalist moralistic discourses.[22] Centering immigrant women as mothers, "Bring Our Mothers Home" argues that these women should be given asylum in the US because they are motivated by a moral imperative that carves a place for them in the US national family. In the rhetoric of motherly duty, women are positioned as those who not only bear the children that will inhabit the nation but also, through the passage of beliefs, values, and traditions, create good citizens to populate the state. As Natalie Fixmer-Oraiz contends, "motherhood and nation are deeply enmeshed and mutually constitutive."[23] The moralistic nationalist rhetoric of motherly duty—built primarily on the heteropatriarchal idea that women have essential moral duties centered on the family—invokes dominant associations about a mother's duty to reproduce the nation, both biologically and culturally.[24] As Fixmer-Oraiz writes, however, not all mothers are celebrated. Women of color are often subject to "a deeply racialized and classed notion of pathological motherhood"[25]; their low-income bodies of color come to be understood as unruly reproductive bodies and as threats to the nation.

To avoid the racialized and classed discrimination against low-income mothers of color, the NIYA video defines the immigrant women's motherly identity by their adherence to a universalized notion of motherly duty. The immigrant mothers' moral obligations to their families attempt to make these women acceptable to the nation in opposition to other imaginings of Latinx women who are deemed troublesome and unacceptable, including the hypersexual Latina and the immigrant mother of the anchor baby.[26] In contrast with these two rhetorical figures, the acceptable immigrant mother as outlined by the rhetorics of motherhood is self-sacrificing and respectable.

The rhetoric of motherly duty is introduced by the first woman who speaks in the video, Elvira Arellano, and then reproduced in the other women's motherly narratives.[27] Arellano is an undocumented woman from Mexico who became a vocal advocate for the rights of immigrant families after taking up sanctuary in the Adalberto United Methodist Church in Chicago when she was issued a deportation order.[28] Arellano was eventually arrested in August 2007 when she left the church to attend an immigration rally in Los Angeles, California. She was deported back to Mexico shortly after, where she continued her activist work with migrant women.[29] During the Obama years, Arellano was seen as an icon for the family reunification and sanctuary movements in the US. She represented the archetypal immigrant mother who would do anything for her children. Her struggles to reunite with her US-born son inspired a resurgence in the religious sanctuary movement in the US, an echo of the 1980s sanctuary movement that sought to help Central Americans fleeing violent conflict. By including Arellano's story as the video's opener and the hashtag #WeAreElvira in the video's title, NIYA activists highlight that for women the claim to US belonging is legitimated through their identities as mothers. As a mother, Arellano becomes the representative of all undocumented immigrant women trying to return to the US.[30]

Motherly duty is the vehicle with which the rhetorics in the video rationalize the mothers' multiple border crossings. When immigration is explained as driven by family love, undocumented border crossing may sit better with an audience that prioritizes family values. Yet this rhetorical move also legitimizes patriarchal gender hierarchies by portraying motherhood as immigrant women's only valuable subject position.[31] I argue, however, that a decolonial reading may unveil the rhetorics' more radical function. Instead of seeing Arellano as a mother-subject in service of the nation-state, through a decolonial reading she is made visible as an example of resistant motherhood. The idea of resistant motherhood expands on work by feminist geographer Melissa Wright, who explores how rhetorics of motherhood were deployed by the Madres de la Plaza de Mayo in Buenos Aires in order to legitimize their protest against their children's disappearance at the hands of the military dictatorship of the 1970s and '80s.[32] The Madres highlighted their identities as mothers in order to subdue claims that they were politically subversive women on the streets. Emphasizing women's role in the private realm, the Madres framed their rage against the dictatorship as a mother's duty to look after her children. Thus, they gained visibility for their cause while protecting themselves from persecution from the state.

I propose that rhetorics of motherhood do more for Arellano and the other undocumented Latinx women in Reforma 150 than frame their activism as motherly duty in order to understate their critique of state policies. I read the rhetorics of motherhood as closely connecting immigrant mothering with practices of resistance. I contend that in "Bring Our Mothers Home," the mothers' resistance is motivated by a politics of desire: the desire to be with their children is presented as the force that motivates their activism. Black feminist scholar Patricia Hill Collins writes that "physical and/or psychological separation of mothers and children, designed to disempower individuals, forms the basis of a systematic effort to disempower racial ethnic communities."[33] The separation of mothers and children, which for women of color began with colonization and slavery, is reproduced via immigration policies and practices that split families across human-made borders. Thus, the immigrant mother's desire to be next to her children reflects not only a personal will but also a collective struggle for resistance and survival.[34]

Rhetorically, Arellano is never far away from her children. In images of Reforma 150, she is seen crossing the border with her two sons, fifteen-year-old Saul, who is a US citizen, and her four-month-old son, who was born in Mexico during her exile from the US. While Saul was the driving force for her initial sanctuary claim in Chicago, rhetorical attention now shifts to the infant son she carries with her as she makes her way to the Otay Mesa port of entry. Arellano's need to be close to her sons is presented as the impetus for her participation in this act of resistance. Chicana feminist scholar Emma Perez argues that when we shift the frame of analysis, we can imagine women of color as agents who "cast their own fantasies."[35] In BTH's rhetorics of motherhood, what becomes visible is Arellano's fantasy of closeness and attachment to her child, perhaps even a child's imagined return to the womb where he can be protected and loved without (or with limited) state intervention. Seeing Arellano's activism via a decolonial feminist lens unveils how her desire for her children is framed differently from notions of motherly duty prescribed by white heteropatriarchal discourses of family and even by white feminist theories.[36] Her activism does not reflect her self-sacrifice but her desire for proximity. This shift in view is crucial to a feminist analysis of the mother's video that understands the Latinx immigrant mothers as not only objects of rhetoric but subjects with rhetorical agency. Arellano, as a rhetorical actor, exemplifies mother-as-desiring-subject, mother-as-resister. She becomes an activist when a deportation order threatens to take her away from her son. In her activism, she voices her desire to be with her son above all else. This desire drives her to not only take personal risks but to also confront the might of one of the largest law enforcement agencies in the Western Hemisphere—the US Border Patrol. Her motherhood is feminist defiance.

This resistant motherhood is additionally illustrated in an image Dreamer activists created and circulated in support of Reforma 150 (Figure 1). The image features a black-and-white cut-out of Arellano, the only color on her body coming from stitched pink roses that have been superimposed on her shirt. Behind Arellano, we see a blurred image of Border Patrol agents at the border. Above her head is the flaming sacred heart that is associated with Catholic iconography. This heart looks different, however, from the traditional sacred heart. While the Catholic sacred heart represents the heart of Jesus Christ, the burning heart in the image of Arellano is decidedly feminine and feminist. The flames on the heart seem angry, yet they are patterned with flowers. The heart is red and raw, the color of life. Its central location in the image highlights its power. This is not the heart of Jesus. It is the heart of the mother raging with flagrant defiance. Perhaps it is this defiant feminist mother that immigrant women need as an icon, rather than the paternalistic sacred heart. Read this way, this image and the portrayal of Arellano in Reforma 150 rhetorically reinscribe motherhood for decolonial feminist aims against state oppression and patriarchal forces.[37]

Ethnic studies scholar Evelyn Nakano Glenn argues that "mothering, like other relationships and institutions, is socially constructed, not biologically inscribed."[38] When mothering is characterized by dutiful self-sacrifice, women's agency is subverted in exchange for the family's well-being. However, that same relationship can be rhetorically articulated as resisting state-sanctioned family separation, desiring of physical family bonds, and reproducing not the national(ist) project but subjects of dissent. Chicana feminist Ana Castillo writes that "women are serving the needs of *la patria* when giving birth,

Figure 1. *Reform Starts with Us*, illustration by the National Immigrant Youth Alliance.

producing labor and brainpower for global corporations and fodder for the wars that protect their interests."[39] I admit that the rhetorics of motherhood that Dreamer organizers invoked during Reforma 150 capitalize on framing immigrant women as able to reproduce the heteropatriarchal US nation-state. I argue, however, that there is more to these rhetorics at work. While the image of the virtuous and selfless mother helped to craft a space for the acceptance of immigrant women into the nation-state, the children of the immigrant mother do not fit normative imaginings of the US as a white Anglo-Saxon Protestant nation. Instead, the immigrant women involved in Reforma 150 reproduce a Latinx nation, a nation of those who will disrupt the status quo, who will perhaps be activists and dissenters. Hidden underneath the surface of the rhetorics of motherhood is the claim that Latinx immigrant mothers may indeed reproduce revolutionary subjects, the Indigenous and mestizo children who will decolonize this stolen land. These mothers reproduce not just the citizen but also the dissident. This is their motherly resistance. Describing the Aztec women of Mesoamerica, Castillo writes, "Because of her ability to give birth and nourish her offspring with her milk, woman for centuries was both feared and revered."[40] Perhaps like these Aztec warrior women, immigrant mothers should be feared. Maybe those invested in white nationalist normativity should indeed be scared.

CROSS-BORDER MOTHERWORK: WHISPERS OF EMOTIONAL LABOR AND COALITION

While the gendered rhetorics of Reforma 150 seem to at times directly propose a homogenized version of mothering based on self-sacrifice, there are whispers in the rhetorics that quietly posit something quite different. Even though their overt expressions adhere to the mainstream rules of acceptability and respectability, the mothers' narratives also quietly tell of how their mothering practices—their motherwork—resist patriarchal invisibilization. "Motherwork" is a Black feminist term describing the mothering practices of women of color. A portmanteau of mothering and working, motherwork challenges the private/public dichotomy by arguing that mothering is work that not only influences the realm of the home but also greatly impacts the community.[41] Hill Collins proposes that motherwork functions along three related themes: survival, as in ensuring the physical survival of one's children and the children of the community; empowerment, as in working to empower the community to fight against oppression; and identity, which Hill Collins describes as "trying to foster meaningful racial identity in children within a society that denigrates people of color."[42] Motherwork recognizes that the individual and the community are inherently connected, and that "individual survival, empowerment, and identity require group survival, empowerment, and identity."[43]

As the rhetorics illustrate, the motherly narratives of Reforma 150 have their patriarchal connotations, but they also whisper evidence of resistant motherwork. I invoke whispering here to connote the ways that the rhetorics of those who have been continually silenced by the patriarchal state, whose desires and ideas have been most often subsumed under those of the patriarch—be it a father, male partner, husband, brother, or son—who have been repeatedly told to keep their heads down and be silent in the face of injustice, can have quiet yet powerful meanings beneath the surface. For Latinx women, as for many other women in the world, our hopes and desires are often conscripted by the power of the patriarchy. Unable to voice our preferences and ideas, we are left to whisper to each other in hallways, kitchens, and bedrooms, as we share with each other *en voz baja*, the *secretos* that substantiate our lives. Whispering to each other is the secret code by which we survive.

As I look at the rhetorics in the "Bring Our Mothers Home" video, I hear the whispers of immigrant women who, knowingly or not, evidence their noncompliance with patriarchal expectations of their behavior. Yes these narratives portray motherhood as a woman's main legitimizing role and as a self-sacrificing and homogeneous practice. However, if we pay close attention to the rhetorics at work, we can unveil the practices of survival, empowerment, and identity that immigrant women perform every day. We can also hear the emotional labor that motherwork involves, particularly for immigrant women who are separated from their children. Through the whispered rhetorics of motherwork, the "Bring Our Mothers Home" video creates alternative definitions of motherhood that reflect the realities of immigrant lives and evidence the strategies of survival and resistance that immigrant women and children practice to resist their oppression.

One of the main aspects of immigrant motherwork that subtly permeates this text is the fact that many of these immigrant women were compelled to leave their children in home countries to ensure their survival. Sociologist Leah Schmalzbauer, who has done empirical research on transnational families from Latin America living in the US, notes that "in the global south, motherwork increasingly mandates migration."[44] By crossing the border north, immigrant women are able to provide for their children. Mothers trying to send money home to pay for food and/or schooling may have to leave their children with what Schmalzbauer refers to as "other-mothers," networks of women who are left in charge of mothering children whose parents are working in the

US. This sacrifice is an important part of immigrant women's motherwork, and it weaves into agentive definitions of motherhood that acknowledge how immigrant women act in the face of life-threatening difficulties.

Such practices can be gleaned in the narrative of the second woman who speaks in the "Bring Our Mothers Home" video.[45] Holding her young daughter on her lap, the woman describes the difficult decision she made to return to Mexico, her country of origin, when her mother was diagnosed with cancer and could no longer take care of the woman's son. She states, "*Pero un día, mi mamá me habló llorando que ella estaba enferma de cáncer y que yo tenía que volver para hacerme cargo de mi hijo que necesitaba ser operado. Esa fue una decisión muy fuerte para mi, pero lo hice porque primero soy madre.*"[46] ("But one day, my mother called me crying [telling me] she was sick with cancer and that I had to return to take care of my son who had to have surgery. This was a very tough decision for me, but I did it because I am first a mother.")

The idea that women are first of all mothers helps to frame immigrant women as acceptable to the nation. The rhetorics of motherhood look to build identification among women across difference so that all can make a claim for national belonging. This move rhetorically eliminates other differences that women may have across cultures, races, nationalities, etc. The statement of "*primero soy madre*" subsumes other possible identities that this woman may have and clouds any disparaging association that a US audience may have with this woman (for example, as a so-called illegal alien). Furthermore, these rhetorics of motherhood seem to assume a universal experience of motherhood, obscure the heterogeneity within this identity, and privilege motherhood as immigrant women's main valuable subject position. However, if we listen to what is left unsaid, at what is only hinted at, we can hear evidence of Latinx women's resistant motherwork. First, while the woman does not specifically explain it, her narrative whispers the story of a mother who left her son in the care of an *abuela* so that she could move to the US and earn money to send back home. As Schmalzbauer writes, "Material and economic remittances are rooted in the values of motherwork."[47] The need to ensure the survival of their children prompts women to take actions that separate them.

The motherhood rhetorics here make an argument about the ways in which immigrant motherwork under a capitalist world order demands that women make impossible decisions: the woman in the video has to choose between being there to physically care for her son and her ill mother and being able to provide for her son (and perhaps for her mother) financially. In emphasizing the difficulty of the woman's decision to return, this video segment rhetorically highlights the push and pull of immigrant motherwork and the capitalist state's role in family separation. These transnational motherhood practices also underscore the emotional labor of motherwork for immigrant women.[48] Immigrant mothers who are separated from their children must bear the emotional weight of that separation, of being unable to fulfill their own and society's expectations of in-person nurturing and care, and of the decisions they must continue to make to ensure their children's survival.

The next woman who speaks in the "Bring Our Mothers Home" video similarly demonstrates the impossible decisions of transnational motherwork. This woman tells her story of leaving the US to return to her country of origin to help her daughter who was very ill. She states, "*Yo regresé a mi país de origen en el 2011. Me vi en la gran necesidad de hacerlo porque mi hija se encontraba muy grave, debatiéndose entre la vida y la muerte. Y yo hice lo que cualquier madre hubiese hecho en ese momento de desesperación y angustia de salir a estar al lado de ella en esos momentos difíciles de su vida en los cuales ella se encontraba.*"[49] ("I returned to my country of origin in 2011. I found myself with the great need to do so because my daughter was very ill, wavering between life and death. And I did what any mother would have done in that moment of despair and anguish, going to her in those difficult moments of life in which she found herself.")

Significantly, this woman's rhetorics also illustrate how motherwork can function as a coalitional gesture for community empowerment. Looking straight into the camera, the woman seeks a connection among all mothers, stating that she did "what *any mother* would have done." With these words she seems to appeal to a universalized code of motherhood where all mothers are compelled to act in the same commonsensical way. Here, her rhetorics help to make the argument that she and the other immigrant women share a common core of beliefs around motherly duty—a set of core beliefs that should be familiar to mothers across difference. In this way, the woman's rhetorics assume a universal experience of motherhood and thus obscure the heterogeneity within this identity.

Yet, because the experience of motherhood is differentiated by race, class, national origin, language proficiency, and education, to name but a few criteria, the words "what any mother would have done" may be read as a whispered coalitional gesture that seeks to connect immigrant mothers with other mothers who struggle. Read this way, the woman's words are not speaking to and about *all* mothers. She is speaking to and thus gesturing coalition with other mothers whose motherwork incorporates the fear of state-sanctioned separation and precarity. I draw here on queer migrations scholar Karma Chávez's definition of coalition. Building on Lugones, Chávez writes that "coalition is a present vision and practice that is oriented toward others and a shared commitment to social and political change."[50] While coalition can be a temporary joining of forces, it can also denote "the horizon of possibility," a space of engagement where "the distinction between entities blends and blurs."[51] I read a gesture of coalition in the woman's words: a signal of "we are in this together."

By evoking the idea that *any* mother in her position would have done the same, the rhetoric addresses other immigrant mothers and connotes, "I see you, and I'm asking you to see me." After all, not just *any* mother is faced with the decision of crossing a man-made border, risking detention, and uprooting her life to help her ailing daughter. This woman's words create the space for coalition with other immigrant mothers who face or fear facing such impossible situations, as well as with other women of color who face similar obstacles to their ability to mother. Her words constitute the possibility for togetherness, commiseration, collective empowerment, and action.

QUEER MOTHERING, REVOLUTIONARY MOTHERING

As undocumented immigrants attempt to counter the narratives of criminalization and demonization coming from mainstream media and politicians, they may find that identifying as members of the heteronormative family could perhaps help them seem more acceptable to the US. Cacho writes, "In fact, both undocumented Latinas/os and un(der)employed African American citizens are required to provide evidence that their intimate relationships are proper embodiments of heteronormativity and respectable domesticity" in order to gain state recognition and assistance.[52] In the rhetorics of Reforma 150, the focus on the family frames immigrant women as heteronormative and consequently reproduces heteropatriarchal family values. Indeed, there is a noticeable assumption of heteronormativity in the rhetorics used in the "Bring Our Mothers Home" video and in a second video introducing the story of another immigrant mother who would take part in Reforma 150.

The ways these immigrant rhetorics reproduce heteronormativity are particularly evident in the story of the last woman who speaks in the "Bring Our Mothers Home" video. We first see a still image of her and her family: the woman and her presumed male partner with their two daughters stare at the camera with polite smiles. The narrative of heteronormativity is visually implied by the image's composition of the family unit alongside the video's plea to "bring our mothers home." The assumption is that this woman, Estela Martinez, is indeed the mother in this heteronormative family unit. While this may very well be the case, I want to problematize the assumption of undocumented immigrant women as always already heteronormative objects of patriarchal politics. This assumption of heteronormativity not only detracts from the opportunity for the activist rhetorics of Reforma 150 to more deeply critique oppressive family structures but also reduces the possibility of empowerment for the women who are understood in the rhetorics through their roles as mothers and wives, in other words, through their relation to someone else.

After the picture of her family fades, we hear and see Estela, who describes how her family returned to Mexico because in the US they faced discrimination and feared ICE would separate them. Once in Mexico, however, their fear of separation remained. I provide a transcript and translation of the narrative in its entirety with my analysis to follow:

> *Nos tuvimos que regresar de Arizona por las leyes anti-inmigrantes porque andábamos en la calle o trabajando y la demás gente nos echaba la policía por vernos hispanos y teníamos miedo a que en vez de la policía, llegara la, este, el ICE. Y, este, por miedo de separarnos de nuestras niñas nos tuvimos que regresar a México. Y ahora pues me arrepiento porque está muy feo; la delincuencia, asaltos, asesinatos, secuestros, y no quiero que en una de esas a mis niñas me las secuestren. No aguantaría yo eso, que me arrebataran a mis niñas. Como ahorita le quitaron la niña a mi esposo, se la arrebataron. Yo no sé por qué, porque es su hija. Y la tienen en un centro de detención. Están separados y no es justo que esté separada de su papa. Por favor, al presidente, que nos ayude en esto, a estar las familias unidas. Que no nos separen más. Gracias. Ayúdanos por favor.*[53]
>
> We had to return [to Mexico] from Arizona because of the anti-immigrant laws, because we were on the street or working and other people would call the police on us because we looked Hispanic and we were afraid that instead of the police, ICE would arrive. And because of this fear of being separated from our girls we had to return to Mexico. Now I regret it because it is very ugly here; the crime, assaults, murders, kidnappings, and I don't want that one of these times my girls get kidnapped. I would not be able to bear it if my girls got snatched. Like now, one of the girls was taken away from my husband, they snatched her. I don't know why, because she's his daughter. And they have her in a detention center. They are separated and it isn't fair that she is separated from her dad. Please, to the president, help us with this, to be united as families. Don't separate us anymore. Thank you. Please help us.

About halfway through her monologue, Estela begins to cry and has to stop to compose herself. She places her left hand on her chest and shakes her head as she speaks of being unable to bear separation from her daughters. Between tears, she states, "I would not be able to bear it if my girls got snatched." Viewers hear the fear and sadness in Estela's speech. Her shaky voice divulges her weariness and her desire to be safe and together with her family. Her emotional performance serves to rhetorically constitute Estela as fitting what McKinnon describes as the "ancestral narrative of True Womanhood:" "including allegiance to family, sentimentality, domesticity, purity, frailty, and the perfect outward demonstration of femininity through demeanor and mannerism."[54] The video then transitions to an image of Estela's male partner and one of their daughters, presumably the one who has been separated from her father in the US. The juxtaposition of Estela's narrative of True Womanhood and the father-daughter image forwards the assumption of heteronormativity and reproduces the emotion/reason binary that has long been an instrument of women's subjugation. Estela is the suffering mother; she cries, she looks uncertain. She provides the strongest emotional appeal for this already emotionally saturated video. The father, on the other hand, is present only as an image. He is literally unmoving, stoic. While Estela represents emotion, he represents reason. Despite his absence, the father is still positioned on the dominant side of the emotion/reason binary simply by Estela's presence in the emotional realm.

In addition, the video's framing of her family's separation reproduces patriarchal power by empowering the male subject. Estela states, "One of the girls was taken away from my husband, they snatched her. I don't know why, *because she's his daughter.*"[55] While Estela is claiming that a child should not be removed from either of her parents, her rhetorical focus on her husband's role as the father along with the father-daughter image that accompanies this portion of her narrative has the rhetorical effect of giving him sole claim over the girl. She's *his* daughter. She is not their daughter together. Estela repeats this rhetorical move when she states, "They are separated and it isn't fair that *she is separated from her dad.*"[56] It is important to remember that Estela is filming this video from Mexico, while her daughter and male partner are in the US. As she is saying these words, Estela is miles away from her daughter. Yet this distance doesn't figure in this narrative. While Estela voices her anguish at the thought of being separated from her daughters, she is not allowed to claim the child in this text. Her motherhood is subjugated to the father's claim over the children. It is as if, ultimately, her wishes and feelings are secondary. The gendered rhetorics in this moment subjugate her and disempower her as it pertains to her children's fate. In her final words, Estela continues to empower the father figure when she pleads to Obama, "Please, to the president, help us with this." The president, the ultimate patriarch, must come to the rescue.

Such an emphasis on the heteronormative family eclipses the complex configurations of immigrant families who are just as often separated by immigration laws, economic conditions, and other societal stressors. In actuality the family unit is often torn apart and made unrealizable for undocumented immigrants. I propose next a different reading of the immigrant family structure presented in these texts in order to highlight the state's role in their separation as well as the possibilities of resistance and empowerment for immigrant mothers. I develop this alternative reading through an analysis of another video, this one telling the story of Isabel Martinez (no known relation to Estela) and her efforts to reunite with her daughter Sarai, a US citizen. Isabel and Sarai lived in Chicago when Isabel was deported to Mexico. Isabel attempted to cross back into the US to reunite with Sarai seven times without success.[57] Before taking part in the Reforma 150 action, Isabel told her story in a video montage posted on YouTube. In the text, Isabel talks about Sarai and about her own desire to return to the US to be with her young daughter. The montage incorporates Isabel's narration in Spanish, subtitles in English, still images, and music. Viewers are provided brief information about Reforma 150, as well as a link to find out more at the end of the text.

While the video creates a heteronormative image of the immigrant family, Isabel's text also demonstrates how Dreamer rhetorics can fracture the hegemony of heteronormativity in the family unit. By highlighting family separation and the struggles these mothers go through to remain with their children, the impossibility of the immigrant family unit becomes evident. Immigrant families have long been separated by capitalist immigration policies that encourage the migration of the father and discourage that of the mother and children, or that encourage the migration of the parents who are forced to leave the children behind with *abuelas* or *tías*. Migration patterns, influenced by legislation and economic practices, force the absence of the male and therefore break heteronormative family coherence. The women are left to mother on their own or, I venture, with each other. This is visually evident in the "Bring Our Mothers Home" video through the visual impact of a room full of mothers and their children, with no adult male figures present. Throughout the video the women look at each other, hearing each other's narratives. They are present for each other: Latinx immigrants mothering together. The immigrant family becomes not quite heteronormative. It is in this fracture—this interstice between what is presumed (heteronormativity) and what is possible (not quite heteronormativity)—that a queer(ed) immigrant family becomes legible.

Queering the immigrant family makes visible the sorts of revolutionary mothering practices that immigrant women adopt in the face of persisting attacks on multiple fronts. I propose that reading Isabel's story as an example of queer(ed) mothering rhetorics uncovers the ways undocumented immigrant women persist and resist not only the state but also the patriarchy. As queer Black feminist Alexis Pauline Gumbs proposes: "We say that mothering, especially the mothering of children in oppressed groups, and especially mothering to end war, to end capitalism, to end homophobia and to end patriarchy is a queer thing. . . . Those of us who nurture the lives of those children who are not supposed to exist, who are not supposed to grow up, who are revolutionary in their very beings are doing some of the most subversive work in the world."[58]

Queer revolutionary mothering can be seen as mothering against patriarchy. I am drawn to Gumbs's definition of queer as "that which does not reproduce the status quo,"[59] and I venture to see not only Isabel but the rest of the immigrant mothers presented in the Reforma 150 videos as representing queer(ed) mother subjects. According to Gumbs, queer revolutionary mothering is "an investment in the future that requires a person to change the status quo of their own lives, of their community and of the society as a whole again and again and again in the practice of affirming growing, unpredictable people who deserve a world that is better than what we can even imagine."[60] I argue that the undocumented women of Reforma 150 are actively seeking to change their lives in order to build a better world for their children and for the immigrant community at large. Indeed, there is something radical in the mothering practices of undocumented women, something that is visible if one looks deep in the rhetorics.

The following pages differ somewhat from my previous analysis of Dreamer rhetorics in that I claim that the rhetorics of BTH reflect the actions and desires of its participants. I propose that while I can't assume what the women's mothering practices are actually like, reading the rhetorics through a Black queer feminist frame allows me to see the women as rhetorical agents against the patriarchy. In these pages I begin to employ an analytical approach of radical imagining that I will continue to practice in the following chapter. By radical imagining I mean that my method of rhetorical analysis seeks to push the boundaries of what is (im)possible. In this way, my work moves from examining what *is* to imagining what *can be*. I dare to radically imagine the rhetorics as evidencing a different world for these mothers, one where their motherhood is queer(ed) and resistant. I see this new world reflected in the rhetorics of motherhood of BTH.

Drawing on Gumbs's work on queer revolutionary mothering, I have identified two ways in which the motherhood rhetorics of Isabel's story make immigrant queer(ed) mothering practices visible:

Queer Mothering as Futurity

In a world in which the children of undocumented immigrants are always already seen as anchor babies, foreign invaders, and/or future gang members, mothering can be a radical act that dismantles these assumptions by working toward an immigrant future. Gumbs writes, "To answer death with utopian futurity, to rival the social reproduction of capital on a global scale with a forward-dreaming diasporic accountability is a queer thing to do. A strange thing to do. A thing that changes the family and the future forever."[61] I argue that the mothering practices of undocumented women can be read as a commitment to the future, to survival and prosperity for Latinxs in the US. This fight for a future counters national(ist) discourses and practices that are invested in the capitalist exploitation of undocumented labor and in the social death of undocumented Latinx immigrants.

Such tenacity characterizes the queer revolutionary mothering of undocumented women. As such, the *fuerza* with which they face the struggle of family separation and legal precarity, and with which they work to counter the stereotypes about the undocumented Latinx community, permeates their rhetorics. Tenacity becomes a rhetorical trope repeated throughout Isabel's narrative; this trope helps to weave examples of her queer revolutionary mothering in what otherwise could be read as a heteronormative family story. In popular use the concept of tenacity refers not only to determination in a task but also to persistence in continuing to exist. Both of these aspects of tenacity are present in the rhetorics of Isabel's story as the narrative illustrates her and her daughter's resolve to continue to live life fully, rather than to be beaten down by the overwhelming forces that separate them. Isabel herself is a mothering warrior, whose seven foiled attempts to cross the border illustrate her determination to be reunited with Sarai. Describing her fifth attempt to cross, which she claims was the most difficult out of the seven, Isabel tells of being cuffed at the wrists and ankles and tied to a fence by Mexican military who found her riding a train as an undocumented immigrant from Guatemala. In the video she remembers the humiliation of this moment: "*Sentía como si fuera la peor persona, como si hubiera hecho lo mas malo. Como si fuera una criminal, que hubiera matado a alguien, peor que eso.*"[62] ("I felt as if I were the worst person, as if I had done the worst thing. As if I were a criminal, as if I had killed someone, or worse.") Despite her humiliation, Isabel attempted to cross two more times before joining Reforma 150 for her final attempt to reunite with Sarai. Her tenacity shows how immigrant mothering is not a relationship of subservience and self-sacrifice bolstered by patriarchal dominance but a powerful (albeit difficult) practice of revolutionary love that rages in the face of repeated impediments.

Tenacity also shows up in Isabel's description of Sarai. In one particular phrase Isabel shows Sarai's unapologetic lust for life: "*Entre su sonrisa, entre que es muy exagerada cuando se rie de algo.*"[63] ("In her smile, in that she is very exaggerated when she laughs at something.") Isabel laughs a little bit when she describes Sarai's bravado. Sarai is bold. She laughs loudly and exaggeratedly. She is determined to be heard, to exist. Sarai's tenacity is indeed revolutionary. In a society that does not prioritize her happiness, her defiant and exaggerated laugh is a challenge to those who would deny her joy. Again, from Gumbs: "Because we were never meant to survive and here we are creating a world full of love."[64] Despite state forces that seek to silence her voice, Sarai continues to live tenaciously and to create a world in which she can love and be loved.

Mothering as Collaborative Practice

Queer revolutionary mothering helps to understand mothering as a collaborative practice among multiple generations of women, among many similarly situated women, and even among women and their children. Gumbs writes, "Part of the project of seeing mothering as a queer collaboration with the future has to do with transforming the parenting relationship from a property relationship to a partnership in practice."[65] The parent-child relationship has long been rhetorically framed as a relationship of ownership where the parent has ultimate power over the child. This model frames motherhood through a capitalist lens in which the child is the private property of the parent.[66] Drawing on the 1979 National Third World Lesbian and Gay Conference, Gumbs invites queer revolutionary mothers to embrace a mothering practice "where children are not individual property but rather reminders of the context through which community exists."[67] While this idea was specifically referring to queer subjects as parents in the late 1970s and early 1980s, this idea of community mothering also makes sense for undocumented immigrant women who are joined by the challenges they face to their ability to mother. Mothering can be seen as a collaborative practice, instead of as a defense of private property. Since the children of Latinx immigrants will often continue the fight for community survival, it is to the benefit of all Latinxs to mother them. Queer revolutionary mothering fights against collective oppression with collective actions of love.

This sort of community mothering can be read in the introductory slide of Isabel's video narrative. The text reads as follows: "In the hopes of reuniting with those they love, 150 people seeking asylum crossed through Tijuana as part of the NIYA Bring Them Home campaign. This is the story of one of those people."[68] Instead of reading this text as a universalizing statement about Reforma 150 participants, I read it as a practice of community making through mothering as a partnership. I am particularly drawn to the words "reuniting with those they love." I imagine that "those they love" are not one or two people but the undocumented community in general. This generalized motherly love connotes a commitment to the future of the immigrant community and an act of empowerment and collective strength.

Mothering as partnership also destabilizes the power dynamic of mother-child and instead reflects on how immigrant women and children care for each other. Isabel tells of the ways that Sarai cared for her when they were together and how she continues to do so when separated by the border. She states in between tears and laughter, "*Ella es muy cariñosa, y me daba un beso. . . . y siempre me decía, 'Descanza mami. Estás muy cansada porque fuiste a trabajar.'*"[69] (She is very loving, she would kiss me. . . . and she would always say to me, 'Rest mami. You are very tired because you went to work.'") There is a role reversal in the rhetorics here. This role reversal, in which Sarai mothers Isabel, recognizes that mothering is not a one-way street. It is a partnership in which both mother and child labor for the sake of the other. Despite their separation, Sarai is looking out for her mother. Isabel states that Sarai "*me dice que me quiere, que me extraña. . . . que me cuide, que coma bien. Que me tiene una sorpresa.* (laughs) *Que no me va a decir, pero que me tiene una sorpresa.*"[70] (She tells me that she loves me, that she misses me. . . . to take care of myself, to eat well. That she has a surprise for me. [laughs] That she's not going to tell me, but that she has a surprise for me.") Even at her young age, Sarai provides emotional support and comfort to Isabel, particularly during the difficult moments of separation. Indeed, she mothers her mother.

A queer(ed) reading of a practice that is on the surface seen as heteronormative can destabilize the patriarchal oppressions that mothering under heteronormative frameworks reproduces. If normative gender roles are part of the colonial project—the coloniality of gender—then by queering motherhood the rhetorics make a decolonial gesture. Yet I must also note the fear and precarity that these mothers and children experienced, even as I frame their practices as powerful. We cannot forget that the children in these texts were ripped apart from their parents. In her narrative Isabel makes the viewers confront some of the implications of this separation. One minute and eight seconds into the video, the music suddenly becomes more dramatic. What had been a syncopated beat becomes one sustained grave violin note. Accompanying this change in sound, the images also change. After featuring images of happy families, the screen is filled with a picture of a little girl glancing over her shoulder and looking piercingly into the camera. The image remains on the screen while Isabel talks about her separation from Sarai: "*Lo que más me asusta es de que ella pueda sufrir algún daño de alguna mala persona, o que la traten mal porque no está con familia. . . . Tengo mucho miedo también pues de que los intentos que estoy haciendo para poder reunirme con ella, pues me pase algo y no volver a verla.*"[71] ("What scares me most is that something bad could happen to her because of a bad person, or that someone would mistreat her because she is not with her family. . . . I'm also very afraid that in these attempts I have made to try and get back to her, something could happen to me and I would never see her again."). This heartbreaking revelation is a reminder of the nightmare that undocumented immigrant mothers must live through when they have been separated from their children. While motherhood for undocumented women can be a source of tenacity, love, and support, it is also a source of state-sanctioned suffering.

CONCLUSION

The rhetorics of Reforma 150 illustrate how Dreamer rhetorics expanded its diversity and range over the years. While Dreamer rhetorics started with a somewhat narrow focus, it became clear in Reforma 150 that their aims had changed to incorporate other people, other positionalities, and other rhetorical constraints. In this chapter I refer to the rhetorics of Reforma 150 as "Dreamer rhetorics" because, as my analysis demonstrates, Dreamers were still at the center of these rhetorics as innovators, creators, and organizers. Even though Reforma 150 did not solely involve Dreamers and their path to legalization, it was a moment in which Dreamers acted and spoke in the name of others. Nevertheless, as is usually the case, in acting and speaking for others, they risked minimizing or simplifying the identities and life experiences of those being spoken for. Such minimization is evident in the ways the rhetorics of Reforma 150 play on patriarchal yet emotionally evocative tropes of motherhood, such as innocence, vulnerability, and suffering.

Yet acting for others also shows the Dreamers' selflessness and care, as well as their desire to demonstrate how the entire system of immigration needs reformation. This was a big change for Dreamers. As I show in chapter 1, Dreamer rhetorics were initially characterized by the claim that comprehensive immigration reform needed to be deprioritized to support smaller, piecemeal reform like the DREAM Act. In Reforma 150, however, Dreamers demonstrate their acknowledgment that the entire US system of immigration needs to change. The rhetorics of Reforma 150 also illustrate the Dreamers' implied belief that the US government is an unreliable agent of change. Reforma 150 and the rest of the Bring Them Home campaign show how Dreamers moved away from legislative approaches to protecting immigrant lives, including the DREAM Act and other possible laws that depend on Congress to act, and instead looked for cracks in the US immigration system that would allow them to ease the suffering of some undocumented folks.

The motherhood rhetorics of Reforma 150 make visible the motherhood experiences of Latinx undocumented immigrants and, with that, help to reappropriate motherhood for radical and decolonial ends. Latinx feminist scholar Dorsía Smith Silva writes that "all too often [Latinx mothers'] experiences are rendered invisible in societies that only recognize them as economic commodities—nannies, domestic workers, and migrant helpers."[72] Through rhetorical moves that emphasize the motherwork of undocumented women, the rhetorics of Reforma 150 produce a notion of mothering that is powerful, queer, and revolutionary.

The rhetorics of motherhood in Reforma 150 reclaimed motherhood from the state and argued that, yes, undocumented women *are indeed* mothers but not the kind of mothers defined by (white) normative discourses of femininity. Gumbs writes, "Immigrant mothers are often excluded from 'motherhood' as motherhood is a category of citizenship and as we can see from the many parents and children who are being deported away from each other, right now, rights to motherhood are not respected for non-citizens."[73] The rhetorics of motherhood in Reforma 150 show *how* immigrant women mother; the choices they make, priorities they set, relationships and bonds they create redefine motherhood to reflect the particular ways that immigrant women choose to and/or are compelled to care for their children. Motherhood is often seen as a self-sacrificing practice in discourses of popular culture, a domestic role in patriarchal discourses, and an isolating confinement in white feminist discourses. The immigrant motherhood rhetorics of Reforma 150 turn all of this on its head. Yes, the women have to sacrifice to care for their children; yet this is not necessarily the sacrifice of the doting mother. Immigrant women often sacrifice by choosing to leave children behind in order to ensure their survival. The sacrifice is leaving them behind knowing that crossing the border to see them could threaten their lives. In addition, for immigrant women, motherwork is not necessarily only domestic. Working outside of the home is an important part of motherwork, as it has been for women of color for centuries. The motherwork of the women of Reforma 150 disrupts the public/private binary and attests that women of color have always had a place in both the public and the private spheres. Furthermore, unlike white feminist discourses of mothering as isolation,[74] the isolation that undocumented immigrants experience is often caused by being separated *from* their children, not *with* them. In this way the rhetorics of Reforma 150 also reclaim motherhood from white feminists by redefining motherhood and by reaffirming that motherhood, just like womanhood, is not a universal experience.

Finally, the rhetorics of Reforma 150 reclaim motherhood from the coloniality of gender. The dichotomous limits of the coloniality of gender not only defined gender as binary but also positioned women in the subjugated category. In addition, under the coloniality of gender, women of color (i.e., colonized women) were unable to claim gender and, consequently, humanity. By claiming motherhood, and a specific type of motherhood at that, the rhetorics of Reforma 150 disrupt the coloniality of gender. This reappropriation, however, works within the binary confines of the coloniality of gender—it still reproduces the binary—but enacts female power and agency from within it. Thus, it ruptures the totalizing power of coloniality. In the next chapter, I look at how Dreamer rhetorics continued to challenge gender binaries. In subsequent activism, Dreamers purposefully incorporated queer subjects and queer rhetorics, made arguments based on intersectionality, and demonstrated that they were not confined by the coloniality of gender and its binary definitions of gender and sexuality. As they continued to evolve, the Dreamers' rhetorical aims demonstrated a growing awareness of the intersectionality of oppression and an increasing commitment to widespread justice.

4

Queer and Undocumented

Resistance at the Intersections

Even though young people living at the intersection of being undocumented and being queer were discouraged from expressing their queer identities in initial mainstream activism,[1] the intentional separation of queer perspectives from mainstream Dreamer organizing would prove unsustainable. Because Dreamers often engaged in activism in addition to the fight for immigrant rights (e.g., queer rights, labor organizing, and climate change action), they began to see the ways in which many of the different issues they were fighting for were interrelated. Queer Dreamers talked about carrying a double stigma and about having to "come out" twice: as queer and as undocumented.[2] The activism of queer undocumented youth grew to reflect their imperative to "make sure the public [was] aware that immigrant rights and queer rights are not two separate issues; they are one issue that is very much at the heart of undocumented queer people's lives."[3]

As I described in chapter 1, queer youth have always been central to the Dreamer movement as leaders of and participants in different actions. For some queer Dreamers, it was actually their queer identities that provided the urgency for their immigrant activism. Mohammad Abdollahi, the leader of the NIYA, who was arrested during the Dreamer sit-in in John McCain's office, stated to the *New York Times* that returning to his birth country of Iran as an openly queer man would mean certain persecution from the state.[4] Queer activist tactics were also crucial to the Dreamer movement: most notably, as I mention in chapter 1, the Coming Out of the Shadows campaign drew inspiration from activist and leader Harvey Milk's call for gay people to "come out of the closet" in the late 1970s.

Activism at the intersections of queer and undocumented identities highlighted the specific challenges faced by queer undocumented folks during the Obama years. For example, before the US Supreme Court decided in 2015 to uphold the legality of same-sex marriage in *Obergefell v. Hodges*, people in same-sex couples were denied the possibility of legalizing their status through marriage to a US citizen—a course of action generally available to undocumented people in heterosexual relationships. In addition, like Abdollahi, many queer undocumented folks feared being deported to their birth countries because of the stigma and/or violence they could face due to their queer identities. Finally, queer and trans undocumented people experienced and continue to experience disproportionate amounts of harassment and abuse from ICE, from police, and while in detention.[5]

As a way to address the intersectionality of oppression that queer undocumented people (later to be known as undocuqueer[6]) experienced, the Queer Immigrant Project was launched as part of United We Dream during the organization's 2011 conference.[7] I see this as an important moment in the rhetorical story of Dreamer activism: the official and purposeful recognition of queer undocumented perspectives in the Dreamer movement. The strategic proliferation of the undocuqueer identity marker among Dreamer activist circles helped to bring the concerns and strengths of queer undocumented folks into the foreground of immigrant activism and to grow this new branch of the movement. After the creation of QUIP, undocuqueer youth had a ready-made community to draw on, as well as institutional support for their activist efforts.

This chapter highlights the ways undocuqueer activists mobilized by using art and creative cultural productions to reach people outside and inside the undocuqueer community. I focus on art in activism—or "artivism"—because art played a central role in the undocuqueer community's engagement with Dreamer activism and in their mobilization and success.[8] Undocuqueer artivists have used visual arts, poetry, video, and other creative cultural productions to challenge normative Dreamer narratives and push the immigrant community to reflect on its own sexism, homophobia, and transphobia. Queer artist collaboratives like Culture Str/ke and Dreamers Adrift, artists like Julio Salgado, Ella Mendoza, and Adriana Elena Ortiz-Carmona, and web series like *Undocumented Tales* and *Osito*, to name but a few, have disseminated the voices of the undocuqueer community throughout the world and continue to be strong rhetorical forces in crafting new narratives about undocumented youth. Undocuqueer artivism crosses boundaries of homonormativity to position queer undocumented youth in a new rhetorical space that is driven by queer lives and desires.

In this chapter I analyze two examples of artivism at the intersections of queer and undocumented identities in order to provide a glimpse of this complex and rhetorically innovative branch of the Dreamer movement. While the term "undocuqueer" has often been central to this sort of activism, I illustrate how queer undocumented youth also imagined possibilities for representation beyond this identity label. I argue that just like other branches of Dreamer activism, undocuqueer activism is not monolithic. It is complex, changing, and responsive to the rhetorical needs of its time. It is found both within institutions and in creative undergrounds. The activism that I analyze illustrates how undocuqueer youth during the Obama years worked not only to advocate for themselves and their communities but also to find new rhetorical ways to engage with hostile publics, ways that rejected immigrant oppressions and the neoliberal immigrant rhetorics that characterized the Obama era.

The texts I analyze in this chapter highlight the queer in the *nepantla* rhetorics employed by young Dreamers. The flexibility of undocuqueer rhetorics is not just about being neoliberal and radical at the same time but about pushing boundaries to imagine new queer worlds out of neoliberal realities. These rhetorics create new paths out of oppression—a *caminante* that forges new *caminos* as she travels. I connect here to what Anzaldúa terms "*movimientos de rebeldía*" or movements of rebellion—where queer folks mobilize aspects of themselves that have been vilified, in this case undocuqueer sexuality, in order to create something new, to "put feathers on this particular serpent."[9] Through undocuqueer rhetorics, these undocuqueer artivists express the beauty and strength in their undocuqueer sexualities.

The work I analyze in this chapter shows the range in queer undocumented activism, the importance of art and creative expression to the movement, and its connection to a politics of the erotic—a queer of color way of being and knowing. The first text I discuss is a video posted on YouTube titled "The Undocuqueer Manifesto." The video and manifesto were created by the Queer Undocumented Immigrant Project (QUIP), "a program of United We Dream [that] seeks to organize and empower Undocumented, Lesbian, Gay, Bisexual, Transgender and Queer immigrants . . . and allies to address social and systemic barriers that affect themselves and the broader LGBTQ and immigrant community."[10] While QUIP is concerned with immigrant rights and queer rights, the intersection of both is at the heart of QUIP's mission. The "UndocuQueer Manifesto" is a bilingual video montage of various presumably undocuqueer young people reciting the manifesto alongside sentimental guitar music. This decidedly Latinx text doesn't just code-mesh English and Spanish effortlessly; it also utilizes concepts that are common in the queer Latinx community, such as *jotería*—a queer Chicanx concept of empowerment—and *familia*. Significantly, the manifesto's repetition of the theme of love throughout the text highlights the important role of community, positivity, and support for the undocuqueer movement. In my analysis of the "UndocuQueer Manifesto," therefore, I focus on how love is used as a rhetorical frame through which QUIP youth make their argument for inclusion and acceptance. The theme of love helps the QUIP youth to demonstrate the care and affection of their undocuqueer community, to ask to be loved by the nation-state, and to imagine a queer utopian future[11] in which undocuqueer youth no longer experience exclusion, persecution, and violence.

The second example that I analyze in this chapter is the 2016 artivism by undocuqueer artivist Julio Salgado. I propose that Salgado's artwork evidences a rhetoric of queer pleasure that moves away from the desire for recognition, inclusion, and love, and toward confident self-affirmation and a desire-driven pleasure politics. As I examine Salgado's artivism, particularly the work created in the lead-up to the 2016 US presidential election, I see a critique not only of the exclusion of undocumented people from the US but also of national borders, systemic oppression, and attempts at immigration reform that includes some immigrants at the expense of others. Salgado's rhetoric of queer pleasure intimates an assertive presentation of a queer Latinx self as a desire-driven political subject—an unapologetic dissident of state politics and mainstream Dreamer activism.

The erotic plays out in the rhetoric of these examples in multivariate ways. In the "UndocuQueer Manifesto," the erotic appears as a connection to love and the desire to be loved, a rhetorical position of vulnerability, empathy, and acceptance. Love is mobilized rhetorically toward coalitional efforts with the goal of building hope out of oppression. The undocuqueer youth of QUIP present themselves as motivated by love and act politically in its name. In Salgado's work, on the other hand, the erotic is present in its embodiment of antinormative pleasure: the kinky, the promiscuous, the insubordinate. The desire for the pleasure derived from being boisterously undocuqueer and unapologetic drives the art's rhetorical force.

Women of color feminists have long argued for the value of centering the erotic in theory and praxis. Audre Lorde signals specifically to the epistemic potential of the erotic, which she defines as "the nurturer or nursemaid of all our deepest knowledge."[12] Lorde claims the erotic for all aspects of life—not just the sexual—as the driving force of action against oppression. The erotic is a source of power and information[13]; the suppression of the erotic perpetuates the oppression of woman and queer folks. The erotic is the bridge that connects the spiritual and the political.[14] The queer undocumented activism that I examine in this chapter rhetorically reconnects the spiritual, the sensual, and the emotional to the political in order to make political arguments from a place of erotic embodiment. As Lorde argues, getting in touch with the erotic makes "our acts against oppression become integral with self, motivated and empowered from within."[15] The analysis that follows illustrates how queer undocumented activism is inspired from personal experiences of oppression, as well as from a source of power that is within the self. It is the power of the erotic that, as Lorde contends, moves us toward social transformation rather than acceptance into existing structures.[16] As a rhetoric, the erotic allows queer undocumented youth to make claims based on body, emotion, and desire, while also demanding and working toward radical change.

QUEER, UNDOCUMENTED, UNDOCUQUEER

Before getting to the case study analyses, I will outline two ways in which Dreamer activism intersected with queer activism during the Obama years. First, as mentioned above, the Dreamer movement adopted and adapted activist strategies and language from the LGBT activist movement, most notably, the coming-out strategy famously called for by Milk. Queer migrations scholar Karma Chávez writes,

> Using Harvey Milk to express the importance of coming out is central to the way that [undocumented] activists position their movement. During the first action in Chicago, one [Immigrant Youth Justice League] activist, Tania, gave a speech called "Coming Out," designed to introduce other youth to the idea of coming out and also to inspire them to do so. Tania said, "What does it mean to come out? *¿Qué quiere decir, salir de las sombras?* Coming out means telling a friend, a loved one, a classmate, a teacher something that otherwise you would have kept private. It is using our lives, our stories as a political tool for change. For us, it is being undocumented and we are inspired by a legacy of other movements, from past immigrant rights marches, to civil rights, to gay liberation. Brothers and sisters, we must come out, said Harvey Milk in 1978."[17]

Coming out for queer people during Milk's time was a way to force the general public to confront the effects of homophobia on their family members, friends, neighbors, and coworkers. By coming out, queer people were arguing that they were integral parts of their communities, putting a face and a name to what many mainstream US citizens saw as a distant and insignificant statistic. In turn, coming out made sense as a strategy for undocumented youth for many of the same reasons. Undocumented youth wanted to show the US mainstream that they are their neighbors, coworkers, and friends; the goal was to argue for the urgency of immigration reform and to advocate for tolerance and acceptance of undocumented youth. Because their US upbringing meant that they could often "pass" as US citizens, coming out helped undocumented youth to increase their visibility and demand change.[18] Yet, as Chávez argues in her insightful analysis of "coming out" rhetoric in Dreamer activism, coming out as a coalitional gesture relies on a logic of citizenship rights that syllogistically negates the possibility for undocumented immigrants to make arguments for justice.[19] Therefore, even in their use of "coming out" as an activist strategy, Dreamers differed greatly from LGBT activists who could claim that, as US citizens, they deserved rights.

Dreamer activism also intersected with queer activism in that because queer youth had been so central to the Dreamer movement, there was a need and desire to express intersectional identities. The identity label "undocuqueer" served this purpose: in the years since its creation, it has become shorthand for this intersectional identity and the communities that have grown around it. In this section of the chapter, I expand on the development of this intersectional construct in Dreamer activism and discuss its role in the Dreamer movement at large.

First, however, I define how I am using the word "queer" in this chapter. Since I am using it to describe Dreamer activism at the intersections of queer and undocumented identities, I draw on what undocumented youth themselves have said about the term. In an interview with cultural anthropologist Hinda Seif, undocuqueer artivist Julio Salgado said: "The word queer within Latino communities, it's still pretty new. A couple of years ago, I would have said 'gay.' But the more I find out and experience what the word 'gay' means to the mainstream—this idea of clean, white, male, white picket fence ideal. Gay marriage. That's what I think when I hear the word 'gay.' And that doesn't necessarily represent who I am. While I understand the idea of gay marriage—everyone should be able to marry who they want—there is more to my identity. . . . Using the word 'queer' embodies more than this one identity that the mainstream has. Ellen DeGeneres. Will and Grace."[20]

As Salgado states, the word "queer" helps to identify a racialized intersectional identity that differs from the homonormative[21] white, cis-gendered, citizen mainstream gay identity. Chávez describes her use of the word: "I use 'queer' in two primary ways. First, 'queer' refers to LGBT people and others such as prostitutes or 'welfare mothers,' who fail to conform to the conventions of heternormativity. I also use 'queer' to describe something as abjected, othered, and out of place."[22] As evident in Chávez's use of the word, the term "queer" not only connotes a rejection of heteronormativity (and of normativity in general) but also demonstrates how queer folks are those often marginalized, dehumanized, and criminalized. Queer migrations scholar Eithne Luibhéid writes that the word "queer" as related to immigration "is used to mark the fact that many standard sexuality categories were historically formed through specific epistemologies and social relations that upheld colonialist, xenophobic, racist, and sexist regimes."[23] This means that the word "queer" not only denotes a rejection of heterosexuality but also acknowledges that categories of sexuality are connected to colonialism, imperialism, and exclusion.

In turn, the term "undocuqueer" also has a complexity of origins and meanings. Contrary to popular belief, Salgado did not coin the term.[24] Indeed, its origins are unclear, which is appropriate, since this identity label was developed in a diffused community taking shape throughout the US, transnationally, and virtually. Just like the word "Dreamer," the term "undocuqueer" has activist connotations. As immigration scholar Mara Pieri writes, the term was first used to refer to young people who "engaged in intersectional practices of activism based on being undocumented and queer."[25] Undocuqueer activists used this new identity label to create visibility for themselves and their communities in a way that "resembles the emergence of queer subjects at the beginning of the 70s."[26] The undocuqueer label helped to build community for undocumented queer youth in the immigrant rights fight, creating visibility for the movement while simultaneously giving these young people a rhetorical construct with which to express their arguments for acceptance and inclusion.[27]

Importantly, the leadership and visibility of queer youth in the Dreamer movement also challenged assumptions that Latinx social movements (and Latinx communities at large) marginalize the perspectives of queer folks and women.[28] Just as Dreamers have become an important part of the way in which Latinx identity is understood in the US, so have undocuqueer youth. In this way, this identity label not only pushes the US mainstream to see the role of undocumented youth in the nation but also prompts the Latinx community to confront its own heterosexisms.

DESIRE AS INVENTION FOR A NEW POLITICAL MOMENT

In both the "UndocuQueer Manifesto" and Salgado's 2016 images, desire creates a point of invention for a rhetoric that constitutes undocuqueer subjects as it challenges the oppressive discourses and practices of the moment. It is important to note the keen awareness of the rhetorical situation that both of these texts exhibit. The shift in the form and function of the erotic in the activist texts in this chapter—from loving and beautiful to playful and disruptive—signals how the overtly anti-immigrant political discourses of 2016 created a new exigence among undocumented queer youth, an urgency to stop participating in democratic and state-sanctioned ways of living in the present or imagining the future.

While immigrant dehumanization and criminalization are par for the course in US immigration policy, it is worth noting the changing ideological landscape denoted by Trump's immigration rhetoric, a shift that signaled something different and newly concerning in Trump's immigration agenda. While under Obama the number of deportations reached an unprecedented height, his immigration policies were underlain by neoliberal models of acceptable heterogeneity that sought to include some exceptional undocumented folks—those that would best serve the needs of the capitalist state—to present an image of tolerance to his liberal constituents and to the world.[29] Obama made family reunification and the status of Dreamers foci of his immigration agenda, implying that hardworking parents and innocent youth had a place in the nation. While undocuqueer youth were largely excluded from this framework of acceptability, the linchpin of Obama's immigration rhetoric was the good immigrant/bad immigrant binary "in which certain [immigrants] are positioned as acceptable to the state and deserving of its protection while others are read as threats to the nation and, therefore, undeserving."[30] This binary left room for arguments based on humanity, and the QUIP manifesto embraces this rhetorical terrain by emphasizing the love, creativity, and community of undocuqueer youth.

On the other hand, Trump seemed to make no distinctions between "good" and "bad" immigrants. If anything, through his speeches while presidential candidate and via his executive orders at the beginning of his presidency, Trump continued to expand the "bad immigrant" category so that no "good immigrants" remain to be accepted into the nation-state. Shortly after Trump signed an anti-immigrant executive order,[31] just five days after being sworn in as the forty-fifth president of the US, the effects of this larger "bad immigrant" category started to be felt across undocumented communities. On February 10, 2017, ICE arrested and threatened to deport Daniel Ramirez Medina in Seattle, Washington, a twenty-three-year-old undocumented immigrant who had received a temporary work permit and deferred deportation under Obama's Deferred Action for Childhood Arrivals (DACA) program. ICE stated that they were putting Ramirez Medina in deportation proceedings because he was a "self-admitted gang member" (a claim that Ramirez Medina vehemently denied), even though he had committed no crime.[32] On March 26, 2017, ICE agents arrested and threatened to deport Francisco J. Rodriguez Dominguez, another DACA recipient, based on a 2016 DUI conviction for which he had served his penalty. And, in a case that gained widespread national attention, Guadalupe García de Rayos, a thirty-five-year-old mother of two who had been in the US since she was fourteen, was deported on February 8, 2017, for being caught working with a fake Social Security number in 2008, even though she had been dutifully reporting to ICE every year as mandated since her arrest. The foci of these arrests and deportations were offenses that under Obama would have gotten little notice. Trump was casting a much wider net of detention and deportation that was meant not only to drive undocumented US residents into the shadows but also to reify his discursive criminalization of undocumented immigrants. The artivism of undocuqueer youth responded to these new sociopolitical realities.

LOVE IN THE "UNDOCUQUEER MANIFESTO"

On October 11, 2013, United We Dream published a YouTube video titled "UndocuQueer Manifesto." The manifesto was drafted by members of the QUIP and the video features some of the queer and trans youth involved in the effort. The purpose of the video is to present an emotional argument for inclusion, tolerance, and love of undocuqueer youth. However, the text is first and foremost a statement of self-representation with which the youth from QUIP express who they are and what they stand for as a community. Accordingly, the text includes many "we are" statements, such as "we are who we are," "we are undocuqueers in solidarity," and "we are all *gente*."[33] The manifesto thus constitutes the undocuqueer community as it states its beliefs and positions.

The QUIP's "UndocuQueer Manifesto" is part of the rhetorical tradition of queer migration manifestos that Chávez documents in her book *Queer Migration Politics*. As is characteristic of the genre, the "UndocuQueer Manifesto" presents a utopian future as it ruptures the normative conditions of dominant discourses of migration and of mainstream Dreamer activism. In her analysis of the rhetorics of queer migrations manifestos of the early 2000s, Chávez defines manifestos as "statements that dramatically emphasize the necessity of the 'now.'"[34] Indeed, QUIP's "UndocuQueer Manifesto" is a passionate statement about the urgent spiritual and political needs of queer and trans undocumented Latinx youth. It was created at a time when Dreamer activism was considering intersectional rhetorical approaches and it worked to center some of the most vulnerable voices and positionalities in the immigration debate. Adopting the "usually visceral and excessive . . . form, style, and content" of queer migrations manifestos,[35] the "UndocuQueer Manifesto" uses an overly sentimental and perhaps even melodramatic style, with a melancholic guitar soundtrack and emotional immigrant voices that seem to want to tug at the heartstrings of the viewer.

As a manifesto, the "UndocuQueer Manifesto" also does the work of stating the community's beliefs and intentions. The "UndocuQueer Manifesto," therefore, is not only an emotional argument for inclusion but also works to locate the undocuqueer community of QUIP within an ideological position. As such, like with much of Dreamer rhetoric during the Obama era, an important part of the manifesto's audience is the undocuqueer community itself. Despite statements addressing an external audience directly ["If *you* believe in social justice, then what makes us different than *you*?"[36]], the manifesto does the work of a guiding document for the undocuqueer community: it is a statement of principles. Fittingly, because it is an inward-looking text, it revolves around a rhetoric of love for the undocuqueer community—a rhetoric of undocuqueer love that is presented as a tool for liberation.

Undocuqueer love creates an alternative framework for social justice that pushes the undocuqueer community towards political engagement and creative production. In the "UndocuQueer Manifesto," love is closely connected to desire, as the desire for another and the desire to be loved drive its erotic rhetorical energies. As Queer Chicana Cherrie Moraga writes, "*el amor, el deseo*" can be motivations for political engagement.[37] The authors of the "UndocuQueer Manifeto" tap into the power of the erotic through a rhetoric of undocuqueer love that serves as the manifesto's central theme and organizing structure. QUIP's undocuqueer youth not only "demand the right to love and be loved" but also profess "undocuqueer love, unconditional love, loving, lover, lovemaking and love being."[38] They position love as a vehicle for resistance that doesn't reproduce discrimination and exclusion. Undocuqueer love is presented as a love for self and other. Unlike other manifestos that contain a list of grievances that points to the abuses of particular dominant groups,[39] the "UndocuQueer Manifesto" does not signal to a specific group as the source of their oppression, nor does it list grievances. Instead, it focuses on affirmation of the community and on finding common ground and kinship with the other: "If you believe in social justice, then what makes us different than you? . . . *Somos tu vecin@, hij@, prim@, amig@—tenemos corazón* (We are your neighbor, your child, your cousin, your friend—we have heart). We are human."[40]

While the "UndocuQueer Manifesto" at first seems to be mobilizing mainstream tropes of marriage equality by demanding the right to love, it also turns the exigency around on the viewer by demanding the right to *be* loved. This rhetorical maneuver is part of the manifesto's rhetorical force as it demonstrates the undocuqueer community's love for the other. Demanding the right to *be loved*—not just to love—the manifesto presents an imperative to the other, urging an active engagement in the welfare of undocuqueer youth. Instead of relying on the neoliberal tropes of inclusion and tolerance, the undocuqueer manifesto asks for love—a practice with much more radical potential. Love asks me to imagine the other as part of myself—as having a *place in my heart*. It ties the other's being-in-the-world to my own survival, as the presence of the other drives the blood flowing through my veins. What's more, the undocuqueer youth of QUIP are unsatisfied by just any kind of love. They desire to be loved on their own terms and unconditionally, as "*gente* with different names, cultures, *cuerpos*, desires, roads, and different life philosophies."[41]

Whether you believe in it or not, the idea of unconditional love is a formidable force. Unconditional love asks us to be selfless—whether or not this is an achievable goal. It is a feeling of complete surrender of the self to the interests of another. It disturbs our awareness of ourselves, or at least our self-centered impulses. The idea of unconditional love helps me—no, forces me—to imagine a better future and a more just world for those I love. And, it does not have to be realized or requited for it to have these effects. It is the practice of unconditional love—the trials, the errors, the reattempts—that forces a revision of the types of human connections that are possible. Sara Ahmed, who states her skepticism about unconditional love, still finds radical potential in contemplating it as an idea, even if it is simply to recognize love's failure. She proposes that "in the understanding that love comes with conditions however unconditional it might feel, we can find perhaps a different kind of line or connection between the others we care for, and the world to which we want to give shape."[42] Unconditional love for the immigrant "other" opens up the possibility for society to see how it is caught up with immigrant life, how we depend on each other and should therefore love each other. It is this sort of attachment that creates radical solidarity: the idea that we are in this together, every step of the way, because we love each other.

According to Chela Sandoval, love has decolonizing potential.[43] Love plays an important part of her methodology of the oppressed as it works to trouble awareness and dislodge meaning, making new meanings possible. As a hermeneutic—a methodology for interpretation—love can allow people to enter what Sandoval calls a "third place of meaning": "that which always haunts any other two meanings in a binary opposition. . . . It is an extra, uncategorizable, unnamable meaning haunting all human need to name, classify, order and control."[44] In the rhetoric of the "UndocuQueer Manifesto," undocuqueer love has the potential to trouble the colonial binaries that prohibit justice, such as insider/outsider, citizen/alien, male/female, self/other. Through their rhetorical affirmation of an undocuqueer identity constituted through love, undocuqueer youth present an identity that is more than the sum of its parts. They are constituting an identity that is not undocumented *and* queer, but both and, therefore, more. It is a refusal of neoliberal frameworks of diversity and acceptability in which "the homosexual other is white [and] the racial other is straight."[45] In refusing to be separated into the supposedly mutually exclusive categories of undocumented *and* queer, the rhetoric of undocuqueer love forces a unity and fluidity between the two, so that we cannot think of one without the other. So that we can no longer consider immigration status without also taking sexuality into account.

The rhetorical versatility enabled by the manifesto's rhetoric of undocuqueer love makes room for those undocumented lives that do not fit neatly into binaries of gender or sexuality—specifically trans undocumented youth. While Latinx and undocumented trans folks have long been active in both queer and immigrant social movements, their presence has been purposefully silenced or unintentionally obscured so that their intersectional activist positionalities are erased within the movement. We have but to recall Latina trans activist Sylvia Rivera's speech during the 1973 Christopher Street Liberation Day Rally (the predecessor of today's PRIDE parades) in New York City to realize how trans women of color have been in the front lines of queer liberation, yet this movement has been slow to recognize their labor and advocate for their needs. Rivera, the founder of the Street Transvestite Action Revolutionaries (STAR), who participated in the Stonewall Riots, stated to a hostile audience who was booing her presence on stage: "I have been to jail. I have been raped. And beaten. Many times! . . . But, do you do anything for me? No. You tell me to go and hide my tail between my legs. I will not put up with this shit. I have been beaten. I have had my nose broken. I have been thrown in jail. I have lost my job. I have lost my apartment for gay liberation and you all treat me this way?"[46] And of course there is the case of undocumented trans activist and organizer Jennicet Gutierrez, who was booed and heckled by an audience of queer activists and leaders when she interrupted Obama and asked him to stop the detention of queer and trans undocumented people. These women's silencing is the result of the white, cisgender, homonormative tendencies of the gay rights movement. The "UndocuQueer Manifesto" creates a rhetorical space that empowers and highlights the voices and lives of trans undocumented Latinxs in its rejection of the whiteness, cisgenderism, and homonormativity of the gay rights movement.

The "UndocuQueer Manifesto" highlights the voices and experiences of trans people of color through its multiple references to transition and transformation. Indeed, transition and transformation are not secondary themes but instead are central to the undocuqueer community constituted in the manifesto. Transitions and transformations are crucial parts of undocuqueer love: "Our love, our *jotería,* and transitions have travelled through mountains, rivers, deserts, and oceans and settled in the hearts of open minds. . . . We seek to transform ourselves as we walk hand in hand with our many communities. . . . We are continuously transforming our community and each other."[47]

Emphasizing transition and transformation, the undocuqueer community challenges the idealized notion of the nuclear family and builds a community that is queer and trans: queer in that it incorporates queer folks and queer ways of loving, and trans in that it incorporates trans folks and transitional, nonbinary thinking. The rhetoric of undocuqueer love constitutes an identity that dislodges binary thinking and creates a different kind of coalition with the goal of social transformation. Here, I build on Adela Licona's and Karma Chávez's concept of relational literacies, which they define as the practice of interacting around a text with the goal of shared action. Licona and Chávez write, "Relational literacies imply the labor of making meaning, of shared knowledges, or of producing and developing new knowledges together."[48] The "UndocuQueer Manifesto," therefore, functions as a relational literacy that uses a rhetoric of undocuqueer love to connect multiple disenfranchised communities—undocumented queer and trans Latinx people—with the purpose of building new knowledges and worlds.

As a relational literacy, the "UndocuQueer Manifesto" opens up the "space for new kinds of understanding, interaction, and politics."[49] Through a rhetoric of undocuqueer love, the manifesto evokes affective solidarity and coalition in "*familia de corazón*"—a purposefully chosen family. The manifesto states, "We have created a queer *familia* within the movement because our survival depends on it. Together we rise, we are *jotería, familia de corazón.*"[50] The *familia de corazón* presents a different kind of connection that does not reproduce the heteropatriarchal familial structures of biological family but instead provides undocuqueer kinship with the goal of social justice. The *familia de corazón* imagines new meanings previously unimaginable—familial connection without the heteropatriarchal baggage.

The *familia de corazón* is also the practice of *familia* for survival. Left out of queer and undocumented communities, queer and trans undocumented youth created a *familia* among themselves to help them survive and thrive. This community is not incidental; it is a community ascribed to fate: "We must always be there to support one another because our lives, spirits, and existence didn't cross by accident."[51] This community of border crossers has come together not by coincidence but by destiny. Their connection also extends to the larger Latinx queer community through their use of the term *jotería.* Stemming from derogatory Mexican slang, *jotería* is a reappropriation of a negative term to express the experiences at the intersections of queerness and Chicanidad. *Jotería* is often referred to as a positive and resistant expression of identity—an acknowledgment of intersectionality and a reclaiming of queer Chicanidad as a powerful and beautiful positionality.[52] The manifesto uses the idea of *jotería* to claim undocuqueer power and beauty while connecting to the larger queer Latinx community: "Somos jot@s, div@s, atrevid@s, fabulous queers with a cause fighting for social justice."[53] In naming *jotería,* undocuqueer youth make queer desire central to their social actions and embodiments, appropriate previously derogative terms for their own liberatory means, and grow the intensity of their undocuqueer love through queer desire-driven coalition.

Through the "UndocuQueer Manifesto," the undocuqueer community constitutes itself as strongly connected to desire and love—it is love that constitutes the community, drives their activist motivations, and mobilizes their desire for justice. This innovative rhetoric of love does not turn away from the other but instead offers love for the oppressor in order to build a better world. The undocuqueer community of QUIP also offers itself up to *be* loved—a position of additional vulnerability for already vulnerable subjects. Undocuqueer love is framed as a source of power and unity, and a rhetorical manifestation of *nuevos mundos* based on kinship.

JULIO SALGADO AND A RHETORIC OF RADICAL UNDOCUQUEER PLEASURE

As the Obama years came to a close, undocuqueer people continued to face an uncertain future. While DACA was a step toward making Dreamers' lives more livable, in 2016 a long-term solution to Dreamer illegalization looked ever more unrealizable. Deferred Action for Parents of Americans (DAPA), Obama's 2014 executive order to provide temporary relief from deportation for undocumented parents of US citizens or legal residents, had been blocked by the courts. In 2015, the *Obergefell v. Hodges* Supreme Court decision that guaranteed the right of same-sex marriage seemed like a positive moment for all queer folks. Yet at the same time, then–presidential candidate Donald Trump's anti-immigrant, anti-Mexican, and anti–Latin American rhetoric was rallying the racism of conservative voters and saturating mainstream media. In these volatile times it would be expected for undocuqueer activists to turn away from optimism.

And yet queer undocumented artivists still conveyed a belief in the future, if only a radically different one. With art that centered radical undocuqueer pleasure, undocuqueer artivists expressed their contempt for the current social moment while they worked to build a future of liberation and justice for queer undocumented immigrants. To illustrate this phenomenon, I focus my analysis in the next few pages on Julio Salgado's engagement with a rhetoric of radical undocuqueer pleasure in one piece of art from 2016, a drawing titled *Beyond Dreams* (Figure 2). Building from pleasure activism and queer Latinx performance studies, a rhetoric of radical undocuqueer pleasure centers themes related to desire, ecstasy, and eroticism in order to imagine a thriving future for undocuqueer folks. Importantly, this rhetoric is also highly antagonistic: it takes pleasure in being defiant, in crossing the line of respectability, and in rejecting the status quo. A rhetoric of radical undocuqueer pleasure engages the body, its desires and ecstasies, and prioritizes the pleasure of dismantling oppressive systems and working toward liberation and justice.

In the following pages, I ground the idea of radical undocuqueer pleasure on queer Latinx performance studies and examine a rhetoric of radical undocuqueer pleasure in Salgado's work. I propose that radical undocuqueer pleasure is a rhetorical tool with which queer undocumented Latinx youth expressed their defiance of respectability politics as they also voiced their rage and disgust in the face of continued discrimination, criminalization, and dehumanization of undocumented immigrants. As the Obama years waned, artivism by some undocuqueer folks moved away from the politics of visibility, which had been a prominent theme particularly evident in Salgado's art with the use of "I exit" and "I am undocuqueer" as artivist slogans, and moved toward a more oppositional rhetoric that foregrounded sexuality, desire, and pleasure. In hindsight the rhetoric of radical undocuqueer pleasure in the artivism that I analyze in this section may have provided a preemptive survival strategy for the dark times that were to come for undocumented immigrants, queer and trans folks, and refugees (including all those in the intersections) under the presidency of Donald Trump.

A Rhetoric of Radical Undocuqueer Pleasure

In his landmark book *Cruising Utopia*, José Esteban Muñoz defines queerness as a "utopian formation . . . based on an economy of desire and desiring.

This desire is always directed at that thing that is not yet here, objects and moments that burn with anticipation and promise."[54] That is to say that queerness mobilizes the imagination toward radically new possibilities of liberation. As a rhetoric, radical undocuqueer pleasure can be a source of innovation and invention, a needed break with the hackneyed rhetorical tropes of hope and inclusion. The rhetoric of radical undocuqueer pleasure that is evident in undocuqueer artivism emerges out of a weariness with the anti-immigrant established order and with the perceived homonormativity of mainstream Dreamer activism. It is a rejection of the now and of the future, as they are. But it also holds on to the hope that out of the ashes of today something better can be built.

Muñoz contends that a moment of ecstasy can bring forth "transformative change" by connecting the past, present, and future.[55] He argues that queer ecstasy, which I connect to radical undocuqueer pleasure, challenges straight time and its obsession with reproductive futurity.[56] The focus on radical undocuqueer pleasure becomes a way to look to the past, experience pleasure in the present, and create a better, queerer future. Muñoz gives us the idea of queer utopianism—a belief in a better tomorrow that is not tethered naively to the present's continuation (through procreation) but to a radical departure from the present.

Following Muñoz, I contend that a rhetoric of radical undocuqueer pleasure is a queer utopian formation that imagines and works for a more just future. In his work Salgado constitutes a queer undocumented subject that dares to imagine a radically different tomorrow. Evoking a rhetoric of radical undocuqueer pleasure, Salgado draws out what this future might look like and situates undocuqueer subjects as protagonists of this new universe. In Muñoz's poignant words, "The present is not enough. It is impoverished and toxic for queers and other people who do not feel the privilege of majoritarian belonging, normative tastes, and 'rational' expectations."[57] In response to the toxicity of the present, Salgado uses bold colors and concepts to create new worlds that actually prioritize pleasure for undocuqueer folks.

Indeed, a rhetoric of radical undocuqueer pleasure illustrates how the act of taking pleasure itself can challenge oppression and the precarious living conditions engendered by global capitalism. Pleasure activist adrienne maree brown argues that "pleasure is a measure of freedom," particularly for BIPOC women and queer folks whose pleasure has been circumscribed and/or vilified.[58] brown names this phenomenon as pleasure activism—"the work [BIPOC communities] do to reclaim our whole, happy, and satisfiable selves from the impacts, delusions, and limitations of oppression and/or supremacy."[59] Importantly, brown asks that we "make justice and liberation the most pleasurable experiences we can have on this planet," so that pleasure itself is a practice of freedom.[60] Drawing on brown, I propose that radical undocuqueer pleasure is deeply invested in countering the continued oppressions of settler colonialism and the US racialized hierarchy of citizenship, and on becoming a life force for undocuqueer folks who face rejection, violence, deportation, and death at the intersections of multiple forms of oppression. Performance scholar Juana María Rodriguez writes, "The life chances of so many poor people, children, queers, people of color, elders, people with disabilities, undocumented immigrants, and those who make the streets their home become more precarious every day. Hope has become an exhausted cliché, and *living becomes a conscious act that we must labor to willfully choose*."[61] The rhetoric of radical undocuqueer pleasure is a practice of willful living for undocuqueer folks, despite state forces that would prefer otherwise.

"Fuck Your Borders:" The Radical Undocuqueer Pleasure of Julio Salgado

Julio Salgado came to the US from Mexico with his family in the nineties. He has a BA in journalism from California State University, Long Beach. His art deals with social justice issues, particularly with the plight of undocumented youth. Salgado is one of the most successful undocuqueer artivists in the US. His bright images of undocuqueer youth have been circulated through social media, exhibited in galleries and universities around the US, and written about in books and academic articles. His "I Am Undocuqueer" series has particularly garnered academic and popular attention, as it helped to define for mainstream audiences what the intersectional undocuqueer identity label means.

The "I Am Undocuqueer" project of 2012 sought to highlight the stories and experiences of those identifying as undocuqueer. Salgado describes his process of asking people around the country to write down what "undocuqueer" means for them. Then he put those words alongside portraits of the authors and their first names. The images are colorful and bright, typical of Salgado's artwork. Yet they are also very subdued visually. Each person featured in the images is wearing a white t-shirt and looking straight at the camera. Most of them are smiling. While some of them have raised fists or are holding microphones and megaphones that indicate their activism, there is nothing visually subversive. Only the words are subversive because of their inclusion of the term "undocuqueer," which in 2012 was just beginning to surface in the Latinx immigrant community.[62] In the following years, some of Salgado's art took a decidedly more antagonistic turn. The term undocuqueer was replaced by the phrase "illegal faggots."[63] Instead of arguing for a place in the nation-state, Salgado's art now said, "Fuck your borders."[64]

Because he has been producing art about undocumented youth for more than a decade, Salgado's work evidences the ways that artivism by queer undocumented young people has evolved over the years. In an interview with KQED, the Bay Area's National Public Radio member, Salgado talks about this change:

> For many years . . . the message for a lot of us—was to show this country that we're good immigrants. The whole premise of the narrative around the DREAM Act was to convince the U.S. that, "Look! You could potentially give a green card and a path to citizenship [to people] who are going to college, who are going to pay taxes. We are the good crop. We are the good people you want to have on your team." Now, I think the art that I create is for us. And by "for us," I mean for other queer people, other undocumented people, other people of color, because I want to make art that other people can see themselves in. . . . I want to change the narrative for my people. That means creating art that does not put us in a perfect light, or a perfect immigrant narrative that only shows my good side. It's dangerous for us to show our flaws and so I hope that through my art, I can change that a little bit.[65]

Salgado's art in the second half of the 2010s shows other queer, undocumented, and BIPOC folks that a different future is possible—a future that doesn't reach for the normative and neoliberal American Dream but that troubles the desire for normativity in general. I propose that Salgado's use of a rhetoric of radical undocuqueer pleasure presents a desire-driven politics and a critique of respectability in Dreamer activism in order to imagine other antinormative possibilities.

In 2016 Salgado created a provocative image titled *Beyond Dreams*. The image circulated digitally after the artist posted it on his Instagram page and can be found for sale as a print on the artist's website. *Beyond Dreams* is a self-portrait featuring most of the artist's body centered in front of a maroon half wall. A yellow sky contrasts against the outlines of Blackhawk helicopters flying and a mouth floating to the right of the subject. The mouth is open, reminiscent of the iconic mouth from the queer cult classic *The Rocky Horror Picture Show*. It is drooling slightly, tongue visible, expressing sexual desire. Salgado faces the camera, eyes closed, mouth open, tongue out. Written in all caps on his bare chest are the words: "SOMETIMES I READ.

SOMETIMES I PROTEST. SOMETIMES I DRAW. SOMETIMES I FUCK. SOMETIMES I GET FUCKED."

The rhetoric of radical undocuqueer pleasure in Salgado's image creates tension in its expression of brown and undocumented queerness for its own sake. The image is overtly sexual and queer but not in the "love wins" sort of way that is preoccupied with white cisgendered same-sex marriage. Salgado's seminude brown body, which queer studies scholar Juan Ochoa describes as "husky joto,"[66] keeps this image from fitting into the normative queer white male aesthetic archive. Indeed, as Ochoa describes in his analysis of Salgado's images, the purposeful use of brown subjects in Salgado's art "create[s] a queer brown constellation of *jotería*" that sets his artwork firmly in a countercultural space.[67]

In this image queer pleasure intersects with *jotería* to create a disruption of white hetero- and homonormative discourses via a queer brown body

Figure 2. *Beyond Dreams*, illustration by Julio Salgado.

experiencing desire and pleasure. Rather than the hopeful tone of *jotería* alluded to in the QUIP's "UndocuQueer Manifesto," in *Beyond Dreams, jotería* becomes oppositional and unsettling. I propose that in this self-portrait, Salgado's protagonist is unapologetically experiencing pleasure in being queer, brown, and undocumented. There is no attempt to assimilate into any normative scripts.

Rodriguez claims that radical sexual politics—of which, I argue, radical undocuqueer pleasure is part—move toward critiquing assimilationist politics of respectability by emphasizing sexual desire that makes cis-heterosexual white people uncomfortable.[68] The refusal to curtail the whitestream's discomfort is an ingenious feature of the rhetoric of radical undocuqueer pleasure because it creates a receptive audience by appealing to their discomfort, not to their beneficence or to similarities with the writer/artist/speaker. This refusal to appease is highly productive. *Beyond Dreams* refuses to prioritize the comfort of majoritarian audiences and thus calls out people who would rather undocuqueer folks stay hidden from view, as well as those liberal communities who don't want to be reminded of their complicity in the precarious lives of undocumented immigrants. Importantly, the image also prompts viewers to confront their own pleasure and/or discomfort at sexualized *joto* bodies. The subject's position in the image is a sexual invitation. Salgado stands as if he is performing an erotic dance. His legs are conspicuously open, as is his robe (the graduation gown associated with Dreamer activism; more on this later). He invites the viewer to look at him, to consume him visually, and he claims agency in his ability to be consumed, desired. His physical openness invites audiences to participate in his pleasure but also mocks an audience who might be uncomfortable by the overt expression of undocuqueer sexuality.

Furthermore, Salgado's stance is an invitation for viewers to consume him in the same ways that US liberals consume the stories of exceptional Dreamers. While liberal US politicians, media, and so-called allies brownwash their politics with ideas about exceptional Dreamers being acceptable to the US, they also erase the violence that US immigration and economic policies continue to inflict on brown migrant bodies.[69] The idea that the nation is friendly to immigrants and to diversity, popular in the Obama years, is predicated upon the concept of acceptable (and exceptional) heterogeneity. Only those exceptional Dreamers—the college grad, the valedictorian, the Pulitzer Prize–winner—are acceptable in the nation. These exceptional Dreamers supposedly prove that the nation is a tolerant place. Salgado's image calls out this brownwashing by exposing his undocuqueer body to be seen. He puts his body up for consumption, but not under any measure of normativity. He demands to be taken in as a sexualized queer brown body. His *joto* body confronts US liberal hypocrisy that seeks to accept some immigrants at the expense of others.

With the words "SOMETIMES I FUCK. SOMETIMES I GET FUCKED," Salgado engages the viewers in a deliberation about power and sexuality for undocuqueer youth. In Salgado's queer utopian future, undocuqueer people of color have the power to both fuck and get fucked. The words "SOMETIMES I FUCK" present an argument about the ways in which undocuqueer pleasure fucks things up. These words denote the disruption caused by *jotería*: that *jotos y jotas* will destabilize the heteronormative (and homonormative) world order. It is important to note that the fucking in the image obviously does not refer to reproductive sex. It is nonreproductive sexuality based solely on desire and pleasure—as opposed to heterosexual sexuality that can always have reproductive undercurrents. It is, to use Rodriguez's words, "sexual in the queerest of ways, meant to inspire intense feeling rather than reproduction."[70]

Furthermore, the fucking here is not just sex. It is fucking *with*, as in messing with, the viewer. It queers the viewer's gaze. The words "SOMETIMES I FUCK. SOMETIMES I GET FUCKED" lead the gaze of the viewer down Salgado's stomach to his crotch. Viewers can't help but look at his Speedo-clad groin (*is there a hint of an erection?*). His sexuality is demanding to be seen, to be taken in. His stance directs the gaze of the viewer, in essence having power over the viewer's desires. Salgado presents himself to be devoured; it is the stance of an exotic dancer, making himself available for our consumption but also having power in that positionality.

The rhetoric of radical undocuqueer pleasure in *Beyond Dreams* troubles the US preoccupation with borders, heteronormativity, and homonationalism[71] through an emphasis on antinormative sexual desire and its potential to mock society's heteronormative rhetorical investments. The image disrupts Dreamer exceptionalism, not by providing an image of a different Dreamer but by using a rhetoric of radical pleasure to change the conversation—to focus not on how Dreamers may contribute to and build on existing societal structures but by perhaps positing that through undocuqueer sexuality nothing will ever be the same again. In the image the dancing Salgado wears a hot-pink graduation cap and gown that rhetorically mocks Dreamers and their respectability politics. First the cap and gown are hot pink, a stereotypically feminine color not traditionally seen in graduation regalia. Although his cap is firmly held on his head, both sleeves of his gown are worn off his shoulders and, of course, the gown is open exposing his torso and thighs. While the graduation regalia is normally a conservative outfit that denotes serious academic achievement,

Salgado wears his cap and gown as an exotic dancer would—in the process of taking the gown off in front of the strip club patrons. In lieu of a stripper pole, Salgado leans on a Roman pillar reminiscent of Ivy League university architecture. The gown and the pillar together scoff at the idea of higher education and its role in respectability politics. Salgado's image speaks directly to the dominant claim that Dreamers' worth can be measured only through their college attendance and participation in the labor force.

Here, Salgado engages in the rhetorical practice of disidentification, which Jonathan Alexander and Jacqueline Rhodes describe as "the ways in which one situates oneself both within and against the various discourses through which we are called to identify."[72] Salgado takes on the neoliberal discourses of the meritocracy and the American Dream—discourses that have been mobilized to situate Dreamers within the nation-state—and resignifies them to expose their failures. Muñoz describes disidentification as a process that "scrambles and reconstructs the encoded message of a cultural text in a fashion that both exposes the encoded message's universalizing and exclusionary machinations and recircuits its workings to account for, include, and empower minority identities and identifications."[73] Salgado's recoding of the graduation regalia and the Ivy League pillar calls out the ways undocumented youth continue to be excluded from the so-called American Dream, questions whether the American Dream actually exists for nonnormative people, and empowers undocuqueer youth to make their own dreams.

Finally, I would be remiss if my analysis of this image didn't acknowledge the presence of tongues. Alexander and Rhodes identify the queer tongue as metonym for queer struggle, critique, and possibility: "The queer tongue, long denied its utterances, long disciplined by legislation and normalization, long in the making of critique and the construction of queer identities, of queer particularities, of queer taste. The tongue contains our histories, and our possibilities."[74] It is no coincidence, then, that Salgado includes two tongues in this image, his and the floating mouth's. Following the idea of queer tongue as metonym, I suggest that the tongues here connect *Beyond Dreams* to the histories of undocuqueer life, struggle, and resistance. Through their allusion to pleasure—seeking and giving—the tongues link Salgado's mouth to other queer mouths and tongues that have remained open and desiring despite state attempts to silence them. The undocuqueer tongues in this image are a final demonstration of the pleasure of defiance and the defiance of taking pleasure. With these undocuqueer tongues, Salgado reminds his fellow undocuqueers of the need to continue to, in the words of Alexander and Rhodes, "be mouthy, to spit, to eat fire, to do things that we are not supposed to do with our mouths and tongues."[75] To counter the death created by silence and silencing, Salgado challenges himself and other undocuqueers to continue to *live*.

CONCLUSION

The rhetorics employed by the undocuqueer community, as I illustrate in this chapter, mobilize undocuqueer desire, love, and pleasure to create texts that not only make space for undocuqueer folks in the nation, but reimagine the nation entirely. I propose that these texts work as lifelines for undocuqueer communities by providing a way out of an intolerable present. They are the bricks with which to make new queer homes and new queer worlds where borders are flexible and welcome crossings and transitions. Through their *nepantla* rhetorics, these undocuqueer artivists expand what we dare to imagine and therefore push the boundaries of what sorts of relationships are possible.

Although the two texts that I analyze are quite different, they each appropriately reflect and respond to the changing times and the changing rhetorical situation. While the manifesto was created in 2013, a time when there was hope in the changes that Obama's second term in office could bring in the lives of undocuqueer folks, *Beyond Dreams* was created at the end of the Obama administration, when the torrential clouds of the Trump era were looming. Like a ballad, the manifesto uses gentle persuasion through appeals to love to position undocuqueer folks in a new, more compassionate world. On the other hand, Salgado's rhetoric is forceful, like a punk song that features loud notes and expletives to push the current world into our rearview.

Finally, these examples show the ways art and multimodality functioned in the Dreamer movement. As Sandoval writes, artivism can "seek egalitarian alliances and connections across difference."[76] Through their art, undocuqueer communities were able to reach places where words would not be listened to or actions would not be tolerated. Of course, the examples cited in this chapter are not the only two examples of artivism in the Dreamer movement. There is an abundance of examples that illustrate how artivism in the Dreamer movement engendered coalition, spoke truth to power, and provided an outlet for expression. Art is an important part of the Dreamers' rhetorical story and a good medium with which to work toward rhetorics that will respond to future challenges.

Conclusion

Looking Back to Move Forward: Dreamer Activist Lessons from the Obama Era

Donald Trump's attacks on the undocumented community began shortly after his inauguration as the US's forty-fifth president. On January 25, 2017, Trump signed "Enhancing Public Safety in the Interior of the United States," one of a slew of executive orders designed to slow undocumented immigration into the US and penalize undocumented immigrants already living in the country. The order outlined new deportation guidelines prioritizing undocumented immigrants who have been charged with or convicted of a crime, and even those who have "committed acts that constitute a chargeable criminal offense," even if no charge has been made.[1] Also prioritizing undocumented immigrants who "have engaged in fraud or willful misrepresentation in connection with any official matter or application before a governmental agency,"[2] the order made any undocumented immigrant who'd ever worked with a fake Social Security number or driver's license a priority for deportation. Finally, the executive order gave law enforcement officers the power to enforce immigration laws subjectively by stating that undocumented immigrants who "in the judgment of an immigration officer, otherwise pose a risk to public safety or national security" would also be a priority for detention and deportation.[3] To accomplish these new practices of detention and deportation, Trump empowered state and local law officers to enforce federal immigration laws, commanded that Immigrations and Customs Enforcement (ICE) hire 10,000 additional agents, and threatened funding cuts for sanctuary cities.[4]

The new realities that followed the Obama years not only made life more difficult for undocumented people and their families but also capitalized on white folks' fear of Latin American immigrants through language that reproduced the idea that undocumented immigration presents a great danger to public safety and national security. Trump made his anti-immigrant agenda not only about jobs but also about the safety of the nation, tapping into the already enhanced fear of the brown terrorist in the era of the war on terror.[5] For example, the order gave as its purpose "to ensure the public safety of the American people in communities across the United State,"[6] thus presenting a threat that is clear, tangible, and localized.

This executive order was not based on factual information, as it ignored the wealth of research showing that foreign-born US residents have no effect on crime rates and are actually less prone to criminality than US-born citizens.[7] Without providing any supporting evidence, the order claimed that many undocumented immigrants "present a significant threat to national security and public safety" and "have served time in our Federal, State, and local jails."[8] Trump's executive order was about an idea, and more specifically about planting an idea in the minds of US citizens—that undocumented immigrants from Latin America are real, physical threats to US lives. Indeed, the order even created the Office for Victims of Crimes Committed by Removable Aliens to provide "proactive, timely, adequate, and professional services to victims of crimes committed by removable aliens and the family members of such victims,"[9] thus contributing to Trump's assertion that the US was being overrun by undocumented violent criminals, a narrative that he capitalized on during his presidential campaign and that he continued to deploy as a political tactic to rally his base while in office.

Trump made immigration a central issue of his presidency, with the apparent goals of increasing the criminalization of undocumented immigrants, spreading fear about this population in the mainstream US, and using this fear to mobilize conservative voters in order to maintain power. The narrative of the dangerous undocumented criminal was further ingrained in the structure of the US government through the vast system of reporting that the executive order outlined. The order mandated a weekly "comprehensive list of criminal actions committed by aliens" in sanctuary cities, quarterly reports "studying the effects of the victimization by criminal aliens present in the United States," and quarterly reports on the immigration status of foreign-born inmates in federal, state, and local prisons and jails.[10] This extensive system of reporting not only structured new dynamics of surveillance for undocumented immigrants but also sought to remind the public about the criminality of undocumented immigrants so that they would continue to think of this population as an ongoing threat.[11]

Throughout his presidency Trump capitalized on the panic caused by the often-cited statistic about the looming end of the white majority[12] to portend the doom of white US culture and propose the urgency to protect it.[13] His attacks on immigration (legal and otherwise) were his way of garnering the vote of the 46 percent of whites that believe that having a majority nonwhite population will harm the nation.[14] The discursive emphasis on the dangers of undocumented immigration built on and enhanced popular fears about the threatened nation. Such appeals to personal safety and community security expanded the reach of Trump's anti-immigrant rhetoric. When the fear of undocumented immigration was about losing jobs, those who feared their jobs would be "stolen" by the undocumented immigrant were primarily the targets of anti-immigration rhetoric. These fears were somewhat easily assuaged with the argument that undocumented immigrants worked jobs that US citizens did not want. A concern for national security and public safety, as well as the fear that white people will soon no longer make up the country's majority, set a much larger audience that was particularly receptive within Trump's rhetoric of American carnage.

Despite Dreamer activism during the Obama years, conditions for them under the Trump administration were much more dire. During Trump's first year in office, he signed seven executive orders related to immigration, including "Enhancing Public Safety in the Interior of the United States" and the controversial Muslim ban.[15] He expanded priorities of immigration enforcement to people with no criminal records—a noticeable departure from Obama's approach. The Migration Policy Institute reports that during 2016, Obama's last year in office, 90 percent of people deported had been convicted of "serious crimes." On the other hand, during Trump's first year in office, almost 30 percent of detained undocumented immigrants had no criminal convictions.[16] Trump also moved to phase out DACA[17] for Dreamers and to end Temporary Protected Status for people from countries ravaged by war and natural disaster, including Haiti, Nicaragua, and Sudan.[18]

The Trump administration also gained notoriety through a variety of policies that sought to punish undocumented immigration and decrease legal immigration. In his second year in office, Trump's "zero tolerance" policy gained widespread attention for its inhumane practice of separating children from their parents at the border. In April of 2018, Trump ordered the prosecution of all individuals who entered the US without proper immigration documentation. This meant that when parents were traveling with their children, the parents would be put in detention to face prosecution for illegal entry into the US, while the children would be given to the care of the state. As a result more than 650 children were initially separated from their parents in a two-week period in May 2018.[19] The ACLU reports that as of October 15, 2018, the government estimated that over 2,600 children had been separated from their parents as a result of Trump's zero tolerance policy.[20] Many of these children were held in "tender age" detention centers—immigrant detention centers for children under the age of twelve.[21] More than a year later, at least thirty of the separated children had not been reunited with their parents or released to a sponsor.[22]

While Trump and his administration faced harsh national and international criticism for his zero tolerance policy, other practices of family separation gained less attention. In August of 2019, an immigration raid of seven Mississippi food-processing plants led to the arrest of 680 undocumented immigrants in the "largest single-state workplace enforcement action in US history."[23] Many of the arrested were parents of small children. The *Washington Post* reported that "many children didn't have a loved one or family friend to go home to. Some walked home from school but were locked out because their parents were detained in the raid."[24]

Throughout the chapters of *Dreamer Nation*, I have described the challenges Dreamers and other undocumented immigrants faced under Obama: their criminalization and dehumanization, their fear of detention and deportation, their inability to attend college and get jobs that will provide access to the US middle class. I write now about the realities of undocumented immigration under the Trump administration as a reminder to the reader that the fight for immigrant rights will continue until there is a comprehensive and legislative solution to the status of all undocumented immigrants living in this country. Regardless of what party is in power, this will be a tremendous undertaking that must also encompass a revision of how this country defines citizenship, a racial reckoning that puts a stop to the scapegoating and fearmongering of communities of color by media pundits and politicians, and a widespread change in economic structures so that the prosperity of the US no longer depends on Latin American poverty.

I also want to underscore the personal connection that I have to this research as a Latina, a mother, and an immigrant. As I mentioned in this book's introduction, for those of us engaging in the study of Latinx rhetorics, our research can be quite personal, as it often involves communities of which we are part. It was heartbreaking at times to write about Dreamers in the Obama years while seeing the many injustices that immigrants faced under Trump. The resurgence of white supremacist groups and discourses that accompanied Trump's anti-immigrant agenda made the US a newly hostile place for Latinxs, undocumented immigrants, and people of color in general.[25] In *Dreamer Nation*, I discuss the abjectivity and precarity faced by undocumented immigrants during the Obama years. Still, I can say that those years look mild compared to the onslaught of attacks that the immigrant community faced in four years of Trump.

But, despite the darkness of the post-Obama years, Dreamers continued to fight. I look forward to future research in rhetorical studies that will analyze how Dreamers kept their community alive during these most difficult years and how they adapted their rhetoric to face new exigencies. In spite of the increased risks of detention and deportation, Dreamers remained visible in the fight against Trump's DACA phaseout. In February 2018, for example, eleven Dreamers walked from New York to Washington, DC, to protest Trump's elimination of DACA, using the hashtag #WalkToStayHome.[26] In addition, United We Dream, the Dreamer-led activist network that was central in Obama-era activism, co-organized nationwide protests to close immigrant detention centers along the US-Mexico border. I have no doubt that Dreamers and their allies will continue to fight for the lives of all immigrants.

NEW RHETORICAL PATHWAYS: LESSONS FROM DREAMER RHETORICS

Dreamer Nation brings new understandings of how Dreamers and their allies respond to the criminalization of undocumented immigrants and the ongoing persecution of this already vulnerable population in the US. As I show in this book, in the last decade, undocumented Latinx youth have put themselves in the forefront of the immigrant rights movement, as they use creative and impassioned activism to respond to the xenophobia of heightened nationalisms and the transnational displacements of neoliberalism. My analysis shows how Dreamer rhetorics sought not only to speak truth to power but also to be self-sustaining and life-giving for the undocumented community. Dreamer activism in the Obama years gave valuable nourishment to a community that has continued to be the nation's scapegoat. Dreamers and their allies will need to draw on this strength to continue their fight.

While it would be logical to assume that Dreamer rhetorics need to address first and foremost the US government, which has the power to effect change in Dreamers' legal status, Dreamer rhetorics most often and most successfully addressed undocumented folks with the goal of building and empowering the community. Indeed, one of the most significant lessons of Dreamer rhetorics in the Obama years is that it is at its most successful when aiming inward. The Dreamer community proved the value of rhetoric that is created *by* Dreamers and that speaks to Dreamers instead of about them. Ergo, the main purpose of Dreamer rhetorics during the Obama years was to build and sustain the undocumented community. Activism and other public rhetorical expressions of community identity (such as were visible in the various forms of activism that I detail in this book) are crucial to the life of the undocumented community, not only so that undocumented immigrants will continue to push for immigration reform but also so that they will find a way to endure in a country that fails to recognize them as people. This lesson is particularly important as we think about how Dreamer rhetorics adapted to the Trump years and will adapt to whatever is to follow.

Dreamer rhetorics, however, did not accomplish some of the most immediate goals of Dreamer activism: passage of the DREAM Act, legal pathways to citizenship, and an end to family separation through detention and deportation. This fact complicates the definition of success for contemporary social movements. Sociologist Wayne Santoro, who analyzes the meaning of success when it comes to the US Civil Rights Movement, posits that the definition of movement success must be complicated. In his analysis of surveys documenting Black folks' opinions on the Civil Rights Movement's success, he found that while traditionally the passage of legislation is associated with social movement success, this narrow definition misses entire dimensions of movement success or failure.[27] Indeed, as Santoro demonstrates, many Black people were disappointed by the movement's failures, despite the policy changes that the movement engendered.[28] Similarly, as I show in *Dreamer Nation*, the Dreamer movement during the Obama years calls into question dominant perspectives of social movement success. I argue that the Dreamer movement was indeed successful, regardless of the lack of legislative action or political inclusion. Not only did Dreamer rhetorics help to create and sustain the undocumented community, but they also provided important rhetorical pathways to more critically consider rhetoric and citizenship in the US. In the last few pages of this chapter, I discuss some of these new rhetorical pathways.

1. Dreamer rhetorics illustrate how conflict and contradiction can be productive. Living in a state of constant threat—from the state that wants to lock them up and/or deport them, from people in their communities who want to take advantage of them and/or inflict violence—Dreamers used *nepantla* rhetorics to challenge US power. Their rhetorics did not always seek to create common ground or coalition. Instead, Dreamer rhetorics were often forceful, irreverent, and independent. Indeed, the Dreamers' rhetorical story reminds us that some of the most innovative and powerful rhetorical expressions of our time have come from places of struggle.[29]

2. Dreamer rhetorics dare to imagine something that seems unimaginable: a country in which undocumented immigrants will be regarded as people with rights rather than disposed of whenever the nation needs a scapegoat. Dreamer rhetorics during the Obama years had the audacity to work toward a novel world with new and different ways for people to relate to one another and to culture and place—community connections that have little to do with nationalism, creed, birthright, etc.

3. *Dreamer rhetorics, as the rhetorics of noncitizens, move us away from our reliance on citizenship as the only legitimately recognized form of community connection.* The Dreamers' case calls into question the meaning of citizenship in a US context. Does citizenship indicate love of country? Civic participation? Family history within a nation? Dreamers intimate that US citizenship does not measure any of these but is instead an arbitrary designation for those who happen to be born in the US and for those who have the privilege to access naturalization. In traditional conceptualizations of US citizenship—those associated with love of country, service to country, democratic participation, etc.—it would make logical sense for Dreamers to be recognized as citizens. Dreamers, who have often lived most of their lives in the US, who sometimes believe in the so-called American creed, and who want to work for the future of this country, have no path for legalization. They represent the failure of US citizenship laws.

Importantly, Dreamers' exclusion from US citizenship makes visible the ways that citizenship and immigration controls have more to do with money, race, and access than they have to do with values, love, and culture. As I've written elsewhere, immigration legislation serves to maintain the myth of US racial homogeneity, beginning from the Naturalization Act of 1790, which limited naturalized citizenship to "free white persons."[30] Deportation policies and practices also have a clear racial component, starting with the first deportation law—the Page Act of 1875—that specifically targeted Chinese immigrants, and following with the Chinese Exclusion Act of 1882 and Mexican repatriation of 1929. The ways Dreamers and their loved ones, a population that is overwhelmingly Latinx, have been detained and deported is but another rung in the ladder of racialized exclusion undergirded by immigration law. In 2019 Trump issued a new rule (which was rescinded by President Joe Biden in his first one hundred days in office) that would have based green card decisions on what the *New York Times* termed "an aggressive wealth test."[31] The *New York Times* reported, "Poor immigrants will be denied permanent legal status, also known as a green card, if they are deemed likely to use government benefit programs such as food stamps and subsidized housing. Wealthier immigrants, who are designated as less likely to require public assistance, will be able to obtain a green card."[32] Since obtaining a green card is an important step in the path toward US citizenship, this new "public charge rule" would have ensured that in the years to come, naturalized US citizenship would be safeguarded for immigrants from wealthy nations, which in our current world order means nations from the global North populated primarily by people who would fit US conceptualizations of whiteness.

US citizenship therefore continues to prove its reliance on the exclusion of a particular type of subject, and this "unacceptable" subject is designated along lines of race, national origin, sexual orientation, language, and even wealth. US citizenship has been a horizon for Dreamers that has simultaneously driven their activism and maintained their exclusion. As feminist scholar Amy L. Brandzel reminds us, "citizenship will always claim to be aspirational—to include the excluded eventually, once they are marked as deserving or human enough. But this is nothing less than an illusion, because according to citizenship, there will always be, *there must be,* (an)Other who experiences the full force of the exclusionary technologies of citizenship."[33] The struggle of Dreamers during the Obama years shows how the enduring promises of citizenship kept them fighting to be recognized, while the same promises undergirded the exclusions of Latinx undocumented immigrants from the US civic body.

4. *Dreamer rhetorics illustrate the violence of persuasion,* since for Dreamers, what is most persuasive is not always what is most humane, just, or equitable. Advocating for family reunification, for example, without acknowledging the disservice this causes to some of the most vulnerable—particularly, to queer and trans undocumented immigrants—reproduces violence toward those populations. While family reunification may be persuasive to a "family values" nation, it only reproduces inequality if not accompanied by radical critique of heteronormative assumptions of family configurations.

Confronting the limits of persuasion may not necessarily be a brand-new lesson for rhetorical studies. However, I propose that the field needs to more explicitly trouble the romanticization of persuasion in rhetorical studies, especially when it comes to considering BIPOC ways of knowing and being. If we continue to deify and romanticize persuasion, or to uncritically assume its importance, then we fail to take into account how persuasion can hurt communities of color. I call on rhetoric scholars to ask, How much rhetorical violence has been done to communities of color in the name of persuasion? The harm of silencing queer immigrant lives in the name of persuasive coherence, the damage of criminalizing the parents of Dreamers in the push for the DREAM Act, the violence of reproducing conservative notions of womanhood to appeal to a heterosexist nation, all of these are examples of the perils of persuasion.

FINAL THOUGHTS

One of my aims in writing *Dreamer Nation* has been to acknowledge and value the rhetorical power and innovation of Dreamers and to position Dreamer rhetorics within the history of rhetoric. I hope this book prompts readers to consider how our understanding of rhetoric at large should take into account the rhetorical choices and practices of the undocumented young people who are in a fight for their lives.

In *Dreamer Nation,* I've written about brave moments of activism and the ruthless policies and practices that motivated them. As I mentioned earlier in this chapter, this book has not been easy to write. It has been an emotional, heart-wrenching journey that at times forced me to stop and separate myself from the writing for a few days before being able to return to it. I acknowledge the privilege I've had as a researcher of being able to distance myself from what I was writing, to distract myself and think about something else in order to lessen my emotional connection to the moments I was writing about. This distancing was always accompanied by the reminder that Dreamers do not have such privilege. They must live every day with the risk of deportation as they listen to the hatred spewed from the mouths of conservative members of the country they call home. Yet I feel it is important to end this book on a hopeful note, because Dreamers, despite it all, largely remain hopeful, if not for a path toward legalization, for the ability to live their lives and express themselves fully in this country.

As queer migrations scholar Eithne Luibhéid reminds us, "Immigration and citizenship controls function in a double sense: as the means to delimit the nation, citizenry and citizenship and, conversely, as the loci for contesting and reworking these limits."[34] Despite the racialized exclusions engendered by immigration and citizenship controls, these same elements can serve as the sites for questioning and challenging what constitutes the nation and who makes up its citizenry. Attending to the limitations of the US immigration system unveils two inevitable conclusions: the first is that global patterns of migration cannot and will not be stopped, not by a wall along the US-Mexico border, not by discriminatory state policies, not by practices of detention and deportation. While none of these actions are insignificant, and each has real material consequences for people migrating to save their lives, none of them together or separately can stymie global patterns of migration. The unequal distribution of power, wealth, and resources produced by colonialism, capitalism, and neoliberalism have created the necessity for migration. Those on whose backs the global North has built its empires have been left with little choice but to seek aid from their oppressors, to take back even just a little of what was taken from them. Leaders of the global North who are exasperated with the droves of migrants at their borders are simply reaping what they and their predecessors sowed. Human beings will continue to migrate to save their lives. As the common saying goes, you show me a fifty-foot wall and I'll show you a fifty-one-foot ladder.

The second inevitable conclusion from attending to border rhetorics and their political implications is that citizenship as a monolithic idea has always been a faulty concept. Indeed, citizenship has never just meant one thing. It has always been a flexible and contested concept. It is only those who naively hang on to a supposedly better long-gone past, to the "good old days" of an ostensibly coherent nation, that continue to think that US citizenship was ever easily defined, that the borders of the nation were ever impermeable, and that citizenship controls were ever full-proof. With this realization in mind, it is easier to question citizenship and to see the futility in trying to preserve it as something that was ever and therefore must remain inviolable.

After analyzing the Dreamers and their activism, I agree with Brandzel's provocation that "there is nothing redeemable about citizenship, nothing worth salvaging or sustaining in the name of 'community,' practice, or belonging."[35] The Dreamers' fight for rights and recognition provides the sites from which to wage challenges to citizenship. Dreamers exemplify the rupture in the imagined idea of the nation's wholeness. Their actions can teach us to see what we have often been unable to see on our own: that the nation was never one, was never whole. In this way, Dreamers are the future, not just of the US, but of the world. They forecast how citizenship, belonging, and community will be reworked to account for new global realities and possibilities.

Notes

Introduction

1. While DACA provided respite from the threat of deportation, many Dreamer activists were skeptical of its implementation. DACA required its recipients to either attend college or serve in the military, the former a difficult option in a time of rising costs in higher education, and the latter a dangerous one in a time of continued US military involvement around the world. Many Dreamers also believed that those requirements fractured the Dreamer community by benefiting only a relatively small group of Dreamers while leaving other undocumented folks in the same situation, including their parents and loved ones who were not eligible for DACA. Some even felt anxious about providing the government their information in order to enroll in DACA. What would happen to that information if Congress failed to find a more permanent solution to their status? Would the government then in essence have a Dreamer deportation list?

2. Roberto G. Gonzales and Leo R. Chavez, "'Awakening to a Nightmare': Abjectivity and Illegality in the Lives of Undocumented 1.5-Generation Latino Immigrants in the United States," *Current Anthropology* 53, no. 3 (2012): 255–81.

3. Julia Preston, "Illegal Immigrant Students Protest at McCain Office," *New York Times*, May 17, 2010.

4. BIPOC underscores the differential experiences of Black and Indigenous peoples with oppression, racism, and colonization.

5. Eileen Truax, *Dreamers: An Immigrant Generation's Fight for Their American Dream* (Boston: Beacon Press, 2015).

6. Christine Garcia writes that the term "Latinx" reflects a rejection of gendered language practices and of the colonial gender binary. My use of "Latinx" here and elsewhere in this book is meant as a challenge to the patriarchy of language and as a gesture of inclusion to all people, regardless of gender identity. Christine Garcia, "In Defense of Latinx," *Composition Studies* 45, no. 2 (2017): 210–11.

7. Walter Nicholls, *The DREAMers: How the Undocumented Youth Movement Transformed the Immigrant Rights Debate* (Stanford, CA: Stanford University Press, 2013).

8. In June 2020 the Supreme Court of the United States ruled that the Trump administration could not begin to phase out the DACA program for procedural reasons, leaving open the possibility of ending the program in the future.

9. Miriam Jordan, "Most Americans Want Legal Status for 'Dreamers.' These People Don't," *New York Times*, January 25, 2018.

10. I write "US American" here and in the rest of this book to refer to people from the United States and to reject the hegemonic use of "America" and "American" when referring to the United States and its people.

11. See Sarah Bishop, *Undocumented Storytellers: Narrating the Immigrant Rights Movement* (Oxford: Oxford University Press, 2019); Lisa King, Rose Gubele, and Joyce Rain Anderson, "Introduction: Careful with the Stories We Tell: *Naming* Survivance, Sovereignty, *and* Story," in *Survivance, Sovereignty, Story: Teaching American Indian Rhetorics* (Logan: Utah State University Press, 2015); Malea Powell et al., "Our Story Begins Here: Constellating Cultural Rhetorics," *Enculturation* 18 (2014), https://enculturation.net.

12. Bishop, *Undocumented Storytellers*, 4.

13. Powell et al., "Our Story Begins Here."

14. See Laura Wides-Muñoz, *The Making of a Dream: How a Group of Young Undocumented Immigrants Helped Change What It Means to Be American* (New York: Harper, 2018); Karla Cornejo Villavicencio, *The Undocumented Americans* (New York: One World, 2019).

15. Bishop, *Undocumented Storytellers.*

16. Karma Chávez, *Queer Migration Politics: Activist Rhetoric and Coalitional Possibilities* (Urbana: University of Illinois Press, 2013); Ralph Cintron, *Democracy as Fetish* (University Park: Pennsylvania State University Press, 2019); Kent Ono and John Sloop, *Shifting Borders: Rhetoric, Immigration, and California's Proposition 187* (Philadelphia: Temple University Press, 2002).

17. Mary Bloodsworth-Lugo and Carmen Lugo Lugo, *Projecting 9/11: Race, Gender, and Citizenship in Recent Hollywood Films* (London: Rowman and Littlefield, 2014).

18. Bloodsworth-Lugo and Lugo Lugo. *Projecting 9/11.*

19. Cornel West, "Goodbye, American Neoliberalism: A New Era Is Here." *The Guardian*, November 17, 2016.

20. Jeffrey St. Onge, "Neoliberalism as Common Sense in Barack Obama's Health Care Rhetoric," *Rhetoric Society Quarterly* 47, no. 4 (2017): 295–312.

21. St. Onge, "Neoliberalism as Common Sense," 295.

22. See Nicholls, *DREAMers*; Claudia Anguiano and Karma Chávez, "DREAMers' Discourse: Young Latino/a Immigrants and the Naturalization of the American Dream," in *Latina/o Discourse in Vernacular Spaces: Somos de Una Voz?*, ed. Michelle Holling and Bernadette Calafell (Lanham, MD: Lexington Books, 2011); Stacey Sowards and Richard Pineda, "Immigrant Narratives and Popular Culture in the United States: Border Spectacle, Unmotivated Sympathies and Individualized Responsibilities," *Western Journal of Communication* 77, no. 1 (2013): 72–91; and Cintron, *Democracy as Fetish.*

23. Gloria Anzaldúa, "Now Let Us Shift . . . the Path of Conocimiento . . . Inner Work, Public Act," in *This Bridge We Call Home: Radical Visions for Transformation*, ed. Gloria E. Anzaldúa and Analouise Keating (New York: Routledge, 2002), 541.

24. Anzaldúa, "Now Let Us," 544.

25. Gloria Anzaldúa, "Let Us Be the Healing Wound: The Coyolxauhqui Imperative—la Sombra y el Sueño," in *The Gloria Anzaldúa Reader*, ed. AnaLouise Keating (Durham, NC: Duke University Press, 2009), 310.

26. Anzaldúa, "Let Us Be," 310.

27. Chela Sandoval, *Methodology of the Oppressed* (Minneapolis: University of Minnesota Press, 2000), 43.2.

28. Sandoval, *Methodology*, 57.8.

29. Anzaldúa, "Let Us Be," 310.

30. Sarah de los Santos Upton, "Nepantla Activism and Coalition Building: Locating Identity and Resistance in the Crack between Worlds," *Women's Communication Studies* 42, no. 2 (2019): 135–39.

31. Anzaldúa, "Now Let Us," 549.

32. See Nicholls, *The DREAMers*; Hinda Seif, "'Coming Out of the Shadows' and 'Undocuqueer': Undocumented Immigrants Transforming Sexuality Discourse and Activism," *Journal of Language and Sexuality* 3, no. 1 (2014): 87–129; Roberto Gonzales, *Lives in Limbo: Undocumented and Coming of Age in America* (Oakland: University of California Press, 2016); Veronica Terriquez et al. "Intersectionality as a Multipurpose Collective Action Frame: The Case of the Undocumented Youth Movement," *Ethnicities* 18, no. 2 (2018): 260–76, Bishop, *Undocumented Storytellers*; Chávez, *Queer Migration*; among others.

33. See Chávez, *Queer Migration*; Josue David Cisneros, *The Border Crossed Us: Rhetorics of Borders, Citizenship, and Latina/o Identity* (Tuscaloosa: University of Alabama Press, 2014); Kent Ono and John Sloop, *Shifting Borders*; Lisa Flores, "Constructing Rhetorical Borders: Peons, Illegal Aliens, and Competing Narratives of Immigration," *Critical Studies in Media Communication* 20, no. 4 (2003): 362–87; and Otto Santa Ana, "Like an Animal I Was Treated': Anti-immigrant Metaphor in U.S. Public Discourse," *Discourse and Society* 10, no. 2 (1999): 191–224; among others.

34. Flores, "Constructing Rhetorical Borders," 365.

35. Flores, "Constructing Rhetorical Borders," 380.

36. William V. Flores and Rina Benmayor, "Constructing Cultural Citizenship," in *Latino Cultural Citizenship: Claiming Identity, Space, and Rights*, ed. William V. Flores and Rina Benmayor (Boston: Beacon Press, 1997), 15.

37. William V. Flores, "Citizens vs. Citizenry: Undocumented Immigrants and Latino Cultural Citizenship," in *Latino Cultural Citizenship: Claiming Identity, Space, and Rights*, ed. William V. Flores and Rina Benmayor (Boston: Beacon Press, 1997), 258.

38. Flores, "Citizens vs. Citizenry," 260.

39. Flores, "Citizens vs. Citizenry," 263.

40. Cisneros, *The Border*, 84.

41. Cisneros, *The Border*, 123.

42. Tania Unzueta Carrasco and Hinda Seif, "Disrupting the Dream: Undocumented Youth Reframe Citizenship and Deportability through Anti-deportation Activism," *Latino Studies* 12, no. 2 (2014): 295.

43. Unzueta and Seif, "Disrupting the Dream," 296.

44. Amy L. Brandzel, *Against Citizenship: The Violence of the Normative* (Urbana: University of Illinois Press, 2016), 5.

45. Anguiano and Chávez, "DREAMer Discourse," 98.

46. Unzueta and Seif, "Disrupting the Dream," 280.

47. Elsewhere I have defined "acceptable heterogeneity" as those BIPOC immigrants the US deems acceptable in order to pit them against so-called "bad immigrants," maintain immigrants' subordinate position in white-dominant US, and eclipse histories of racialized violence and border securitization. Ana Milena Ribero, "Acceptable Heterogeneity: Brownwashing Rhetoric in President Obama's Address on Immigration," *Present Tense: A Journal of Rhetoric in Society* 5, no. 2 (2015): n.p.

48. Unzueta and Seif, "Disrupting the Dream," 291.

49. Ono and Sloop, *Shifting Borders*, 30.

50. Otto Santa Ana studies the use of metaphor in news articles in the *Los Angeles Times* that discussed Proposition 187 and finds that the dominant metaphor compares immigrants to animals. While Santa Ana's study does not fit the trend that immigrants are discussed primarily in neoliberal terms, his work is noteworthy because of the ways in which dehumanizing discourse always also plays a part in the nation's understanding of undocumented immigrants.

51. Ono and Sloop, *Shifting Borders*, 31.

52. Sowards and Pineda, "Immigrant Narratives and Popular Culture in the United States."

53. Sowards and Pineda, "Immigrant Narratives," 82.

54. Gonzales, *Lives in Limbo*, 211.

55. Terriquez et al., "Intersectionality as a Multipurpose Collective Action Frame," 4.

56. See Damián Baca, *Mestiz@ Scripts, Digital Migrations, and the Territories of Writing* (New York: Palgrave Macmillan, 2008); Jaime Mejía, "Bridging Rhetoric and Composition Studies"; Cristina Ramirez, *Occupying Our Space: The Mestiza Rhetorics of Mexican Women Journalists and Activists, 1875–1942* (Tucson: University of Arizona Press, 2015).

57. Gloria Anzaldúa, *Borderlands/La Frontera* (San Francisco: Aunt Lute, 1999), 100.

58. Andrea Lunsford, "Toward a Mestiza Rhetoric: Gloria Anzaldúa on Composition and Postcoloniality," *JAC* 18, no. 1 (1998): 1–27.

59. See the Pew Research Center's report on "Key Facts about Unauthorized Immigrants Enrolled in DACA," for more information.

60. Nicholls, *The DREAMers*, 5.

61. Nicholls, *The DREAMers*, 9.

62. Development, Relief, and Education for Alien Minors Act of 2011, S. EAS11295, 112th Cong. 2011.

63. Nicholls, *The DREAMers*, 10.

64. Nicholls, *The DREAMers*, 31.

65. Nicholls, *The DREAMers*, 31.

66. Gayatri Chakravorty Spivak, "Criticism, Feminism and the Institution," *Thesis Eleven* 10/11 (1984/85): 175–87.

67. Spivak, "Criticism, Feminism and the Institution," 184.

68. Truax, *Dreamers*, 5.

69. Seif, "'Coming Out of the Shadows' and 'Undocuqueer.'"

70. Hinda Seif, "Layers of Humanity: Interview with Undocuqueer Artivist Julio Salgado," *Latino Studies* 12, no. 2 (2014): 300–309.

71. Nicholls, *The DREAMers*, 31.

72. Truax, *Dreamers*, 50.

73. Villanueva, "Puerto Rico," 62.

74. I use Michel Foucault's definition of discourse, as he defines it in *Archaeology of Knowledge*, as "made up of a limited number of statements for which a group of conditions of existence can be defined" (117) and which constitute subjectivities and other material phenomena.

75. Sara P. Alvarez et al., "On Multimodal Composing," *Kairos: A Journal of Rhetoric, Technology, and Pedagogy* 21, no. 2 (2017), http://kairos.technorhetoric.net.

76. Licona, *Zines in the Third Space*, 7.

77. Fortier, Anne Marie, "Afterword: Acts of Affective Citizenship? Possibilities and Limitations," *Citizenship Studies* 20, no. 8 (2016): 1038–44.

78. Patricia Hill Collins, "Shifting the Center: Race, Class, and Feminist Theorizing about Motherhood," *Representations of Motherhood*, ed. Donna Basin et al., 371–88 (New Haven: Yale University Press, 1994).

79. Chela Sandoval and Guisela Latorre, "Chicana/o Artivism: Judy Baca's Digital Work with Youth of Color," in *Learning Race and Ethnicity: Youth and Digital Media*, ed. Anna Everett, 81–108 (Cambridge, MA: MIT Press, 2007).

Chapter 1

1. Dominguez Zamorano, Neidi, et al. "DREAM Activists: Rejecting the Passivity of the Nonprofit, Industrial Complex." TruthOut.org, September 21, 2010, original emphasis.

2. Dominguez Zamorano et al., "DREAM Activists," original emphasis.

3. Dominguez Zamorano et al., "DREAM Activists," original emphasis.

4. Sen. Jeff Sessions, "Ten Things You Need to Know about S.3827, the DREAM Act," November 18, 2010.

5. A deeper discussion of Dreamers' *nepantla* rhetorics is in this book's introduction.

6. Nicholas De Genova, "The Deportation Regime: Sovereignty, Space, and the Freedom of Movement," in *The Deportation Regime: Sovereignty, Space, and the Freedom of Movement*, ed. Nicholas De Genova and Nathalie Peutz, 33–65 (Durham, NC: Duke University Press, 2010).

7. Karma Chávez, *Queer Migration Politics: Activist Rhetoric and Coalitional Possibilities* (Urbana: University of Illinois Press, 2013), 8.

8. Chávez, *Queer Migration Politics*, 9, my emphasis.

9. *Diccionario de la lengua española*, 23rd ed., Real Academia Española (Madrid: Planeta, 2014), s.v. "Coyuntura."

10. Chávez, *Queer Migration Politics*, 9.

11. Jorge Mariscal, "Immigration and Military Enlistment: The Pentagon's Push for the DREAM Act Heats Up," *Latino Studies* 5, no. 3 (2007): 362.

12. Dominguez Zamorano et al., "DREAM Activists."

13. "New MPI Estimates: As Many as 2.1 Million Young People Could Be Eligible for the DREAM Act, though Far Fewer Would Meet Its Education or Military Service Requirements for Legalization." MigrationPolicy.org. Migration Policy Institute, February 18, 2014.

14. Dominguez Zamorano et al., "DREAM Activists."

15. In his groundbreaking article "*Brown v. Board of Education* and the Interest-Convergence Dilemma," critical race theorist Derrick Bell describes this idea as "interest convergence." Bell proposes that legislative advancements in civil rights occurred only when they also benefited the US government. Specifically, he writes that "the interest of blacks in achieving racial equality will be accommodated only when it converges with the interests of whites." Derrick Bell, "*Brown v. Board of Education* and the Interest-Convergence Dilemma," *Harvard Law Review* 93, no. 3 (1980): 523.

16. Tamara K. Nopper, "Why I Oppose Repealing DADT & Passage of the DREAM Act," in *Against Equality: Don't Ask to Fight Their Wars*, edited by Ryan Conrad (Lewiston, ME: Against Equality Publishing Collective, 2011), 36.

17. Dominguez Zamorano et al., "DREAM Activists."

18. Dominguez Zamorano et al., "DREAM Activists."

19. Dominguez Zamorano et al., "DREAM Activists," my emphasis.

20. Banu Bargu, *Starve and Immolate: The Politics of Human Weapons* (New York: Columbia University Press, 2014).

21. Adalberto Aguirre Jr. and Jennifer K. Simmers, "The DREAM Act and Neoliberal Practice: Retrofitting Hispanic Immigrant Youth in US Society," *Social Justice* 28, no. 3 (2012): 12.

22. Johanna Siméant and Christophe Traïni, *Bodies in Protest: Hunger Strikes and Angry Music* (Amsterdam: Amsterdam University Press, 2016), 22.

23. Siméant and Traïni, *Bodies in Protest.*

24. Kirk Semple, "3-day Fast Is Latest Call to Overhaul Immigration," *New York Times*, June 2, 2010.

25. Kimberly Brown, "Hunger Strikes Used by Immigration Reform Advocates," *ABC News*, June 7, 2010.

26. Kirk Semple, "Immigrants' Hunger Strike Ends with 'Die-In,'" *New York Times*, June 10, 2010.

27. Brown, "Hunger Strikes Used," my emphasis.

28. Leslie Berestein Rojas, "Emotional Rally Ends DREAM Act Hunger Strikes," KPCC, August 5, 2010.

29. Carlos Amador, "This Is Our Country Too: Undocumented Immigrant Youth Organizing and the Battle for the DREAM Act," *National Association of Social Workers*, Summer 2011.

30. Berestein Rojas, "Emotional Rally Ends."

31. Seth Freed Wessler, "Hunger-Strike DREAMers: 'Our Future Is on the Line,'" *Colorlines*, December 1, 2010.

32. Seth Freed Wessler, "Dozens of DREAMers Join Texas Hunger Strike," *Colorlines*, November 24, 2010.

33. Vivian Weinstein, "DREAM Act Hunger Strikers to End Strike after 40 Days," *People's World*, December 20, 2010.

34. Freed Wessler, "Hunger-Strike DREAMers," my emphasis.

35. Weinstein, "DREAM Act Hunger Strikers."

36. Melissa Ludwig, "Mayor Asks Hunger Strikers to Eat, but DREAMers Refuse," *San Antonio Express-News*, December 7, 2010.

37. For more, see this book's introduction.

38. Bargu, *Starve and Immolate*, 14.

39. Bargu, *Starve and Immolate*, 15, my emphasis.

40. Bargu, *Starve and Immolate*.

41. OED Online (Oxford: Oxford University Press, 2020), s.v. "Extortion."

42. Gerard A. Hauser, *Prisoners of Conscience: Moral Vernaculars of Political Agency* (Columbia: University of South Carolina Press, 2012).

43. James Chase Sánchez, "Preaching behind the Fiery Pulpit: Rhetoric, Public Memory, and Self-Immolation," PhD diss., Texas Christian University, 2017, 114.

44. Hauser, *Prisoners of Conscience*, 123.

45. Hauser, *Prisoners of Conscience*, 123.

46. Freed Wessler, "Dozens of DREAMers," my emphasis.

47. Hauser, *Prisoners of Conscience*, 127.

48. Bargu, *Starve and Immolate*, 6.

49. See, for example, Karma Chávez's fascinating analysis of the rhetorical form and function of the concept of the shadows, Hinda Seif's discussion of the epistemology of the shadows, or Jesus Cisneros and Christian Bracho's study on undocuqueer folks' visibility strategies. Chávez, *Queer Migrations Politics*; Seif, "'Coming Out of the Shadows' and 'Undocuqueer'"; Jesus Cisneros and Christian Bracho, "Coming Out of the Shadows and the Closet: Visibility Schemas among Udocuqueer Immigrants," *Journal of Homosexuality* 66, no. 6 (2018): 715–34.

50. De Genova, "Deportation Regime."

51. Unzueta and Seif, "Disrupting the Dream," 287.

52. I discuss coming out as an activist strategy with roots in the LGBT liberation movement in chapter 4.

53. Mikaela Shwer, *Don't Tell Anyone* (No le digas a nadie), September 21, 2015.

54. For a fascinating analysis of Dreamer agency and subjectivity in the Coming Out of the Shadows event in Chicago, see René Galindo, "Undocumented & Unafraid:

The DREAM Act 5 and the Public Disclosure of Undocumented Status as a Political Act," *Urban Review* 44, no. 5 (2012): 589–611.

55. Yen Le Espiritu, *Home Bound: Filipino American Lives across Cultures, Communities, and Countries* (Berkeley: University of California Press, 2003), 47, my emphasis.

56. Gonzales and Chávez, "Awakening to a Nightmare," *Current Anthropology* 53, no. 3 (2012): 255–81.

57. Espiritu, *Home Bound*, 48.

58. One poignant example of the sorts of abuses facilitated by the deportation regime was documented by the New Orleans Workers' Center for Racial Justice in their report "And Injustice for All: Workers' Lives in the Reconstruction of New Orleans." In this report the NOWCRJ outlines how in post-Katrina New Orleans, undocumented workers were forced to endure toxic work conditions, wage theft, violence, and police harassment under the threat of being reported to immigration authorities.

59. "Coming Out of the Shadows / Saliendo de las Sombras," YouTube, uploaded by Edy Anxeli, March 11, 2010.

60. "Coming Out of the Shadows / Saliendo de las Sombras."

61. "Coming Out of the Shadows / Saliendo de las Sombras."

62. De Genova, "Deportation Regime."

63. "Coming Out of the Shadows 3.10.10," YouTube, uploaded by edia12, March 13, 2010.

64. "Coming Out of the Shadows 3.10.10."

65. "Coming Out of the Shadows 3.10.10," YouTube, uploaded by edia12, March 13, 2010. This video contains the same file name as above but was posted separately and has a unique URL.

66. Dominguez Zamorano et al., "DREAM Activists."

67. Dominguez Zamorano et al., "DREAM Activists."

Chapter 2

1. Luís León, "Luís's Story," guest lecture at the University of Portland, Portland, Oregon, November 14, 2013.

2. León, "Luís's Story."

3. León, "Luís's Story."

4. León, "Luís's Story."

5. León, "Luís's Story."

6. Perla Trevizo, "Dreamers Released from Custody," *Arizona Daily Star*, August 8, 2013.

7. I draw on Sharon Yam's use of "affect," which she describes as "a bodily intensity and potentiality that eludes signification . . . an embodied prelinguistic sensation and intensity." Sharon Yam, *Inconvenient Strangers: Transnational Subjects and the Politics of Citizenship* (Columbus: Ohio State University Press, 2019).

8. National Immigrant Youth Alliance, "About National Immigrant Youth Alliance," Facebook.

9. Griselda Nevarez, "150 Undocumented Immigrants to Enter US in Border-Crossing Demonstration." *HuffPost Latino Voices*, TheHuffingtonPost.com, March 11, 2014.

10. Truax, *Dreamers*.

11. Michael Di Gregorio and Jessica L. Merolli, "Introduction: Affective Citizenship and the Politics of Identity, Control, Resistance," *Citizenship Studies* 20, no. 8 (2016): 933–42.

12. Yam, *Inconvenient Strangers*.

13. Danielle Allen, *Talking to Strangers: Anxieties of Citizenship since* Brown v. Board of Education (Chicago: University of Chicago Press, 2004), xxii.

14. Yam, *Inconvenient Strangers*, 3.

15. Sarah Ahmed, *Strange Encounters: Embodied Others in Post-Coloniality* (London: Routledge, 2000), 21, original emphasis.

16. Anne Marie Fortier, "Afterword: Acts of Affective Citizenship? Possibilities and Limitations," *Citizenship Studies* 20, no. 8 (2016): 1041.

17. Siobhan B. Somerville, "Notes toward a Queer History of Naturalization," *American Quarterly* 57, no. 3 (2005): 9.

18. Jose Antonio Vargas, "Not Legal Not Leaving," *Time*, June 25, 2012.

19. Vargas, "Not Legal," 40.

20. Vargas, "Not Legal," 44.

21. All the Dream 9 participants were born in Mexico.

22. Chandra Tapalde Mohanty, *Feminism without Borders: Decolonizing Theory, Practicing Solidarity* (Durham, NC: Duke University Press, 2003), 90.

23. Claudia Amaro, "Claudia," YouTube, uploaded by the National Immigrant Youth Alliance, July 22, 2013.

24. Amaro, "Claudia."

25. Amaro, "Claudia."

26. Amaro, "Claudia."

27. Amaro, "Claudia."

28. *Pocho* is a Mexican slang term used to refer to Mexican Americans who exhibit traces of US culture and accent. Although some Latinx scholars have worked to reclaim *pocho* (see Medina, *Reclaiming Poch@ Pop*), the word continues to have a negative connotation. In Gloria Anzaldúa's popularly anthologized essay "How to Tame a Wild Tongue," she describes common perceptions of *pocho* as "cultural traitor, you're speaking the oppressor's language by speaking English, you're ruining the Spanish language."

29. León, "Luís's Story."

30. Anayansi Diaz-Cortes, "Can the Dream 9 Change Immigration Policy in the US?" *Sonic Trace*, KCRW, Los Angeles, October 8, 2013, emphasis added.

31. Nicholas De Genova, *The Deportation Regime: Sovereignty, Space, and the Freedom of Movement* (Durham, NC: Duke University Press, 2010).

32. León, "Luís's Story."

33. Diaz-Cortes, "Can the Dream 9?"

34. National Immigrant Youth Alliance, "Bring Them Home," livestream video, Ustream, July 22, 2013.

35. See Josue David Cisneros, "(Re)Bordering the Civic Imaginary: Rhetoric, Hybridity, and Citizenship in *La Gran Marcha*," *Quarterly Journal of Speech* 97, no. 1 (2011): 26–49; Nicholls, *Dreamers*.

36. Amaro, "Claudia."

37. Ceferino Santiago, "Ceferino Santiago," YouTube, uploaded by the National Immigrant Youth Alliance, July 22, 2013, emphasis added.

38. Lizbeth Mateo, "Bring Them Home: Lizbeth Mateo Checking in from Oaxaca, Mexico," YouTube, uploaded by the National Immigrant Youth Alliance, July 17, 2013.

39. Somerville, "Notes," 661.

40. Wendy Brown, *Undoing the Demos: Neoliberalism's Stealth Revolution* (New York: Zone, 2015), 31.

41. René Galindo, "Undocumented & Unafraid: The DREAM Act 5 and the Public Disclosure of Undocumented Status as a Political Act," *Urban Review* 44, no. 5 (2012): 590.

42. León, "Luís's Story."

43. Ana Milena Ribero, "Acceptable Heterogeneity: Brownwashing Rhetoric in President Obama's Address on Immigration," *Present Tense: A Journal of Rhetoric in Society* 5, no. 2 (2015).

44. De Genova, *Deportation Regime*, 39.

45. De Genova, *Deportation Regime*, 58, my emphasis.

46. Marco Saavedra, "Bring Them Home: Marco Saavedra Checking in from Mexico," YouTube, uploaded by the National Immigrant Youth Alliance, July 18, 2013.

47. Mateo, "Bring Them Home."

48. Lulu Martinez, "Bring Them Home: Lulu Martinez Checking in from Mexico City," YouTube, uploaded by the National Immigrant Youth Alliance, July 20, 2013.

49. Martinez, "Bring Them Home."

50. Saavedra, "Bring Them Home."

51. Mateo, "Bring Them Home."

52. Martinez, "Bring Them Home."

53. Mateo, "Bring Them Home."

54. María Hinojosa, Antonia Cerejido, and Marlon Bishop, "The Dream 9," *Latino USA*. NPR, New York, Februaary 3, 2017.

55. The Eloy Detention Center is notorious for having the highest number of deaths of any immigrant detention center in the US, according to Perla Trevizo, "Report: ICE Complicit in Hiding Maltreatment at Eloy Center," *Arizona Daily Star*, Tucson.com, October 15, 2015.

56. Maria Inez Peniche, "Maria Checks in from Detention; #BRINGTHEMHOME," YouTube, uploaded by the National Immigrant Youth Alliance, July 26, 2013.

57. Hinojosa et al. "The Dream 9."

58. Claudia Amaro, "A Call from the Eloy Detention Center: Claudia Amaro," You-Tube, uploaded by the National Immigrant Youth Alliance, July 29, 2013.

59. Karma Chávez, *Queer Migration Politics: Activist Rhetoric and Coalitional Possibilities* (Champaign: University of Illinois Press, 2013), 8.

60. The song "El pueblo unido jamás será vencido" ("The people united will never be defeated") was first written and performed in Chile during the popular tumult that ended in a military coup deposing President Salvador Allende, according to Fernanda Paúl, "'¡El pueblo unido jamás será vencido!' La historia de emblemático himno de protesta que vuelve a ser protagonista en Chile," *BBC News*, December 16, 2019, https://www.bbc.com/mundo/noticias-america-latina-50809666.

61. Anil Kalhan, "Rethinking Immigration Detention," *Columbia Law Review* 110 (2010): 44.

62. "Find a Facility," *CoreCivic*, https://www.corecivic.com/facilities.

63. Kalhan, "Rethinking Immigration Detention," 46.

64. Kalhan, "Rethinking Immigration Detention," 49.

65. Kalhan, "Rethinking Immigration Detention," 43.

66. Kalhan, "Rethinking Immigration Detention," 47.

67. *In Their Own Words: Enduring Abuse in Arizona Immigration Detention Centers* (Phoenix: ACLU of Arizona, 2011).

68. María Inés Taracena, "Eloy Detention Center Hunger Strike: Tucson Teen Demands to Speak to Her Father," *Tucson Weekly*, June 16, 2015.

69. Kalhan, "Rethinking Immigration Detention," 44.

70. Lizbeth Mateo, "Lizbeth Mateo: 'I Don't Know What They've Done to the Women Here . . .'—Eloy Prison," YouTube, uploaded by the National Immigrant Youth Alliance, July 30, 2013.

71. Amaro, "Call from Eloy."

72. Juan Escalante, "Opinion: Attention Immigration 'Allies'—Stop Silencing DREAMers," NBC Latino, November 14, 2012.

73. Thelsa Zelaya Trejo, "Thelsa Zelaya Trejo A# 077–195–967 Translated," You-Tube, uploaded by the National Immigrant Youth Alliance, August 2, 2013.

74. Michel Foucault, *Discipline and Punish: The Birth of the Prison* (New York: Vintage Books, 1995), 232.

75. "Meet the Dream 9," *Latino USA*, October 16, 2015.

Chapter 3

1. David Bennion, "In 2013, the Dream 30 Fought to Come Home," *Open Borders*, December 30, 2013.

2. Roque Planas, "Big Win for Immigrant Activists Who Staged Border-Crossing Protest in Laredo," *HuffPost*, October 1, 2013.

3. Olivia Salcido and Cecilia Menjívar, "Gendered Paths to Legal Citizenship: The Case of Latin-American Immigrants in Phoenix, Arizona," *Law & Society Review* 46, no. 2 (2012): 335–68.

4. JOMO, "Fighting Obama's Deportation Policies without Papers," *The Nation*, April 24, 2014.

5. I use the Spanish "*familia*" instead of "family" to denote that I am not referring to an actual biological family but to a large community of care beyond kinship.

6. Of course, all this was in 2014, four years before President Donald Trump would order the "zero tolerance" immigration policy that would see the forced separation of immigrant children from their parents at the border. Read more about Trump's zero tolerance policy in this book's conclusion.

7. Wendy Hesford, *Spectacular Rhetorics: Human Rights Visions, Recognitions, Feminisms* (Durham, NC: Duke University Press, 2011).

8. Lisa Marie Cacho, *Social Death: Racialized Rightlessness and the Criminalization of the Unprotected* (New York: New York University Press, 2012), 117.

9. Sara McKinnon, "Excavating Gender in Women's Early Claims to Political Asylum in the United States," *Women's Studies in Communication* 33, no. 2 (2010): 91.

10. Maria Lugones, "Methodological Notes toward a Decolonial Feminism," *Decolonizing Epistemologies: Latina/o Theology and Philosophy*, ed. Ada Mara Isasi-Daz and Eduardo Mendieta (New York: Fordham University Press, 2011): 68–86.

11. Amalia Pallares, *Family Activism: Immigrant Struggles and the Politics of Noncitizenship* (New Brunswick, NJ: Rutgers University Press, 2015), 9.

12. See Michelle Tellez, "Personal Is Political: Chicana Motherwork," *Feminist Wire*, March 6, 2014; Hill Collins, "Shifting the Center."

13. Anzaldúa, *Borderlands.*

14. Lugones, "Methodological Notes," 72.

15. Lugones, "Methodological Notes," 73.

16. Lugones, "Methodological Notes," 73.

17. Lugones, "Methodological Notes," 73.

18. Eve Tuck and K. Wayne Yang, "Decolonization Is Not a Metaphor," *Decolonization: Indigeneity, Education, & Society* 1, no. 1 (2012): 1–40.

19. Lugones, "Methodological Notes," 76.

20. Tuck and Yang, "Decolonization," 7.

21. Tuck and Yang, "Decolonization," 18.

22. Chandra Tapalde Mohanty, *Feminism without Borders: Decolonizing Theory, Practicing Solidarity* (Durham, NC: Duke University Press, 2003), 133.

23. Natalie Fixmer-Oraiz, *Homeland Maternity: US Security Culture and the New Reproductive Regime* (Urbana: University of Illinois Press, 2019), 3.

24. Spike Peterson, "Sexing Political Identities/Nationalism as Heterosexism," *Women, States, and Nationalism: At Home in the Nation?*, ed. Sita Ranchod-Nilsson and Mary Ann Tétreault (London: Routledge, 2000), 64.

25. Fixmer-Oraiz, *Homeland Maternity*, 61.

26. Chávez, *Latino Threat.*

27. For an analysis of the concept of family as a frame in Arellano's deportation activism, see Pallares, *Family Activism*, 38–61.

28. N. C. Aizenman and Spencer S. Hsu, "Activist's Arrest Highlights Key Immigrant Issue," *WashingtonPost.com*, August 21, 2007.

29. Pallares, *Family Activism*, 30.

30. See Pallares, *Family Activism*, for an analysis of Arellano's "representativity."

31. Ana Milena Ribero, "'Papá, Mamá, I'm Coming Home:' Family, Home, and the Neoliberal Immigrant Nation in the National Immigrant Youth Alliance's 'Bring them Home' Campaign," *Rhetoric Review* 37, no. 3 (2018): 273–85.

32. Melissa Wright, *Disposable Women and Other Myths of Global Capitalism* (New York: Routledge, 2006).

33. Hill Collins, "Shifting," 54.

34. Fixmer-Oraiz evokes a rhetoric of maternal desire with which (wealthy white) women frame their longing for motherhood and their need for assisted reproductive technologies. The maternal desire that I am discussing in Arellano's case is related to Fixmer-Oraiz's rhetorics of maternal desire in that it expresses the desire to mother. However, immigrant women and other women of color may have not only the desire to become mothers in the face of infertility but also the desire to continue to mother in the face of state-sanctioned separation.

35. Emma Perez, *Decolonial Imaginary: Writing Chicanas into History* (Bloomington: Indiana University Press, 1999), 116.

36. See Adrienne Rich, *Of Woman Born: Motherhood as Experience and Institution* (New York: W. W. Norton, 1976).

37. In *Family Activism*, Pallares writes about Arellano's purposeful use of the image of the Virgin Mary in her activism. While this chapter does not address the Virgin Mary specifically, I think there is room for the Virgin Mary's image to also be read as antipatriarchal (see, for example, Anzaldua's *Borderlands/La Frontera* and Sandra Cisneros's "Guadalupe the Sex Goddess").

38. Evelyn Nakano Glenn, "Social Constructions of Mothering: A Thematic Overview," *Mothering: Ideology, Experience, and Agency*, ed. Evelyn Nakano Glenn, Grace Chang, Linda Rennie Forcey, 1–29 (New York: Routledge, 1994), 3.

39. Ana Castillo, "Toward the Mother-Bond Principle," *Massacre of the Dreamers: Essays on Xicanisma* (Albuquerque: University of New Mexico Press, 2014), 195.

40. Castillo, "Toward the Mother-Bond Principle," 194.

41. Hill Collins, "Shifting the Center," 47.

42. Hill Collins, "Shifting the Center," 57.

43. Hill Collins, "Shifting the Center," 47.

44. Leah Schmalzbauer, "Searching for Wages and Mothering from Afar: The Case of Honduran Transnational Families," *Journal of Marriage and Family* 66, no. 5 (2017): 1320.

45. The names of the second and third women who speak in the "Bring Our Mothers Home #WeAreElvira" video are not given in the text.

46. "Bring Our Mothers Home #WeAreElvira," YouTube, uploaded by FirmeProcess, March 18, 2014.

47. Schmalzbauer, "Searching for Wages," 1326.

48. Pierrette Hondagneu-Sotelo and Ernestine Avila, "'I'm Here, but I'm There': The Meanings of Latina Transnational Motherhood," *Gender and Society* 11, no. 5 (1997): 548–71.

49. "Bring Our Mothers Home," my emphasis.

50. Karma R. Chávez, *Queer Migration Politics: Activist Rhetoric and Coalitional Possibilities* (Champaign: University of Illinois Press, 2013), 7.

51. Chávez, *Queer Migration*, 8.

52. Cacho, *Social Death*, 118.

53. "Bring Our Mothers Home."

54. Sara McKinnon, "Positioned in/by the State: Incorporation, Exclusion, and Appropriation of Women's Gender-Based Claims to Political Asylum in the United States," *Quarterly Journal of Speech* 97, no. 2 (2011): 181.

55. "Bring Our Mothers Home," my emphasis.

56. "Bring Our Mothers Home," my emphasis.

57. "Isabel Martinez Bring Them Home NIYA," YouTube, uploaded by LaMunaMusica, March 19, 2014.

58. Alexis Pauline Gumbs, "M/Other Ourselves: A Black Queer Feminist Genealogy for Radical Mothering," *Revolutionary Mothering: Love on the Front Lines*, ed. Alexis Pauline Gumbs, China Martens, and Mai'a Williams (Oakland, CA: PM Press, 2016), 20.

59. Alexis Pauline Gumbs, "Introduction," *Revolutionary Mothering: Love on the Front Lines*, ed. Alexis Pauline Gumbs, China Martens, and Mai'a Williams (Oakland, CA: PM Press, 2016), 115.

60. Gumbs, "Introduction," 115.

61. Gumbs, "M/Other Ourselves," 21.

62. "Isabel Martinez."

63. "Isabel Martinez."

64. Gumbs, "M/Other Ourselves," 23.

65. Gumbs, "M/Other Ourselves," 29.

66. Shelley M. Park, *Mothering Queerly, Queering Motherhood: Resisting Monomaternalism in Adoptive, Lesbian, Blended, and Polygamous Families* (New York: SUNY Press, 2013).

67. Gumbs, "M/Other Ourselves," 23.

68. "Isabel Martinez."

69. "Isabel Martinez."

70. "Isabel Martinez."

71. "Isabel Martinez."

72. Dorsía Smith Silva, "Introduction: Conceptualizing Latina/Chicana Mothering," *Latina/Chicana Mothering* (Bradford, ON: Demeter Press, 2011), 3.

73. Gumbs, "Introduction," 115.

74. Rich, *Of Woman Born*.

Chapter 4

1. Nicholls, *DREAMers*, 127.

2. Truax, *Dreamers*, 172–74.

3. Motta, "Activism, Visuality," 128.

4. Preston, "Illegal Immigrant Students."

5. Chávez, *Queer Migration*, 73.

6. In this chapter, I primarily use the uncapitalized "undocuqueer" to avoid giving precedence to one identity over another and to signal the fluidity between these identities. I use "UndocuQueer" and other possible capitalizations when I am referring to texts that were written as such.

7. Truax, *Dreamers*, 74.

8. "Artivism" is a portmanteau of "art" and "activism," which denotes art in the service of activism. Sandoval and Latorre, "Chicana/o Artivism."

9. Anzaldúa, *Borderlands/La Frontera*, 42.

10. "LGBTQ Justice," UnitedWeDream.org.

11. José Esteban Muñoz, *Cruising Utopia* (New York: NYU Press, 2009).

12. Audre Lorde, "Uses of the Erotic," *Sister Outsider* (Berkeley, CA: Crossing Press, 1984), 56.

13. Lorde, "Uses of the Erotic," 54.

14. Lorde, "Uses of the Erotic," 56.

15. Lorde, "Uses of the Erotic," 58.

16. Lorde, "Uses of the Erotic," 59.

17. Chávez, *Queer Migration*, 94.

18. Seif, "Coming Out," 96.

19. Chávez, *Queer Migration*, 95.

20. Seif, "Layers," 304.

21. Lisa Duggan, "The New Homonormativity: The Sexual Politics of Neoliberalism," in *Materializing Democracy: Toward a Revitalized Cultural Politics*, ed. Russ Castronovo and Dana Nelson (Durham, NC: Duke University Press, 2002): 175–94.

22. Chávez, *Queer Migration*, 153.

23. Eithne Luibhéid, "Introduction: Queering Migration and Citizenship," in *Queer Migration: Sexuality, US Citizenship, and Border Crossings*, ed. Eithne Luibhéid and Lionel Cantu Jr. (Minneapolis: University of Minnesota Press, 2001), xi.

24. Seif, "Layers," 304.

25. Mara Pieri, "Undoing Citizenship: Undocumented Queer Activism and Practices of Rights," *Remhu* 24, no. 48 (2016): 106.

26. Pieri, "Undoing Citizenship," 115.

27. In her chapter in the 2020 collection *We Are Not Dreamers*, Maria Liliana Ramirez critiques the label UndocuQueer because it portrays identity as fixed and rejects the fluidity of the self. Ramirez also shows how some queer undocumented youth reject the label as an imposed identity category that reflects activism by older generations. Maria Liliana Ramirez, "Beyond Identity: Coming out as UndocuQueer," *We*

Are Not Dreamers, ed. Leisy Abrego and Genevieve Negrón-Gonzales (Durham, NC: Duke University Press, 2020): 146–67.

28. Seif, "Coming Out," 94.

29. Ribero, "Acceptable Heterogeneity."

30. Ribero, "Acceptable Heterogeneity."

31. See this book's conclusion for an analysis of Trump's executive order "Enhancing Public Safety in the Interior of the United States."

32. Derek Hawkins, "Immigration Agents Illegally Detain Obama Program 'Dreamer,' Lawsuit says," *Washington Post*, February 15, 2017.

33. "UndocuQueer Manifesto," YouTube, uploaded by United We Dream, October 11, 2013.

34. Chávez, *Queer Migration*, 23.

35. Chávez, *Queer Migration*, 26.

36. "UndocuQueer Manifesto," emphasis added.

37. Cherrie L. Moraga, *Loving in the War Years* (Cambridge, MA: South End Press, 2000), xi.

38. "UndocuQueer Manifesto."

39. Chávez, *Queer Migration*, 26.

40. "UndocuQueer Manifesto."

41. "UndocuQueer Manifesto."

42. Sara Ahmed, "In the Name of Love," in *Cultural Politics of Emotion* (New York: Routledge, 2015), 141.

43. Chela Sandoval, "Love as a Hermeneutics of Social Change, a Decolonizing *Movida*," in *Methodology of the Oppressed* (Minneapolis: University of Minnesota Press, 2000).

44. Sandoval, "Love as a Hermeneutics," 143.

45. Jasbir Puar, *Terrorist Assemblages* (Durham, NC: Duke University Press, 2007), 32.

46. Sylvia Rivera, "Y'all Better Quiet Down," speech at Christopher Street Liberation Day Rally, New York, 1973.

47. "UndocuQueer Manifesto."

48. Adela Licona and Karma Chávez, "Relational Literacies and Their Coalitional Possibilities," *Peitho Journal* 18, no. 1 (2015): 96.

49. Licona and Chávez, "Relational Literacies," 97.

50. "UndocuQueer Manifesto."

51. "UndocuQueer Manifesto."

52. Juan D. Ochoa, "Shine Bright like a Migrant: Julio Salgado's Digital Art and Its Use of Jotería," *Social Justice* 42, no. 3–4 (2015): 184–99.

53. "UndocuQueer Manifesto."

54. Muñoz, *Cruising Utopia*, 26.

55. Muñoz, *Cruising Utopia*, 25.

56. Muñoz, *Cruising Utopia*, 22.

57. Muñoz, *Cruising Utopia*, 27.

58. adrienne maree brown, *Pleasure Activism: The Politics of Feeling Good* (Chico, CA: AK Press, 2019), 3.

59. brown, *Pleasure Activism*, 13.

60. brown, *Pleasure Activism*, 13.

61. Juana María Rodríguez, *Sexual Futures, Queer Gestures, and Other Latina Longings* (New York: NYU Press, 2014), 9, my emphasis.

62. Seif, "Layers," 304.

63. Julio Salgado, *I Read, I Create, I Mess Up, I Fall*, illustration, JulioSalgado.com, April 20, 2022, https://www.juliosalgadoart.com/gallery.

64. Julio Salgado, *Fuck Your Borders, Pt. 2*, illustration, Instagram, April 20, 2022, https://www.instagram.com/p/BUHjYhjFIHs/?hl=en.

65. Harrick Wu, "'Undocu-Queer' Artist Julio Salgado on Creative Resistance," KQED, July 5, 2018.

66. Ochoa, "Shine," 193.

67. Ochoa, "Shine," 185.

68. Rodriguez, *Sexual Futures*, 2.

69. Ribero, "Acceptable Heterogeneity."

70. Rodriguez, *Sexual Futures*, 1.

71. Puar, *Terrorist Assemblages*.

72. Jonathan Alexander and Jacqueline Rhodes, "Queer Rhetoric and the Pleasure of the Archive," *Enculturation* (2012), http://enculturation.net/queer-rhetoric-and-the-pleasures-of-the-archive.

73. Muñoz, *Cruising Utopia*, 31.

74. Alexander and Rhodes, "Queer Rhetoric."

75. Alexander and Rhodes, "Queer Rhetoric."

76. Sandoval and Latorre, "Chicana/o Artivism," 83.

Conclusion

1. "Enhancing Public Safety in the Interior of the United States," Executive Order No. 13768, 82 Fed. Reg. 8799 (January 30, 2017). *Federal Register*.

2. "Enhancing Public Safety."

3. "Enhancing Public Safety."

4. "Enhancing Public Safety."

5. Lugo-Lugo and Bloodsworth-Lugo, "Anchor/Terror Babies."

6. "Enhancing Public Safety."

7. See Kristin F. Butcher and Anne Morrison Piehl, "Cross-City Evidence on the Relationship between Immigration and Crime," *Journal of Policy Analysis and Management* 17, no. 3 (1998): 457–93; Walter A. Ewing, Daniel E. Martinez, and Rubé G. Rumbaut, *The Criminalization of Immigration in the United States* (Washington, DC: American Immigration Council Special Report, July 2015); Thomas Miles and Adam Cox, "Does Immigration Enforcement Reduce Crime? Evidence from Secure Communities," *Journal of Law and Economics* 57, no. 4 (2014): 937–73; Graham Ousey and

Charis Kubrin, "Exploring the Connection between Immigration and Violent Crime Rates in US Cities, 1980–2000," *Social Problems* 56, no. 3 (2009): 447–73.

8. "Enhancing Public Safety."

9. "Enhancing Public Safety."

10. "Enhancing Public Safety."

11. The executive order was blocked by federal injunction on November 21, 2017 and rescinded by President Joe Biden on January 20, 2021.

12. The Census Bureau's 2015 analysis states that the US will become "majority-minority" in 2044. For a full report, see Sandra L. Colby and Jennifer M. Ortman, "Projections of the Size and Composition of US Population: 2014–2060," *US Census Bureau*, US Department of Commerce (March 2015).

13. Another illustrative result of this rhetoric is the January 6, 2021, insurrection in the US Capitol.

14. See Kim Parker, Rich Morin, and Juliana Menasce Horowitz, "Looking to the Future, Public Sees an America in Decline on Many Fronts," *Pew Research Center: Social & Demographic Trends*, March 21, 2019.

15. See Kahled Beydoun, "Acting Muslim," *Harvard Civil Rights-Civil Liberties Law Review* 53, no. 1 (2018): 1–64, for a fascinating discussion on the ban and its implications for the performance of Muslim identity in the US.

16. Sarah Pierce and Andrew Selee, "Immigration under Trump: A Review of Policy Shifts in the Year since the Election," Migration Policy Institute, December 2017.

17. In June 2019 the US Supreme Court agreed to review legal challenges to DACA during its next session, with a decision on DACA expected before June 2020.

18. Pierce and Selee, "Immigration."

19. Miriam Valverde, "What You Need to Know about the Trump Administration's Zero-Tolerance Immigration Policy," PolitiFact, the Poynter Institute (June 6, 2018).

20. "Family Separation by the Numbers," ACLU, October 2, 2018, https://www.aclu.org/issues/family-separation.

21. Caitlin Dickerson and Manny Fernandez, "What's behind the 'Tender Age' Shelters Opening for Young Migrants," *New York Times*, June 20, 2018.

22. Ashley Fetters, "At Least 30 Migrant Children Have Been Separated from Their Parents for More than a Year," *The Atlantic*, July 13, 2019.

23. Angela Fritz and Luis Velarde, "ICE Arrested Hundreds of People in Raids. Now 'Devastated' Children Are without Their Parents," *Washington Post*, August 7, 2019.

24. Fritz and Velarde, "ICE Arrested Hundreds."

25. On August 3, 2019, a white twenty-one-year old male (I withhold his name to avoid granting him the notoriety that many mass shooters seek) drove ten hours to a Walmart store in El Paso, Texas, armed with an AK-47 and killed twenty-two people, mostly of Mexican and Latin American ancestry. The killer admitted to the police that he was targeting Mexicans. An online manifesto titled "The Inconvenient Truth," has been linked to the shooter and claims that the attack was "a response to the Hispanic invasion of Texas." See Tim Arango, Nicholas Bogel-Burroughs, and Katie Benner,

"Minutes before El Paso Killing, Hate-Filled Manifesto Appears Online," *New York Times,* August 3, 2019.

26. Joe McCarthy, "DACA Dreamers Walk 250 Miles to Capital to Protest Inaction," *Global Citizen,* March 1, 2018.

27. Wayne A. Santoro, "Was the Civil Rights Movement Successful? Tracking and Understanding Black Views," *Sociological Forum* 30, no. S1 (2015): 644.

28. Santoro, "Was the Civil Rights Movement Successful?," 631.

29. For relevant work making this claim, see Jacqueline Jones Royster, *Traces of a Stream* (Pittsburgh: University of Pittsburgh Press, 2000); Malea Powell, "Rhetorics of Survivance: How American Indians Use Writing." *College Composition and Communications* 53, no. 3 (2002): 396–434.

30. Ana Milena Ribero, "Citizenship," *Decolonizing Rhetoric and Composition Studies: New Latinx Keywords for Theory and Pedagogy,* es. Iris Ruiz and Raúl Sanchez (New York: Palgrave Macmillan, 2016), 35.

31. Michael D. Shear and Eileen Sullivan, "Trump Policy Favors Wealthier Immigrants for Green Cards," *New York Times,* August 12, 2019.

32. Shear and Sullivan, "Trump Policy."

33. Brandzel, *Against Citizenship,* 5, original emphasis.

34. Luibhéid, "Introduction," xi.

35. Brandzel, *Against Citizenship,* 5.

Bibliography

Aguirre, Adalberto Jr., and Jennifer K. Simmers. "The DREAM Act and Neoliberal Practice: Retrofitting Hispanic Immigrant Youth in US Society." *Social Justice* 28, no. 3 (2012): 3–16.

Ahmed, Sara. "In the Name of Love." *Cultural Politics of Emotion*. New York: Routledge, 2015.

———. *Strange Encounters: Embodied Others in Post-Coloniality*. London: Routledge, 2000.

Aizenman, N. C., and Spencer S. Hsu. "Activist's Arrest Highlights Key Immigrant Issue." *Washington Post*, August 21, 2007. http: WashingtonPost.com.

Alexander, Jonathan, and Jacqueline Rhodes. "Queer Rhetoric and the Pleasure of the Archive." *Enculturation*. January 16, 2012. http://enculturation.net.

Allen, Danielle, *Talking to Strangers: Anxieties of Citizenship since* Brown v. Board of Education. Chicago: University of Chicago Press, 2004.

Alvarez, Sara P., et al. "On Multimodal Composing." *Kairos: A Journal of Rhetoric, Technology, and Pedagogy* 21, no. 2 (2017).

Amador, Carlos. "This Is Our Country Too: Undocumented Immigrant Youth Organizing and the Battle for the DREAM Act." *National Association of Social Workers*, Summer 2011.

Amaro, Claudia. "A Call from the Eloy Detention Center: Claudia Amaro." YouTube, uploaded by The National Immigrant Youth Alliance, July 29, 2013.

———. "Claudia." YouTube, uploaded by The National Immigrant Youth Alliance, July 22, 2013.

Anguiano, Claudia, and Karma Chávez. "DREAMers' Discourse: Young Latino/a Immigrants and the Naturalization of the American Dream." In *Latina/o Discourse in Vernacular Spaces: Somos de Una Voz?*, edited by Michelle Holling and Bernadette Calafell, 81–99. Lanham, MD: Lexington Books, 2011.

Anzaldúa, Gloria, *Borderlands/La Frontera*. San Francisco, Aunt Lute, 1999.

———. "Let Us Be the Healing Wound: The Coyolxauhqui Imperative—La Sombra y el Sueño." *The Gloria Anzaldúa Reader*, edited by AnaLouise Keating, 303–18. Durham, NC: Duke University Press, 2009.

———. "Now Let Us Shift . . . the Path of Conocimiento . . . Inner Work, Public Act." In *This Bridge We Call Home: Radical Visions for Transformation*, edited by Gloria E. Anzaldúa and Analouise Keating, 540–78. New York: Routledge, 2002.

Arango, Tim, Nicholas Bogel-Burroughs, and Katie Benner. "Minutes before El Paso Killing, Hate-Filled Manifesto Appears Online." *New York Times*, August 3, 2019.

Baca, Damián. *Mestiz@ Scripts, Digital Migrations, and the Territories of Writing*. New York: Palgrave Macmillan, 2008.

Bargu, Banu. *Starve and Immolate: The Politics of Human Weapons*. New York: Columbia University Press, 2014.

Bell, Derrick. "*Brown v. Board of Education* and the Interest-Convergence Dilemma." *Harvard Law Review* 93, no. 3 (1980): 518–33.

Bennion, David. "In 2013, the Dream 30 Fought to Come Home." *Open Borders*, December 30, 2013.

Berestein Rojas, Leslie. "Emotional Rally Ends DREAM Act Hunger Strikes." *KPCC*, August 5, 2010.

Beydoun, Kahled. "Acting Muslim." *Harvard Civil Rights-Civil Liberties Law Review* 53, no. 1 (2018): 1–64.

Bishop, Sarah. *Undocumented Storytellers: Narrating the Immigrant Rights Movement*. Oxford: Oxford University Press, 2019.

Bloodsworth-Lugo, Mary, and Carmen Lugo Lugo. *Projecting 9/11: Race, Gender, and Citizenship in Recent Hollywood Films*. London: Rowman and Littlefield, 2014.

Brandzel, Amy L. *Against Citizenship: The Violence of the Normative*. Champaign: University of Illinois Press, 2016.

"Bring Our Mothers Home #WeAreElvira." YouTube, uploaded by FirmeProcess, March 18, 2014.

brown, adrienne maree. *Pleasure Activism: The Politics of Feeling Good*. Chico, CA: AK Press, 2019.

Brown, Kimberly. "Hunger Strikes Used by Immigration Reform Advocates." *ABC News*, June 7, 2010.

Brown, Wendy. *Undoing the Demos: Neoliberalism's Stealth Revolution*. New York: Zone, 2015.

Browne-Dianis, Judith et al. "And Injustice for All: Workers' Lives in the Reconstruction of New Orleans." *New Orleans Workers' Center for Racial Justice*, March 1, 2010.

Butcher, Kristin F., and Anne Morrison Piehl. "Cross-City Evidence on the Relationship between Immigration and Crime." *Journal of Policy Analysis and Management* 17, no. 3 (1998): 457–93.

Cacho, Lisa Marie. *Social Death: Racialized Rightlessness and the Criminalization of the Unprotected*. New York: New York University Press, 2012.

"Can the Dream 9 Change Immigration Policy in the US?" *Sonic Trace*. KCRW, Los Angeles, October 8, 2013.

Castillo, Ana. "Toward the Mother-Bond Principle." *Massacre of the Dreamers: Essays on Xicanisma*, 191–217. Albuquerque: University of New Mexico Press, 2014.

Chávez, Karma R. *Queer Migration Politics: Activist Rhetoric and Coalitional Possibilities*. Champaign: University of Illinois Press, 2013.

Chávez, Leo R. *The Latino Threat: Constructing Immigrants, Citizens, and the Nation*. Stanford, CA: Stanford University Press, 2013.

Cintron, Ralph. *Democracy as Fetish*. University Park: Pennsylvania State University Press, 2019.

Cisneros, Jesus, and Christian Bracho. "Coming Out of the Shadows and the Closet: Visibility Schemas among Undocuqueer Immigrants." *Journal of Homosexuality* 66, no. 6 (2018): 715–34.

Cisneros, Josue David. *The Border Crossed Us: Rhetorics of Borders, Citizenship, and Latina/o Identity*. Tuscaloosa: University of Alabama Press, 2014.

———. "(Re)Bordering the Civic Imaginary: Rhetoric, Hybridity, and Citizenship in *La Gran Marcha*." *Quarterly Journal of Speech* 97, no. 1 (2011): 26–49.

Cisneros, Sandra. "Guadalupe the Sex Goddess." In *Goddess of the Americas: Writings on the Virgin of Guadalupe*, edited by Ana Castillo, 46–51. New York: Riverhead Books, 1996.

Colby, Sandra L., and Jennifer M. Ortman. "Projections of the Size and Composition of US Population: 2014–2060." US Census Bureau, US Department of Commerce (March 2015).

"Coming Out of the Shadows 3.10.10," YouTube, uploaded by edia12, March 13, 2010. https://www.youtube.com/watch?v=Z88LNt8sPGU.

"Coming Out of the Shadows 3.10.10," YouTube, uploaded by edia12, March 13, 2010, https://www.youtube.com/watch?v=wx66g_wp9mk.

"Coming Out of the Shadows / Saliendo de las Sombras," YouTube, uploaded by Edy Anxeli, March 11, 2010.

Cornejo Villavicencio, Karla. *The Undocumented Americans*. New York: One World, 2019.

Costanza-Chock, Sasha. *Out of the Shadows, into the Streets! Transmedia Organizing and the Immigrant Rights Movement*. Cambridge, MA: MIT Press, 2014.

Development, Relief, and Education for Alien Minors Act of 2011, S. EAS11295, 112th Cong., 2011.

De Genova, Nicholas. *The Deportation Regime: Sovereignty, Space, and the Freedom of Movement*. Durham, NC: Duke University Press, 2010.

de los Santos Upton, Sarah. "Nepantla Activism and Coalition Building: Locating Identity and Resistance in the Cracks between Worlds." *Women's Communication Studies* 42, no. 2 (2019): 135–39.

Diaz-Cortes, Anayansi. "Can the Dream 9 Change Immigration Policy in the US?" *Sonic Trace*. KCRW, Los Angeles, October 8, 2013.

Dickerson, Caitlin, and Manny Fernandez. "What's behind the 'Tender Age' Shelters Opening for Young Migrants." *New York Times*, June 20, 2018.

Di Gregorio, Michael, and Jessica L. Merolli. "Introduction: Affective Citizenship and the Politics of Identity, Control, Resistance." *Citizenship Studies* 20, no. 8 (2016): 933–42.

Dolmage, Jay. "Disabled upon Arrival: The Rhetorical Construction of Disability and Race at Ellis Island." *Cultural Critique* 77 (2011): 24–69.

Dominguez Zamorano, Neidi, et al. "DREAM Activists: Rejecting the Passivity of the Nonprofit, Industrial Complex." TruthOut.org, September 21, 2010.

Duggan, Lisa. "The New Homonormativity: The Sexual Politics of Neoliberalism." *Materializing Democracy: Toward a Revitalized Cultural Politics*, edited by Russ Castronovo and Dana Nelson, 175–94. Durham NC: Duke University Press, 2002.

"Enhancing Public Safety in the Interior of the United States," Executive Order No. 13768, 82 Fed. Reg. 8799 (January 30, 2017). *Federal Register.*

Escalante, Juan. "Opinion: Attention Immigration 'Allies'—Stop Silencing DREAMers." NBC Latino, November 14, 2012.

Espiritu, Yen Le. *Home Bound: Filipino American Lives across Cultures, Communities, and Countries*. Berkeley: University of California Press, 2003.

Ewing, Walter A., Daniel E. Martinez, and Rubén G. Rumbaut. *The Criminalization of Immigration in the United States.* Washington, DC: American Immigration Council Special Report, July 2015.

"Family Separation by the Numbers." ACLU. October 2, 2018. https://www.aclu.org/issues/family-separation.

Fetters, Ashley. "At Least 30 Migrant Children Have Been Separated from Their Parents for More than a Year." *The Atlantic*, July 13, 2019.

"Find a Facility." CoreCivic. https://www.corecivic.com/facilities.

Fixmer-Oraiz, Natalie. *Homeland Maternity: US Security Culture and the New Reproductive Regime*. Urbana: University of Illinois Press, 2019.

Flores, Lisa. "Constructing Rhetorical Borders: Peons, Illegal Aliens, and Competing Narratives of Immigration." *Critical Studies in Media Communication* 20, no. 4 (2003): 362–87.

Flores, William Vincent, and Rina Benmayor. *Latino Cultural Citizenship: Claiming Identity, Space, and Rights*. Boston: Beacon, 1997.

Fortier, Anne Marie. "Afterword: Acts of Affective Citizenship? Possibilities and Limitations." *Citizenship Studies* 20, no. 8 (2016): 1038–44.

Foucault, Michel. *The Archaeology of Knowledge*. New York: Pantheon Books, 1972.

———. *Discipline and Punish: The Birth of the Prison*. New York: Vintage Books, 1995.

Freed Wessler, Seth. "Dozens of DREAMers Join Texas Hunger Strike." *Colorlines*, November 24, 2010.

———. "Hunger-Strike DREAMers: 'Our Future Is on the Line.'" *Colorlines*, December 1, 2010.

Fritz, Angela, and Luis Velarde. "ICE Arrested Hundreds of People in Raids. Now 'Devastated' Children Are without Their Parents." *Washington Post*, August 7, 2019.

Galindo, René. "Undocumented & Unafraid: The DREAM Act 5 and the Public Disclosure of Undocumented Status as a Political Act." *Urban Review* 44, no. 5 (2012): 589–611.

Gamber-Thompson, Liana, and Arely M. Zimmerman. "DREAMing Citizenship:

Undocumented Youth, Coming Out, and Pathways to Participation." In *By Any Media Necessary: The New Youth Activism*, edited by Henry Jenkins, Sangita Shresthova, Liana Gamber-Thompson, Neta Kligler-Vilenchik, and Arely Zimmerman, 186–218. New York: New York University Press, 2016.

Garcia, Christine. "In Defense of Latinx." *Composition Studies* 45, no. 2 (2017): 210–11.

Gladwell, Malcolm. "Small Change: Why the Revolution Will Not Be Tweeted." *New Yorker*, September 27, 2010.

Glenn, Evelyn Nakano. "Social Constructions of Mothering: A Thematic Overview." *Mothering: Ideology, Experience, and Agency*, edited by Evelyn Nakano Glenn, Grace Chang, and Linda Rennie Forcey, 1–29. New York: Routledge, 1994.

Gonzales, Roberto. Lives in Limbo: Undocumented and Coming of Age in America. Oakland: University of California Press, 2016.

Gonzales, Roberto G., and Leo R. Chavez. "'Awakening to a Nightmare': Abjectivity and Illegality in the Lives of Undocumented 1.5-Generation Latino Immigrants in the United States." *Current Anthropology* 53, no. 3 (2012): 255–81.

Gumbs, Alexis Pauline. "Introduction." In *Revolutionary Mothering: Love on the Front Lines*, edited by Alexis Pauline Gumbs, China Martens, and Mai'a Williams, 19–31. Oakland, CA: PM Press, 2016.

———. "M/Other Ourselves: A Black Queer Feminist Genealogy for Radical Mothering." In *Revolutionary Mothering: Love on the Front Lines*, edited by Alexis Pauline Gumbs, China Martens, and Mai'a Williams, 115–16. Oakland, CA: PM Press, 2016.

Harlow, Summer, and Lei Guo. "Will the Revolution Be Tweeted or Facebooked? Using Digital Communication Tools in Immigrant Activism." *Journal of Computer-Mediated Communication* 19, no. 3 (2014): 463–78.

Hauser, Gerard A. *Prisoners of Conscience: Moral Vernaculars of Political Agency*. Columbia: University of South Carolina Press, 2012.

Hawkins, Derek. "Immigration Agents Illegally Detain Obama Program 'Dreamer,' Lawsuit Says." *Washington Post*, February 15, 2017.

Hesford, Wendy. *Spectacular Rhetorics: Human Rights Visions, Recognitions, Feminisms*. Durham, NC: Duke University Press, 2011.

Hill Collins, Patricia. "Shifting the Center: Race, Class, and Feminist Theorizing about Motherhood." In *Mothering: Ideology, Experience, and Agency*, edited by Evelyn Nakano Glenn, Grace Chang, and Linda Rennie Forcey, 45–65. New York: Routledge, 1994.

Hinojosa, María, Antonia Cerejido, and Marlon Bishop. "The Dream 9." *Latino USA*. NPR, New York, February 3, 2017.

Hondagneu-Sotelo, Pierrette, and Ernestine Avila. "'I'm Here, but I'm There': The Meanings of Latina Transnational Motherhood." *Gender and Society* 11, no. 5 (1997): 548–71.

In Their Own Words: Enduring Abuse in Arizona Immigration Detention Centers. Phoenix: ACLU of Arizona, 2011.

"Isabel Martinez Bring Them Home NIYA," YouTube, uploaded by LaMunaMusica, March 19, 2014.

JOMO. "Fighting Obama's Deportation Policies without Papers." *The Nation*, April 24, 2014.

Jones Royster, Jacqueline. *Traces of a Stream*. Pittsburgh: University of Pittsburgh Press, 2000.

Jordan, Miriam. "Most Americans Want Legal Status for 'Dreamers.' These People Don't." *New York Times*, January 25, 2018.

Kalhan, Anil. "Rethinking Immigration Detention." *Columbia Law Review* 110 (2010): 42–58.

King, Lisa, Rose Gubele, and Joyce Rain Anderson, eds. "Introduction: Careful with the Stories We Tell: *Naming* Survivance, Sovereignty, *and* Story." In *Survivance, Sovereignty, Story: Teaching American Indian Rhetorics*, 3–16. Logan: Utah State University Press, 2015.

León, Luís. "Luís's Story." Guest lecture at the University of Portland, Portland, Oregon, November 14, 2013.

"LGBTQ Justice." UnitedWeDream.org.

Licona, Adela, and Karma Chávez. "Relational Literacies and Their Coalitional Possibilities." *Peitho Journal* 18, no. 1 (2015): 96–107.

Licona, Adela C. *Zines in the Third Space: Radical Cooperation and Borderlands Rhetoric*. New York: State University of New York Press, 2012.

Lipsitz, George. *The Possessive Investment in Whiteness: How White People Profit from Identity Politics*. Philadelphia: Temple University Press, 2009.

López, Gustavo, and Jens Manuel Krostad. "Key Facts about Unauthorized Immigrants Enrolled in DACA." *Pew Research Center*. September 25, 2017.

Lorde, Audre. "Uses of the Erotic." *Sister Outsider*, 53–59. Berkeley, CA: Crossing Press, 1984.

Ludwig, Melissa. "Mayor Asks Hunger Strikers to Eat, but DREAMers Refuse." *San Antonio Express-News*, December 7, 2010.

Lugo-Lugo, Carmen R. "'So You Are a Mestiza': Exploring the Consequences of Ethnic and Racial Clumping in the US Academy." *Ethnic and Racial Studies* 31, no. 3 (2008): 611–28.

Lugo-Lugo, Carmen R., and Mary Bloodsworth-Lugo. "'Anchor/Terror Babies' and Latina Bodies: Immigration Rhetoric in the 21st Century and the Feminization of Terrorism." *Journal of Interdisciplinary Feminist Thought* 8, no. 1 (2014): 1–21.

Lugones, Maria. "Methodological Notes toward a Decolonial Feminism." In *Decolonizing Epistomologies: Latina/o Theology and Philosophy*, edited by Ada Mara Isasi-Daz and Eduardo Mendieta, 68–86. New York: Fordham University Press, 2011.

Luibhéid, Eithne. "Introduction: Queering Migration and Citizenship." In *Queer Migrations: Sexuality, US Citizenship, and Border Crossings*, edited by Eithne Luibhéid and Lionel Cantu Jr., ix–xlvi (Minneapolis: University of Minnesota Press, 2001).

Lunsford, Andrea. "Toward a Mestiza Rhetoric: Gloria Anzaldúa on Composition and Postcoloniality." *JAC* 18, no. 1 (1998): 1–27.

Mariscal, Jorge. "Immigration and Military Enlistment: The Pentagon's Push for the DREAM Act Heats Up." *Latino Studies* 5, no. 3 (2007): 362.

Martinez, Lulu. "Bring Them Home: Lulu Martinez Checking in from Mexico City." YouTube, uploaded by the National Immigrant Youth Alliance, July 20, 2013.

Mateo, Lizbeth. "Bring Them Home: Lizbeth Mateo Checking in from Oaxaca, Mexico." YouTube, uploaded by the National Immigrant Youth Alliance, July 17, 2013.

———. "Lizbeth Mateo: 'I Don't Know What They've Done to the Women Here . . .—Eloy Prison." YouTube, uploaded by the National Immigrant Youth Alliance, July 30, 2013.

McCarthy, Joe. "DACA Dreamers Walk 250 Miles to Capital to Protest Inaction." *Global Citizen*, March 1, 2018.

McKinnon, Sara. "Excavating Gender in Women's Early Claims to Political Asylum in the United States." *Women's Studies in Communication* 33, no. 2 (2010): 79–95.

———. "Positioned in/by the State: Incorporation, Exclusion, and Appropriation of Women's Gender-Based Claims to Political Asylum in the United States." *Quarterly Journal of Speech* 97, no. 2 (2011): 178–200.

Medina, Cruz. *Reclaiming Poch@ Pop: Examining the Rhetoric of Cultural Deficiency*. New York: Palgrave Macmillan, 2014.

"Meet the Dream 9." *Latino USA*, Oct. 16, 2015.

Mejía, Jaime. "Bridging Rhetoric and Composition Studies with Chicano and Chicana Studies: A Turn to Critical Pedagogy." In *Latino/a Discourses: On Language, Identity, and Literacy Education*, edited by Michelle Hall Kells, Valerie Balester, and Victor Villanueva, 51–73. Portsmouth, NH: Boynton/Cook, 2004.

Miles, Thomas, and Adam Cox. "Does Immigration Enforcement Reduce Crime? Evidence from Secure Communities." *Journal of Law and Economics* 57, no. 4 (2014): 937–73.

Mohanty, Chandra Tapalde. *Feminism without Borders: Decolonizing Theory, Practicing Solidarity*. Durham, NC: Duke University Press, 2003.

Moraga, Cherrie L. *Loving in the War Years*. Cambridge, MA: South End Press, 2000.

Motta, Carlos. "Activism, Visuality, and the Needs of Queer Youth." *Journal of Visual Culture* 15, no. 1 (2016): 118–30.

Muñoz, José Esteban. *Cruising Utopia*. New York: NYU Press, 2009.

National Immigrant Youth Alliance. "About National Immigrant Youth Alliance." Facebook.

———. "Bring Them Home." Livestream video. Ustream. July 22, 2013.

Nevarez, Griselda. "150 Undocumented Immigrants to Enter US in Border-Crossing Demonstration." *HuffPost Latino Voices*, March 11, 2014. TheHuffingtonPost.com.

"New MPI Estimates: As Many as 2.1 Million Young People Could Be Eligible for the DREAM Act, though Far Fewer Would Meet Its Education or Military Service

Requirements for Legalization." MigrationPolicy.org. Migration Policy Institute, February 18, 2014.

Nicholls, Walter. *The DREAMers: How the Undocumented Youth Movement Transformed the Immigrant Rights Debate*. Stanford, CA: Stanford University Press, 2013.

Nopper, Tamara K. "Why I Oppose Repealing DADT & Passage of the DREAM Act." In *Against Equality: Don't Ask to Fight Their Wars*, edited by Ryan Conrad, 33–44. Lewiston, ME: Against Equality Publishing Collective, 2011.

Ochoa, Juan D. "Shine Bright like a Migrant: Julio Salgado's Digital Art and Its Use of Jotería." *Social Justice* 42, no. 3–4 (2015): 184–99.

Ono, Kent, and John Sloop. *Shifting Borders: Rhetoric, Immigration, and California's Proposition 187*. Philadelphia: Temple University Press, 2002.

Ousey, Graham, and Charis Kubrin. "Exploring the Connection between Immigration and Violent Crime Rates in US Cities, 1980–2000." *Social Problems* 56, no. 3 (2009): 447–73.

Pallares, Amalia. *Family Activism: Immigrant Struggles and the Politics of Noncitizenship*. New Brunswick, NJ: Rutgers University Press, 2015.

Park, Shelley M. *Mothering Queerly, Queering Motherhood: Resisting Monomaternalism in Adoptive, Lesbian, Blended, and Polygamous Families*. New York: SUNY Press, 2013.

Parker, Kim, Rich Morin, and Juliana Menasce Horowitz. "Looking to the Future, Public Sees an America in Decline on Many Fronts." *Pew Research Center: Social & Demographic Trends*. March 21, 2019.

Paúl, Fernanda. "'¡El pueblo unido jamás será vencido!' La historia de emblemático himno de protesta que vuelve a ser protagonista en Chile." *BBC News*, December 16, 2019.

Peniche, Maria. "Maria Checks in from Detention; #BRINGTHEMHOME." YouTube, uploaded by the National Immigrant Youth Alliance, July 26, 2013.

Perez, Emma. *Decolonial Imaginary: Writing Chicanas into History*. Bloomington: Indiana University Press, 1999.

Peterson, Spike. "Sexing Political Identities/Nationalism as Heterosexism." In *Women, States, and Nationalism: At Home in the Nation?*, edited by Sita Ranchod-Nilsson and Mary Ann Tétreault, 54–80. London: Routledge, 2000.

Pierce, Sarah, and Andrew Selee. "Immigration under Trump: A Review of Policy Shifts in the Year since the Election." Migration Policy Institute. December 2017.

Pieri, Mara. "Undoing Citizenship: Undocumented Queer Activism and Practices of Rights." *Remhu* 24, no. 48 (2016): 105–20.

Planas, Roque. "Big Win for Immigrant Activists Who Staged Border-Crossing Protest in Laredo." *HuffPost*, October 1, 2013. www.huffpost.com.

Powell, Malea. "Rhetorics of Survivance: How American Indians Use Writing." *College Composition and Communications* 53, no. 3 (2002): 396–434.

Powell, Malea, et al. "Our Story Begins Here: Constellating Cultural Rhetorics." *Enculturation*, 18 (2014). https://www.enculturation.net.

Preston, Julia. "Illegal Immigrant Students Protest at McCain Office." *New York Times*, May 17, 2010.

Puar, Jasbir. *Terrorist Assemblages*. Durham, NC: Duke University Press, 2007.

Ramirez, Cristina. *Occupying Our Space: The Mestiza Rhetorics of Mexican Women Journalists and Activists, 1875–1942*. Tucson: University of Arizona Press, 2015.

Ramirez, Maria Liliana. "Beyond Identity: Coming Out as UndocuQueer." In *We Are Not Dreamers*, edited by Leisy Abrego and Genevieve Negrón-Gonzales, 146–67. Durham, NC: Duke University Press, 2020.

Ribero, Ana Milena. "Acceptable Heterogeneity: Brownwashing Rhetoric in President Obama's Address on Immigration." *Present Tense: A Journal of Rhetoric in Society* 5, no. 2 (2015). https://www.presenttensejournal.org.

———. "Citizenship." In *Decolonizing Rhetoric and Composition Studies: New Latinx Keywords for Theory and Pedagogy*, edited by Iris Ruiz and Raúl Sanchez, 31–45. New York: Palgrave Macmillan, 2016.

———. "'Papá, Mamá, I'm Coming Home': Family, Home, and the Neoliberal Immigrant Nation in the National Immigrant Youth Alliance's 'Bring Them Home' Campaign." *Rhetoric Review* 37, no. 3 (2018): 273–85.

Rich, Adrienne. *Of Woman Born: Motherhood as Experience and Institution*. New York: W. W. Norton, 1976.

Rivera, Sylvia. "Y'all Better Quiet Down." Speech at Christopher Street Liberation Day Rally, New York, 1973.

Rodríguez, Juana María. *Sexual Futures, Queer Gestures, and Other Latina Longings*. New York: NYU Press, 2014.

Saavedra, Marco. "Bring Them Home: Marco Saavedra Checking in from Mexico." YouTube, uploaded by the National Immigrant Youth Alliance, July 18, 2013.

Salcido, Olivia, and Cecilia Menjívar. "Gendered Paths to Legal Citizenship: The Case of Latin-American Immigrants in Phoenix, Arizona." *Law & Society Review* 46, no. 2 (2012): 335–68.

Salgado, Julio. *Fuck Your Borders, Pt. 2*. Illustration. Instagram. Accessed April 20, 2022.

———. *I Read, I Create, I Mess Up, I Fall*. Illustration. JulioSalgado.com. Accessed April 20, 2022.

Sánchez, James Chase. "Preaching behind the Fiery Pulpit: Rhetoric, Public Memory, and Self-Immolation." PhD diss., Texas Christian University, 2017.

Sandoval, Chela. *Methodology of the Oppressed*. Minneapolis: University of Minnesota Press, 2000.

Sandoval, Chela, and Guisela Latorre. "Chicana/o Artivism: Judy Baca's Digital Work with Youth of Color." In *Learning Race and Ethnicity: Youth and Digital Media*, edited by Anna Everett, 81–108. Cambridge, MA: MIT Press, 2007.

Santa Ana, Otto. "'Like an Animal I Was Treated': Anti-immigrant Metaphor in U.S. Public Discourse." *Discourse and Society* 10, no. 2 (1999): 191–224.

Santiago, Ceferino. "Ceferino Santiago." YouTube, uploaded by the National Immigrant Youth Alliance, July 22, 2013.

Santoro, Wayne A. "Was the Civil Rights Movement Successful? Tracking and Understanding Black Views." *Sociological Forum* 30, no. S1 (2015): 627–47.

Schmalzbauer, Leah. "Searching for Wages and Mothering from Afar: The Case of Honduran Transnational Families." *Journal of Marriage and Family* 66, no. 5 (2017): 1317–31.

Schmid, Carol. "Challenges at the Periphery of US Citizenship: Birthright Citizenship of Undocumented Immigrants and the Dream Act." In *Citizenship: Practices, Types and Challenges*, edited by Dexter Petty and Clay MacFarland, 47–61. Hauppauge, NY: Nova Science, 2012.

Seif, Hinda. "'Coming out of the Shadows' and 'Undocuqueer': Undocumented Immigrants Transforming Sexuality Discourse and Activism." *Journal of Language and Sexuality* 3, no. 1 (2014): 87–120.

———. "Layers of Humanity: Interview with Undocuqueer Artivist Julio Salgado." *Latino Studies* 12, no. 2 (2014): 300–309.

Semple, Kirk. "Immigrants' Hunger Strike Ends with 'Die-In.'" *New York Times*, June 10, 2010.

———. "3-day Fast Is Latest Call to Overhaul Immigration." *New York Times*, June 2, 2010.

Sessions, Sen. Jeff. "Ten Things You Need to Know About S.3827, the DREAM Act." November 18, 2010.

Shear, Michael D., and Eileen Sullivan. "Trump Policy Favors Wealthier Immigrants for Green Cards." *New York Times*, August 12, 2019.

Shwer, Mikaela. *Don't Tell Anyone (No le digas a nadie)*. September 21, 2015.

Siméant, Johanna, and Christophe Traïni. *Bodies in Protest: Hunger Strikes and Angry Music*. Amsterdam: Amsterdam University Press, 2016.

Smith Silva, Dorsía. "Introduction: Conceptualizing Latina/Chicana Mothering." In *Latina/Chicana Mothering*. Bradford, ON: Demeter Press, 2011.

Somerville, Siobhan. "Notes toward a Queer History of Naturalization," *American Quarterly* 57, no. 3 (2005): 659–75.

Sowards, Stacey, and Richard Pineda. "Immigrant Narratives and Popular Culture in the United States: Border Spectacle, Unmotivated Sympathies and Individualized Responsibilities." *Western Journal of Communication* 77, no. 1 (2013): 72–91.

Spivak, Gayatri Chakravorty. "Criticism, Feminism and the Institution." *Thesis Eleven* 10/11 (1984/85): 175–87.

St. Onge, Jeffrey. "Neoliberalism as Common Sense in Barack Obama's Health Care Rhetoric." *Rhetoric Society Quarterly* 47, no. 4 (2017): 295–312.

Taracena, María Inés. "Eloy Detention Center Hunger Strike: Tucson Teen Demands to Speak to Her Father." *Tucson Weekly*, June 16, 2015.

Tellez, Michelle. "Personal Is Political: Chicana Motherwork." *Feminist Wire*, March 6. 2014.

Terriquez, Veronica, et al. "Intersectionality as a Multipurpose Collective Action Frame: The Case of the Undocumented Youth Movement." *Ethnicities* 18, no. 2 (2018): 260–76.

Trejo, Thelsa Zelaya. "Thelsa Zelaya Trejo A# 077–195–967 translated." YouTube, uploaded by the National Immigrant Youth Alliance, August 2, 2013.

Trevizo, Perla. "Dreamers Released from Custody." *Arizona Daily Star*, August 8, 2013.

———. "Report: ICE Complicit in Hiding Maltreatment at Eloy Center." *Arizona Daily Star*, October 15, 2015. http://Tucson.com.

Truax, Eileen. *Dreamers: An Immigrant Generation's Fight for Their American Dream*. Boston: Beacon Press, 2015.

Tuck, Eve, and K. Wayne Yang. "Decolonization Is Not a Metaphor." *Decolonization: Indigeneity, Education, & Society* 1, no. 1 (2012): 1–40.

"UndocuQueer Manifesto." YouTube, uploaded by United We Dream, October 11, 2013.

Unzueta Carrasco, Tania, and Hinda Seif. "Disrupting the Dream: Undocumented Youth Reframe Citizenship and Deportability through Anti-deportation Activism." *Latino Studies* 12, no. 2 (2014): 295.

Valverde, Miriam. "What You Need to Know about the Trump Administration's Zero-Tolerance Immigration Policy." PolitiFact. Poynter Institute. June 6, 2018. http://politifact.com.

Vargas, Jose Antonio. "Not Legal Not Leaving." *Time*, June 25, 2012.

Velasquez-Potts, Michelle C. "Staging Incapacitation: The Corporeal Politics of Hunger Striking." *Women and Performance* 29, no. 1 (2019): 25–40.

Villanueva, Victor. "Puerto Rico: A Neoliberal Crucible." *Journal of Cultural Economy* 8, no. 1 (2014): 62–74.

Weinstein, Vivian. "DREAM Act Hunger Strikers to End Strike after 40 Days." *People's World*, December 20, 2010.

West, Cornel. "Goodbye, American Neoliberalism: A New Era Is Here." *The Guardian*, November 17, 2016.

Wides-Muñoz, Laura. *The Making of a Dream: How a Group of Young Undocumented Immigrants Helped Change What It Means to Be American*. New York: Harper, 2018.

Wright, Melissa. *Disposable Women and Other Myths of Global Capitalism*. New York: Routledge, 2006.

Wu, Harrick. "'Undocu-Queer' Artist Julio Salgado on Creative Resistance," *KQED*, July 5, 2018.

Yam, Sharon. *Inconvenient Strangers: Transnational Subjects and the Politics of Citizenship*. Columbus: Ohio State University Press, 2019.

Index